RODALE'S

Soups and Salads

COOKBOOK AND KITCHEN ALBUM

RODALE'S
Soups and Salads
COOKBOOK AND KITCHEN ALBUM

Nearly 300 kitchen-tested recipes – plus surprising facts about foods, nutritional tips and entertaining visits with some remarkable cooks

Editor: Charles Gerras

Assistant Editor: Carol Meinhardt Hopkins
Personal Profiles: Carol Meinhardt Hopkins
Recipes: Carole Collier
Additional Recipes and Recipe Testing: JoAnn Benedick and Linda C. Gilbert
Editorial Assistant: Camille Bucci

Color Photography: Carl Doney
Food Stylist: Laura Hendry Reifsnyder
Black and White Photography: Margaret Smyser, Sally Ann Shenk and Fred Smith Associates

Rodale Press, Emmaus, Pennsylvania

Book design by John F. Carafoli and Barbara Field

Printed in the United States of America on recycled paper containing a high percentage of de-inked fiber.

Library of Congress Cataloging in Publication Data

Main entry under title:

Rodale's soups and salads cookbook and kitchen
album.

  Includes index.
  1. Soups. 2. Salads. 3. Cookery. I. Gerras,
Charles. II. Rodale Press.
TX757.R72   641.8′13   81-4644
ISBN 0-87857-332-1 hardcover AACR2
  4 6 8 10 9 7 5   hardcover

Contents

Soups and Salads Have a Value All Their Own

"I could make a meal of it!" People are always saying that about their favorite salad or soup. And it's true. Any one of us could make a meal of the season's first salad made with leaf lettuce and tomatoes grown in our own gardens. Is there a single soul who can't fill up on homemade bread and bowls of a favorite chowder or a steaming thick pea soup? Such dishes are our heritage, our tradition, our security.

The popularity of soups and salads has endured easily from the days of Eden to the fast-food franchises of today. Every place in the world has a favorite version—Japan's miso, America's corn chowder, France's *salade classique*, Germany's potato salad—a fascinating, unending variety that invites experimentation and promises a somehow familiar pleasure. And with the pleasure come some welcome nutritional benefits that elude us in other dishes.

A salad is the one regular encounter most people have with raw food. Take a minute to think of your own daily eating habits and those of your friends, and you will be surprised at how seldom you eat anything raw. Yet health experts tell us that our bodies need the food values that cooking destroys. In today's society, salads are a nutritional oasis!

It takes enzymes to release the nutrients that are locked up in all foods. Raw foods contain plenty of these enzymes—all unfavorably affected by heat. The high temperatures required for boiling or frying, for example, virtually destroy them. Of course, our bodies manufacture enzymes, but never enough to get the most out of the foods we eat.

The fiber in foods—the roughage—so coveted for health, is at its best when the food is raw. Cooking breaks it down and mushes it, and the valuable aid fiber can supply to digestion is severely impaired. Either vitamins and minerals are destroyed outright by cooking, or they leach out into the cooking liquids and are often poured down the drain.

A bowl of homemade soup is loaded with those good things ordinarily lost from vegetables and meats in cooking other dishes. The best chefs regularly salvage the flavorful, nutrition-rich cooking water from green beans or spinach to use in a sauce or a soup. It's one secret to instilling extra body in a soup. And as the soup cooks, the flavors intensify, and the nutrients from all the ingredients meld with the stock. Nothing good escapes (except for some of the vitamin C and those B vitamins that are especially sensitive to heat), for everything in the vegetables and meats is caught by the welcoming liquid and suspended there for the taking.

Why do doctors prescribe clear broth or light soup for patients who have poor appetites, delicate stomachs, or poor digestion? Because soup provides a big nutritional pick-me-up in a small package; it's simple and easy for the body to handle, even when you're too sick to eat anything else—and it tastes wonderful!

The recipes in this book are aimed at making the most of the good qualities inherent in the very concepts of soup and salad. All ingredients in recipes created for and by Rodale are fresh or homemade and unprocessed. No salt or sugar is called for in the recipes, because of strong evidence that these items can have a damaging effect on health. In the few instances where recipes are reproduced from other publications, of course they must appear as originally written, even when the ingredients do not conform to the healthful attitudes this book seeks to encourage.

But healthfulness alone isn't what soup or salad is all about. It's about flavor and hearty satisfaction and alluring combinations of taste and texture. It's atmosphere and remembrance of a happy summertime picnic or a warming wintertime treat around the kitchen table. Of course soups and salads are good for you, but that's not the half of it! Their real appeal is enjoyment and the discovery of a lot from a little.

C.G.

PART-ONE

Soups

Soup Is a
Sensuous Experience

We each have our own sense-memories about soup—and they're all good. If someone asks what soup means to you, you're sure to enjoy contemplating the answer—a steaming bowl of fresh vegetable soup on a chilly fall evening; the traditional prescription of golden chicken soup your mother spooned into you as you sat propped up in bed with a bad cold; your first enthralling encounter with the rich and fragrant bouillabaisse. Soup is comfort, nourishment, security, pleasure. But most of all soup is homemade. Soup—real soup—comes from a pot, not a can.

For some mystical reason, new cooks who will tackle almost anything from complicated sauces to desserts flambe, blanch at the prospect of making soup from scratch. Yet few areas of cooking are less demanding for the beginner. In a sense, making soup is like making tea; the flavoring agent—tomato, chicken, onion—simply pervades the liquid. But unlike tea, prolonged contact of the flavor source with the liquid never makes the soup bitter, only better. The famous French stock pot, *pot au feu*, is a perfect example. It simmers on the back of the wood cookstove literally for years, never cooling off. The cook simply adds to it—more water, the season's new vegetables, meat scraps, bones. The result is a flavorful base for other dishes, or a tasty bowlful by itself, splendid when partnered with a chunk of crusty bread.

If the *pot au feu* formula sounds haphazard, it also suggests just how informal the art of soup making really is. As you read about stocks in the following pages you will soon realize that you make, say, a chicken stock by using whatever chicken bones and scraps you have on hand and adding water to cover. No absolute amounts—you just keep the pot simmering until the resultant liquid tastes good to you. What could be simpler?

The stock—chicken, beef, vegetable, fish—is strained, and the clear liquid serves as the basis for the soup you want to make. Just add the beans or the split peas or the onions or the barley, plus any special flavoring you like, and there you have it—soup!

And, according to an old saying, "A good soup can carry a dinner." The truth is that a hearty soup can *be* the dinner and often is. Satisfying, nutritious, and economical.

There's no better way to learn about making soup than to try it. The attempt will instill confidence and provide an elemental satisfaction you will want to experience again and again. We hope you will want to try a number of the recipes in this book, but we know you will soon be creating your own soup specialties, dishes that guests will request as special treats. It is astounding how quickly one can become an imaginative, expert, totally independent soup maker.

Stock is the foundation of it all. See how soon the mystery suggested by that term evaporates as you read on.

Stocks and Clear Soups

It doesn't matter which name you use: stock, bouillon, consomme, or broth. They all refer to that marvelous, versatile brew obtained by simmering bones, meat, and/or vegetables.

A good, homemade stock is a rich, healthy, often gelatinous liquid that is literally a flavor essence. This is especially important in a kitchen where wholesome, natural seasonings and ingredients are the rule. A stock that has maximum natural flavor impact needs no help from undesirable ingredients. Because of the gentle simmering involved, homemade stocks are perfect for extracting every ounce of goodness and flavor that nature has locked into our most nourishing foods.

Stocks are simply delicious by themselves, but absolutely irreplaceable as a base for other dishes. They can be amplified to enhance leftovers or to create dozens of soups, sauces, casseroles, or stews. They are so functional and easy to make and to store that no serious cook would be without at least one variety "in stock" at all times.

Stock has the added attraction of being low in calories! The meat-base broth is made a day ahead and refrigerated overnight. In the morning, all the fat will have collected on the surface and solidified, so that it can be lifted off easily. This is called "degreasing."

Although there are many varieties of stock, certain principles apply to all of them. Four basic essentials go into every stockpot:

- nourishing ingredients—such as bones, meat, vegetables, poultry, and fish;
- aromatics—certain vegetables such as carrots, onions, and leeks;
- seasonings—spices and herbs such as parsley, thyme, and bay leaves; and
- liquids—water, vegetable cooking water, and pan juices.

By simmering these ingredients over a very low heat *(small bubbles should barely ripple the surface of the liquid),* a delicious and satisfying broth can be extracted over a period ranging from one to several hours. Fish stock is one exception; it will develop a rich, full-bodied broth in less than an hour. The length of time a stock should simmer (it varies) will be discussed later in detail.

INGREDIENTS

Shop around for good soup bones. Most butchers are only too happy to sell them, or you can get them from supermarkets and wholesale meat stores. Of course, bones with some meat remaining are the best, but if they are unavailable or if they seem too expensive, you can still achieve excellent results by using well-trimmed bones and adding a piece of inexpensive stewing meat for more flavor. Bones provide that desirable natural gelatinous quality for a stock. They should always be hacked or sawed into small pieces so that the goodness within is exposed and, of course, so that they will fit more easily into the pot. Unless a recipe specifically calls for them, go easy on pork, lamb, and ham bones in the stockpot, because they yield a very strong stock and dominate the flavor.

Vegetables should be well scrubbed and any blemishes or bad spots cut out. Peeling is not necessary, because the skins add their own goodness and flavor to the broth. One important thing to remember about vegetables is that they should be cut into *large* pieces before adding them to the pot. Otherwise, they tend to fall apart during the long cooking process, and the result is a cloudy stock. Be aware that strongly flavored vegetables such as asparagus, broccoli, cabbage, and turnips can easily over-power the other flavors in the soup, so use them sparingly, or avoid them altogether when subtle flavoring is important.

Use small seeds and spices such as cloves and peppercorns whole rather than ground, or the powdery bits will float around in the finished broth. Herbs and whole seasonings may be tied into a bouquet garni for easy retrieval. Simply place the herbs in a cheesecloth sack and tie it closed. Then attach the sack to a soup bone, or place it underneath one, to prevent the herb pack from floating.

When you start a stock, be sure the water placed in the pot is *cold*. If you start with hot or boiling water, it tends to sear the ingredients, sealing in the juices. Cold water draws the juices from the ingredients soaking in it. As the water heats, it extracts the maximum amount of goodness. The only time to use hot water is when the stockpot needs topping off (that is, adding water if the liquid level in the stockpot is dropping too low). Even then, it's best to take cold water from the tap and heat it in a kettle before adding it to the stock. Hot water from the tap tends to absorb a metallic taste from the pipes.

Although most recipes for stock list a specific amount of water to be placed in the pot, it is always just an approximation. There are so many variables—the size of the pot, the temperature of the simmering liquid, the evaporation rate—that it's just about impossible to determine the exact amount of water. When in doubt, add more water; it can always be reduced once the stock is strained. The important thing to keep in mind is that the ingredients in the pot should always be covered by the water. The order in which ingredients are added to the pot is up to you. Some people prefer to skim the stock before adding the vegetables; others put everything into the pot at once. And that means everything—leftover steak bones, vegetable trimmings, cooking waters, all have value. There is no waste when it comes to making stock, because everything, as long as it is clean and unspoiled, can contribute to the pot.

EQUIPMENT

The tools needed for making stock are basic items you probably own already. Start with a *large, heavy pot* of at least 4- to 6-quart capacity. Stainless steel or enamel are the best materials. A *slotted spoon,* a *large spatula,* or a specially purchased *stock skimmer* are also necessary. (Wrapping a piece of cheesecloth around the utensil you use for skimming will help facilitate the process.) A *large strainer* is important, too. You will notice that many recipes call for lining the sieve before straining the liquid through it. This can be done with several layers of cheesecloth or a clean, loosely woven dish towel wrung out in cold water. (Do not use dampened paper towels or large coffee filters for this purpose; they tend to strip the gelatinous product of its body.) Use a *ladle* for transferring the stock from the pot to the strainer; pouring the stock from the pot tends to churn it up. *Measuring devices, bowls,* and *storage containers* with *tightly fitting lids* should also be on hand. You'll need a *large wire whisk* if you intend to clarify your stock. And finally, an *asbestos burner pad* is essential for diffusing the heat under the stockpot, if you can't turn your burner down low enough barely to simmer the broth.

COOKING THE STOCK

One day when you plan to be occupied at home, put a pot of stock on the stove. Put it on high heat until it comes to a boil, then turn the heat down to very low. The surface of the broth should barely wrinkle. Now all you have to do is watch the pot occasionally for the next 30 minutes.

When you make stock with ingredients that contain albumin, such as meat, milk, eggs, and bones, they release scum that coagulates and floats in the liquid. Although it is not attractive, this scum is rich in protein; many nutritionists feel that it should not be removed from the broth. Traditionally, however, all stocks are thoroughly skimmed during the first half-hour of simmering, when the scum appears. The idea is to keep the broth as clear and appetizing as possible.

Check the water level in the pot every hour or so, and add boiling water if it drops too low. If you are skimming your stock, check it occasionally for any additional foam that might accumulate on the surface.

HOW LONG TO COOK
THE STOCK

Most recipes specify a cooking time for stock, but you can adjust this to suit yourself. Stocks made with meat bones require the longest cooking time—up to six hours—to extract the gelatin from the bones. Poultry bones require only two to three hours, and fish bones give off a full-bodied broth in 30 minutes.

STRAINING AND
REDUCING

When you have finished cooking the stock, the next step is to strain it. Line a large sieve or colander with a damp, loosely woven cloth, and place it over a clean bowl or pan. Ladle the broth into the strainer, and wash out the pot used to cook the stock. The strained stock may then be returned to the pot for further reducing, if desired. Reducing the stock concentrates its body and flavor into a smaller volume, so it's easier to store. To reduce a stock, boil it vigorously, uncovered, until the volume is lessened by one-third to one-half. Skim, if necessary.

Once the stock is strained or reduced, it should be cooled, uncovered, as quickly and thoroughly as possible to prevent any bacteria from growing in the warm liquid. This must be done before refrigerating the stock. One good way to do this is to place the pot in a larger basin or bowl, surround it with ice, and stir the broth until it is completely cool. Another method is to set the pot on blocks in a sink filled with cold water.

STORAGE

Store the cooled stock in covered containers at once. It will keep under refrigeration for about a week. If you wish to have the stock on hand any longer, freeze it. Put it in small, covered containers—they're easier to handle. Or, you might wish to freeze it in ice-cube trays. The frozen cubes can be unmolded and stored in sealed plastic bags. Then they can be used as needed, without defrosting a large quantity of stock. Don't forget to label and date the stock you freeze. It will keep for up to a year. Before using any stock that has been frozen, bring it to a full, rolling boil.

That's all there is to making stock. There is no mystery. Once you understand these basic principles, there's not much work involved, either—most of the time goes into unsupervised simmering. The many varieties of stock are discussed below. You will surely be tempted to try them all.

SIMPLE STOCK

A simple stock is the base for many of the soups, sauces, gravies, and casseroles that are made with meat or vegetables. A good meat stock can literally "beef up" a dish that might otherwise seem monotonous, and it is equally good used on its own to "beef up" one's spirits.

Simple stock is extremely easy to make because the ingredients—the water, bones, meat, vegetables, and seasonings—are just placed in a pan, brought to a boil, lowered to simmering, and allowed to cook, unattended, to the desired concentration.

[*Continued on page* 9]

CRYSTAL CLEAR CONSOMME For this recipe, see page 21

GAZPACHO ASPIC   For this recipe, see page 244

The broth may be skimmed or not, as desired. Merely follow the basic principles of stock making, and you will end up with a delightful pot of an easy, homemade stock.

VEAL STOCK

Veal stock is perhaps the most classic and elegant of the white stocks because of the delectable flavor and texture veal bones bring to it. Hack or saw the knuckles and bones into pieces of about two or three inches to expose the marvelous properties concealed within. It will take at least 3½ hours of slow simmering to extract the best of this. A few chicken parts may be added to the pot for additional flavor. Veal bones are also notorious for the albuminous scum that they exude during cooking.

POULTRY STOCK

This is probably the most familiar of all stocks and also one of the most economical. It's so easy to make and to freeze, and the flavor of this homemade stock is so rich and nourishing that once you've experienced it, you'll never use canned or instant stock again.

Keep a plastic bag in the freezer for collecting leftover poultry bones and trimmings. When you are ready to make the stock, simply place the frozen ingredients in the pot with the other stock makings. They will defrost as you bring the water to a rolling boil. Then drain and rinse the bones and other ingredients and the pot (getting rid of surface scum), cover all again with cold water, and start the long cooking process.

Wing tips, carcasses (raw or cooked), gizzards, and hearts can all be put to good use in a homemade stock. Chicken backs and necks are excellent for stock, and most butchers will part with them quite cheaply. Chicken feet, although difficult to find, are worth seeking out, because they provide a lot of natural gelatin which gives the broth body. Live-poultry markets, farms, and Jewish neighborhood shops are the best sources for these. Blanch them in boiling water for five minutes, and peel or rub off the yellow skin before adding them to the stockpot. The only edible part of the chicken (and other poultry) that should never be used in stock making is the liver. Liver gives off an unpleasant flavor and darkens the stock. Freeze livers in a separate container, and use them for some other purpose.

Hack carcasses and bones into small pieces to expose their interior values. Since poultry bones are more fragile than meat bones, the stock needs to be simmered only 1½ hours to achieve a gelatinous, rich flavor.

BASIC BROWN STOCK

Making a good basic brown stock requires more attention and initial effort than other stocks, but the result is always worth it. The stock takes on an appetizing hue and has a richer flavor because of the cooking method. The mystery behind the brown color lies in roasting bones and meat in a hot oven or in a skillet, until they are nice and brown.

BASIC BROWN STOCK WITH MIXED MEAT

Use beef or veal bones, shanks, or knuckles. These should be sawed into small-enough pieces (about three or four inches) to expose the goodness within them and to allow them to fit easily into your stockpot. If the bones don't have much meat on them, you can always add a piece of chuck or bottom round for flavor. A few chicken wings or backs may also be used in combination for a richer flavor. The bones and meat should be placed in a roasting pan and roasted in a hot oven (425°F) for about an hour, or until they are nicely colored. Turn the bones occasionally to promote even cooking. *Unpeeled* onions and carrots cut into large pieces should be added during the final half-hour of roasting. Leaving the skins on the onions adds more color and sweetness to the broth. Then transfer the roasted bones, meat, and vegetables to the stockpot. Spoon any fat out of the roasting pan and discard it. Then deglaze the pan (rinse it with a little cold water, scrape the brown particles from the pan bottom with a wooden spoon, and pour all into the stockpot). Add water and seasonings to the pot and leave it to simmer gently for at least five to six hours or longer, skimming as necessary.

BROWNED POULTRY STOCK

This is prepared in much the same way as browned meat stock, except that the poultry bones and other ingredients are browned in a skillet on top of the stove where the cook can keep an eye on them. (They tend to burn easily during oven browning.)

Hack any large poultry bones into smaller pieces, no larger than three or four inches. Coat a large skillet with a small amount of oil, and saute the poultry parts until browned.

Using your favorite recipe for poultry stock, place the browned parts into the stockpot. Saute the vegetables (unpeeled onions and carrots cut into large pieces) in the pan drippings. When the vegetables have browned sufficiently, transfer them to the stockpot. Discard any fat in the skillet. Deglaze the skillet, and add the particles to the pot. Add water and seasonings and simmer very gently for two to four hours, skimming as necessary.

MEAT GLAZE (*GLACE DE VIANDE*)

Glaze is meat stock that has been strained and reduced until it is very thick and syrupy. It cools into a firm jelly that is convenient for handling and storage. Two quarts of stock will condense into approximately one cup of glaze.

It takes a bit of patience and some courage to make a meat glaze for the first time. When you think of the effort and quantity of ingredients that go into the making of a good meat stock, you are bound to feel a tinge of doubt at the thought of cooking it all down to such a small amount. However, you simply have to remember that the glaze is a highly concentrated essence that can be used sparingly. Just half a teaspoon is all it takes to enrich a sauce or soup, or to flavor a stew or casserole. A meat glaze can also be reconstituted in hot water and used in place of stock, yet it takes up much less storage space than a quantity of stock.

To make a meat glaze, place two quarts of any meat stock in a medium-size saucepan. Bring the stock to a boil and cook it, uncovered, on medium heat for about one hour, or until it is reduced by half. Strain this through a fine sieve into a smaller pan and continue to cook until this is reduced by half, about 30 minutes longer. Strain once more into an even smaller pan, and turn the heat down to very low. Continue to cook about 20 minutes longer.

At this point it is absolutely essential to maintain the stock at a low temperature and to keep a close watch on the pan so that the reduced stock does not stick to the bottom or burn. It will become thick and syrupy with bubbles on the surface. When the stock will lightly coat a metal spoon, transfer it to a heat-proof bowl, and let it stand until cool.

Cover the cooled glaze and store it in the refrigerator; it will keep there for weeks. The glaze can also be frozen, and it will keep that way for about a year.

If you decide to freeze it, the best way is to turn out the cooled glaze when it has hardened into a firm jelly, and cut it into small pieces. Arrange the small pieces on a cookie sheet and place in the freezer until frozen. Then transfer the cubes to a covered container or a plastic bag for freezer storage.

SIMPLE VEGETABLE STOCK

Simple vegetable stock, properly made, is absolutely delicious. The trick is to achieve a delicate *balance of flavors* without any single one predominating, so the ingredients must be chosen with care and with some thought as to what role each one will play in the finished broth. For example, asparagus, broccoli, cabbage, and cauliflower yield a very strong broth and should be used with discretion. Starchy vegetables such as corn, peas, or potatoes will make a broth cloudy if used in abundance. Parsnips and carrots tend to sweeten the liquid. Yet, used with a sparing touch, any of the above may be just what is needed to heighten the flavor of a broth.

Leftover vegetable trimmings can be used for added flavor. The liquid from canned vegetables, as long as it tastes good, can be used to replace a portion of the water called for in a recipe. This also applies to the reserved liquid in which vegetables have been cooked. Taste-test it first to be sure it isn't overwhelming.

The texture of simple vegetable stock is an important factor in its appeal. Because it is not made with bones, vegetable stock is likely to be short on the body and gelatinous quality that is so prized in other types of stock. Should your broth seem too thin, you can give it more substance by adding a tablespoon of agar-agar for every quart of broth. Simply sprinkle the agar-agar over the top of the simmering liquid, stir it in, and allow it to dissolve—this takes five or ten minutes.

Here are some basic tips you can use in creating the perfect simple vegetable stock:

- Trim off any bad spots or bruises on the vegetables, but do not peel them. Onion skins, especially, should be used in the broth, because they add to its color.
- Cut the vegetables into large chunks. Small pieces tend to break up and disintegrate, making the liquid cloudy.
- Before adding the liquid to the stockpot, put the cut-up vegetables in the pot, and saute them in a small amount of butter for a different, more intense flavor.

GARLIC STOCK

Because of its powerful smell and flavor, garlic inevitably provokes strong likes or dislikes, and its presence in any dish is not easily disguised. Stock, however, is one place you can use a large quantity of garlic and feel sure that it will appeal to almost everyone. The lengthy cooking process subdues the garlic's flavor and gives off an inviting aroma. A large head of garlic will subtly season two quarts of stock. The stock may be cooked down for a more vigorous flavor, or more garlic can be added. The finished broth may be savored on its own, but it is especially delightful when used as a base for tomato soups.

SOY-BASE STOCKS

Tamari soy sauce and miso are essential staples in any kitchen where nonmeat vegetable, grain, and bean soups are served frequently. They provide a rich flavor and the "beefed-up" quality generally attributed to meat stocks.

TAMARI

Real tamari soy sauce is a fermented product made from soybeans, water, whole wheat, and sea salt aged in casks for at least 18 months. The resultant liquid has no kinship with its cheaper imitators, some of which contain caramel coloring and corn syrup.

Simple preparations lend themselves best to the use of tamari soy sauce. For example, you can put one-half cup into four cups of vegetable stock (more or less according to taste), and add to that mixture a limited number of quick-cooking vegetables. The result will be a satisfying soup with the precise individual flavors still apparent. (See Index for Fresh Vegetable Tamari Soup.)

MISO

Tamari soy sauce's older relative, sometimes fermented as long as three years, is miso, a thick, pasty, soybean substance so pervasive in Japanese diets. Three distinctive types are available: *hatcho* miso (just soybeans, water, and salt), *mugi* miso (including rice), and *kome* (containing barley).

Miso broth is more than the basis for a soup; it is a valuable mineral supplement containing calcium, copper, iron, magnesium, phosphorus, potassium, and sulphur. In addition, due to the fermentation process, it possesses many bacteria which work in the intestinal tract to help our bodies assimilate food. Another bonus is that one cup of miso broth supplies four grams of protein.

Never boil miso. High heat will destroy the friendly bacteria it contains, not to mention its unique flavor. For a nourishing broth, mix one teaspoon miso with approximately one-quarter cup of hot water until the paste is dissolved. Then add three-quarters cup of hot water and drink the liquid. As a soup enhancer, dilute several tablespoons of miso in enough water to form a thin paste, then add it to a simple vegetable soup (see Index for Vegetable Miso Soup) after you have removed the pot from the heat. Many of the Sea-Vegetable Soups recipes in this book (see Index) include miso.

WHITE STOCK

White stock forms the base for cream or yogurt soups and sauces. So it must be transparent, or as nearly so as possible, to maintain the pure whiteness of the dairy products. It is prepared exactly as basic meat stock is prepared, except that only veal, chicken, or fish bones are used.

Veal and chicken bones may also be used in combination. Since a brown color is not desired, the bones are not roasted, nor are onion skins used since they tint the stock. Vegetables are added only after the bones and water have come to a boil and the broth has been skimmed.

FISH STOCK

Delicious, nutritious, and economical, this stock is made from the parts of the fish that are normally discarded. Fish heads, for example, are bargain bonanzas in this world of spiraling food costs. Because so many Americans are squeamish about fish heads, the markets usually discard them or give them away. The larger heads, like those from cod, often contain a half-pound of meat or more. It is worth cultivating your fishmonger so that he or she will save these for you. But the bones and trimmings of any lean, white-fleshed fish are desirable. Fatty or oily fish, on the other hand, yield a broth that is too strongly flavored.

Fish stock is very easy and quick to make. Just put everything into the pot at once, and cook the broth for about half an hour. Strain and reduce. Longer cooking can impart a bitter, disagreeable taste to the stock.

Because fish spoils easily, freshness is essential. Of course, if you catch your own fish, you know how fresh it is. However, when shopping in the market, it takes a bit of basic knowledge to determine whether a fish is fresh or not. The fish should look clean and be fresh smelling. Examine the head carefully. Look for eyes that are

JELLIED STOCKS

What could be more alluring in warm weather than a cold, quivering soup, an *oeuf en gelee*, or a slice of poached fish sheathed in shimmering aspic? These are but a few of the delightful specialties that can be achieved with jellied stock. Best of all, jellied stocks are so easy to make. The only tricky part is in obtaining just the right setting consistency for the purpose intended.

Jellied soup should be just firm enough to allow its being broken into soft lumps with a fork prior to serving. Aspics that are set in decorative molds must be stronger, so they will retain their shape when they are unmolded—but not so rigid as to be unpalatable. Aspics that are used for coating or decorating must be glutinous enough to hold foods in place.

Any stock can be made into a jelly by various methods. The classic and most flavorful way is, of course, to make a homemade stock with bones that give off natural gelatin. Veal knuckles, calves' feet, and chicken feet are especially suited to this purpose, but take care not to use too many of them—if you do, the stock will have a gluey consistency. Long, slow simmering (at least six hours) is essential for drawing out the gelatin from the bones. (Saw or crack them into small pieces—about two-inch lengths—to expose their inner goodness.) Be patient. If the stock is boiled too fast, the albumin and fat will incorporate themselves into the liquid and produce a broth that is thick and pasty, instead of one that is rich and clear.

The transparency of the stock is most important. To appear appetizing, a gelatin must have a brilliant sparkle. This cannot be achieved with a cloudy broth. Aesthetically and traditionally, the stock should also be clarified (see Consommes). This step is omitted only when opaque ingredients, such as yogurt, cream, or mayonnaise, are to be mixed into the gelatin base. Naturally, these would cloud the jelly, even if it had been clarified.

If you make the stock a day ahead of time and refrigerate it until it is very cold, you can easily remove all traces of fat that coagulate on the surface when the stock is chilled (degreasing), and you can determine the natural jelling consistency of the stock.

When a stock does not set as firmly as you want it to, you can add some unflavored gelatin powder. Unflavored gelatin is also useful for jelling stocks that completely lack the natural ability to set—those made without bones, for example.

To set a very liquid stock, gelatin should be used in the following proportions:

- For jellied soups (soft set): 1 tablespoon for every 3 cups of liquid
- For molded aspic (firm set): 1 tablespoon for the first 2 cups of liquid; then 1 tablespoon for each additional 1 ⅔ cups of liquid
- For coating and decorating (very firm set): 1 tablespoon for every 1 ⅔ cups of liquid

To set or firm up a loosely jelled stock, use half the above proportions of gelatin.

To use unflavored gelatin, the granules must be softened in cold liquid a few minutes before being dissolved over heat. Measure out ¼ to ½ cup of cold stock for each tablespoon of gelatin that will be used. Sprinkle the gelatin over the stock and let it stand five minutes to soften. The remaining stock may then be heated up and the softened gelatin stirred into it until dissolved, or the container holding the softened gelatin may be placed in a bath of hot water until the gelatin dissolves. The dissolved gelatin may then be stirred into the remaining stock.

It is always wise to test the setting power of a jelly after adding gelatin powder. Simply pour ½ inch of jelly into a small bowl and place it in the refrigerator until set, about 15 minutes. If the jelly is too soft, more gelatin powder should be added and the mixture retested. If the jelly is too firm, it can be diluted with a small amount of unjellied stock or water and then retested.

A third method for jelling stocks will appeal to vegetarians. By using agar-agar, a natural seaweed with jelling properties, vegetable stock can be set to any desired consistency. Then it can be served as a cold jellied soup or used as a base for a gelatin mold or as a decorative coating. Measure agar-agar in the same amounts specified above for gelatin powder. Its setting power should also be tested before use.

clear, unglazed, and bulging, and gills that are bright red or pinkish. As a freshly caught fish begins to age, its gills discolor and darken. Because of the blood that is naturally present in that area, the gills are the first part of a fish to take on off-odors or off-flavors. If your fish is over a day old, it is advisable to remove the gills before cooking.

If possible, when you buy fresh fish, buy the whole fish—head, bones, and all. The head and bones which would be thrown away otherwise can be used in your fish stock.

CONSOMMES

Consomme is, by definition, a crystal-clear, sparkling soup made from very rich stock that has been *degreased* and *clarified* with egg whites and/or crushed egg shells. The egg whites and shells act like a magnet to attract impurities and particles that normally cloud a stock.

It is best to make and strain the stock a day before using so it can chill in the refrigerator overnight. Any fat in the broth will rise to the surface and harden, and be easy to remove. Place degreased, cold stock in a large (at least 4-quart capacity), clean enamel or stainless steel pan, and slowly heat until melted (if jellied) and warm.

At this point, fold or whisk egg whites and crushed shells into the stock so that they come into contact with all the liquid in the pan. Stop whisking as soon as the stock begins to boil. The egg mixture will rise to the top of the pan, and form a crust like a dome. Lower the heat, and allow the stock to barely simmer, undisturbed, until clear (five to ten minutes). You may gently push the coagulated egg whites aside in order to check on the clarity and temperature of the stock, but do not stir it!

When done, turn off the heat. Wring out a clean dish towel in cold water, and

GLOSSARY OF SOUP TERMS

Bisque—a slightly thick, creamy soup made from shellfish.

Borscht—a soup of Russian origin made from stock, beets, and lemon juice that can be served hot or cold.

Bouillabaisse—a fish soup made of saltwater fish and shellfish with vegetables.

Bouillon—a liquid obtained by cooking meat or poultry, bones, and vegetables together. The term is used interchangeably with "broth" and "stock."

Bouquet Garni—a combination of herbs, usually parsley, thyme, and bay leaf, tied together with string and used to flavor soups. If dried herbs are used, they are wrapped in cheesecloth for easy removal.

Bourride—a fish soup, made of saltwater fish, that differs from bouillabaisse in that shellfish is omitted and a garlic mayonnaise is added.

Broth—*see* Bouillon.

Chowder—a soup made from fish or shellfish with diced potatoes, usually creamy.

Consomme—a clear soup made from clarified stock.

Court Bouillon—a fish-poaching liquid, obtained by simmering vegetables and seasonings in water to which wine or vinegar has been added.

Fond de Cuisine—a basic stock, made from meat or fish, bones, and vegetables, used as a base for soups and sauces.

Fumet—a liquid obtained by simmering the heads, bones, and skins of fish with vegetables.

Glaze—stock, bouillon, or broth that has been reduced to a very thick, syrupy liquid.

Liaison—a mixture of heavy cream or *creme fraiche* and eggs, used as a thickener for potage.

Madrilene—a consomme, flavored with tomato, which can be served hot, cold, or jellied.

Marmite—An earthenware pot used for cooking and serving soups or stews, or the soups and stews cooked in such a pot.

Mulligatawny—a thick soup, usually made with chicken stock and seasoned with curry powder.

Petite Marmite—a consomme made of a combination of beef and chicken broth and finely cut vegetables. Petite suggests the vegetables be cut very small. Marmite is the earthenware container.

Potage—a thick soup made from pureed vegetables. The word means garden soup.

Pot-au-Feu—a beef stock which can be served thick (with vegetables) or thin (as a consomme).

Potee—a soup containing pork and vegetables, especially cabbage and potatoes, usually cooked in an earthenware pot.

Reduce—to cook down liquid for more concentrated essence.

Roux—a cooked mixture of butter or fat and flour used to thicken soups.

Simmer—to cook gently just below the boiling point.

Stock—*see* Bouillon.

Vichyssoise—a cold, creamy soup made with potatoes and leeks.

arrange it in a large strainer placed over a deep bowl. Holding the egg-white crust back with a spoon, carefully strain the clarified stock into the bowl. Do not wring out the cloth into the stock.

The correct color of a well-made consomme is light amber. It should be so clear that if there were small print at the bottom of the soup plates it would be legible.

Although not difficult, the consomme process requires careful attention when clarifying and straining. Nevertheless, consommes are certainly worth the effort, because they are so delicious, healthful, and low in calories. They may be served piping hot and totally clear or embellished with various garnishes. A consomme will usually jell when chilled (see Jellied Stocks, above) and may be used as an aspic or served as a cold gelatin soup. In this last case, set off its sparkling beauty by serving it in crystal or glass, rather than china.

The jellied soups are delightful topped with plain yogurt and snipped chives or scallions. Hot consommes should be simply garnished with foods that lend texture, color, or flavor, such as rice, delicate pastas, slivered vegetables, or croutons. Cook these garnishes separately in a small amount of consomme and then add them to the hot consomme in the serving bowl. Serve croutons at the table to insure their being added at the last minute so that they will remain crisp.

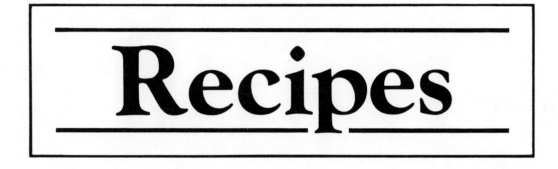

Recipes

Stocks

THE LEGEND OF STONE SOUP

Because of a secret they learned from Stone Soup, the people of one village were delivered from a fear—that of sharing what they had.

The tale begins with three hungry, tired peddlers trudging along a road. As they neared a certain village, townsmen heard of their coming—these were strangers.

Suspecting the hunger of the peddlers and fearing a ravage of what stores they had been able to harvest, the villagers ran to hide their barley, milk, carrots, cabbages, potatoes, and meat.

All they had was hidden.

The peddlers knocked on the doors of the peasants' houses, only to be answered with, "A poor harvest this year." "Our beds are full." "No extra grain." "Too many mouths to feed."

The peddlers talked together and announced their intentions: STONE SOUP! STONE SOUP!

Stone Soup? What was this?

Curiosity had been aroused. The peddlers set about to woo the villagers.

A large iron pot was brought, water was poured into it, and three stones were dropped to the bottom.

"But what is soup without vegetables?" exclaimed the villagers. "What about meat?" "A good idea," answered the peddlers. Reactions came rapidly. The villagers began to uncover hidden wealth; each gave of what he had. A warm, hearty brew soon bubbled above the fire.

When the tables were spread the entire village sat down to a feast—from stones!

That night no one went to bed hungry and the land was no longer strange.

CRYSTAL CLEAR CONSOMME

Yields 6 cups

2 pounds shin beef, cut into chunks
2 pig's feet
12 cups water
2 large unpeeled onions, halved
3 carrots, halved
3 celery stalks, halved
1 leek, halved
10 peppercorns
8 whole cloves
1 bay leaf
6 sprigs parsley
1 sprig thyme
2 egg whites, lightly beaten
2 egg shells, wiped clean and crushed

1. Place all the ingredients, except the egg whites and shells, in a 6-quart soup pot. Bring to a boil, lower heat, and simmer very gently, uncovered, 6 hours. Skim the surface if a scum develops.

2. Soak a 3-layer piece of cheesecloth in cold water and wring it out. Strain the broth through the cheesecloth into another large, clean pot.

3. Add the egg whites and crushed shells, and whisk rapidly until the broth comes to a boil. Stop whisking, lower the heat, and simmer 30 minutes so that the egg whites form a crust at the top of the soup. Be careful not to break this crust.

4. Wring out a clean dish towel in cold water and arrange the cloth over a strainer. Holding back the crust with a spoon, pour the broth through the cloth into a clean pot. Reheat before serving.

FISH STOCK

Yields about 6 cups

2 pounds fish heads, backs, and bones
6 cups water
juice of 1 large lemon
2 large onions, quartered
3 celery stalks, quartered
3 carrots, quartered
1 bay leaf
10 peppercorns
3 sprigs parsley
1 sprig thyme

1. Place all ingredients in a 5-quart soup pot. Bring to a boil, lower heat, and simmer, uncovered, 30 minutes. Skim the surface if necessary.

2. Soak a 3-layer piece of cheesecloth in cold water and wring it out. Strain the broth through the cheesecloth into another large, clean pot.

3. Cool the strained broth, and refrigerate or freeze until needed. If large fish heads are used, remove the meat to use in fish soup or salad.

Note: A richer stock may be made by increasing the cooking time.

Dieters, Dampen Your Appetite with Hot Soup!

Chicken soup will do it—help dieters to diet, that is—but any hot soup will have the same effect. Henry Jordan, M.D., of the University of Pennsylvania, ran a ten-week study involving 10,000 subjects and observed that eating soup at the outset of a meal slows rapid eating and blunts appetite before excessive food is consumed. He concludes that a soup-laden diet can change eating habits and lead to weight loss.

VEAL STOCK

Yields 6 cups

1 pound beef
1 pound raw chicken parts, such as giblets, necks
1 or 2 carcasses of roasted chicken (optional)
1 pound marrow bones, cracked
3 pounds veal knuckles, cracked
16 cups water
2 onions, each stuck with one clove
3 garlic cloves
3 carrots, thickly sliced
3 leeks (white part only), thickly sliced
2 celery stalks with leaves, coarsely chopped

Bouquet Garni (to be tied in cheesecloth)

3 sprigs parsley
2 sprigs thyme
1 bay leaf
2 peppercorns

1. Place the meat and bones in a roasting pan and roast in a 450°F oven 10 to 15 minutes until brown. Turn them occasionally to ensure even browning. Remove the chicken parts and bones before the beef and veal (as soon as they are browned).

2. Transfer all meat and bones to an 8-quart soup pot and cover with the water. Bring to a boil over moderate heat and turn down the heat to a simmer. Skim off any scum that forms on the surface. Add a tablespoon of cold water and continue to skim off any further scum as it rises.

3. Add the remaining ingredients and the bouquet garni. Simmer gently, uncovered, 3½ hours.

4. Cool stock and skim off the fat. Remove the meat if it is a good cut which you intend to serve separately, and strain the stock.

BEEF STOCK

Yields 4 quarts

3 pounds shin beef, cut into chunks
5 large onions, halved
10 medium-size carrots
8 medium-size tomatoes, quartered
16 cups water
½ pound mushrooms
pepper to taste

1. Combine all ingredients in a 6- to 8-quart soup pot. Bring to a boil, reduce heat to low, cover, and simmer 2 hours.

2. Let sit 30 minutes and then strain. Skim the fat off the top of the liquid.

Talk about Powerful!

Garlic was popular everywhere in the Old World, except on board ship. Plutarch was typical of the educated ancients who believed that a whiff of garlic would overcome the magnetism in a lodestone, a vital aid in navigation.

BASIC BROWN STOCK

Yields about 2 quarts

2 pounds meaty beef bones, sawed into small pieces
2 pounds veal shanks, sawed into small pieces
1 pound chicken wings
3 unpeeled onions, quartered
2 carrots, cut into 1-inch pieces
20 cups water
5 sprigs parsley
2 sprigs thyme
1 leek, cut into 1-inch pieces
1 celery stalk, cut into 1-inch pieces

1. Preheat oven to 425°F. Spread the bones, shanks, and wings in a shallow 18 × 12-inch roasting pan. Roast until brown (about 1 hour). Turn them occasionally to promote even cooking. During the last 30 minutes of cooking, add the onions and carrots.

2. Transfer bones and vegetables to a 5-quart soup pot. Add 2 cups of the water to the roasting pan and deglaze it over high heat. Scrape up the brown bits. Add the liquid to the stockpot with the parsley, thyme, leek, celery, and remaining water.

3. Bring to a boil, lower heat, and simmer very gently, uncovered or partially covered, 6 hours. Skim off any surface froth that accumulates during the first 30 minutes of simmering.

4. Strain the stock through a fine sieve. Cool it quickly and then chill it in the refrigerator. Remove the fat that forms on the surface of the cold stock.

VEGETABLE STOCK

Yields 4 quarts

5 large onions, halved
10 medium-size carrots
8 medium-size tomatoes, quartered
1 garlic clove, minced
5 celery stalks
1 bunch parsley
16 cups water

1. Combine ingredients in a 6- to 8-quart soup pot. Bring to a boil, reduce heat to low, cover, and simmer 1 hour.

2. Let sit 30 minutes and then strain. Skim any scum that may form.

GARLIC STOCK

Yields 3 quarts

16 cups water
24 unpeeled garlic cloves, crushed
4 medium-size carrots, halved
4 celery stalks, halved
2 large onions, quartered
2 turnips, quartered
2 sprigs parsley

Combine all ingredients in a 4-quart soup pot. Bring to a boil, lower heat, cover, and simmer 1 hour. Strain.

CHICKEN, DUCK, OR
TURKEY CARCASS STOCK

Yields 5½ to 6 cups

 cooked or uncooked carcass of
  chicken, duck, or turkey,
  broken apart
1 pound veal bones, sawed into
 2-inch pieces
12 cups water
1 large, unpeeled onion, halved,
 each half stuck with 1 clove
1 carrot
1 celery stalk
1 bay leaf
6 sprigs parsley
½ teaspoon dried thyme

1. Place the carcass and veal bone pieces in an 8-quart soup pot with the water. Bring to a boil, lower heat, and skim off the scum that rises to the surface.

2. Add the remaining ingredients and simmer very gently 6 hours.

3. Strain the stock through a fine sieve. Cool it quickly and refrigerate. When cold, remove the surface fat.

CHICKEN STOCK

Yields about 4 quarts

16 cups water
¼ pound mushrooms
2½ pounds chicken wings
6 or 7 carrots, halved
5 celery stalks with leaves
5 medium-size onions, quartered
2 bay leaves
3 sprigs parsley
6 peppercorns

1. Combine all ingredients in a 5-quart soup pot. Bring to a boil and remove scum. Lower heat, cover, and simmer 2 to 3 hours. Stir occasionally.

2. Cool slightly, strain, and refrigerate, then skim congealed fat.

Fruit Soups

Serving a cold soup—perhaps vichyssoise or a fruit soup—is a mark of elegance and sophistication these days. It seems fitting that, according to culinary tradition, the trend got its start in the French court of Louis XIV. But the idea was not born to enhance the glory of France or to promote la belle cuisine. Quite simply, the king's chef was forced to invent chilled soups to keep his job.

Ever-fearful of being poisoned, the Sun King insisted that his food be tasted by several tasters, not just one, before it touched the royal palate. Naturally, hot soup cooled down in the process, often arriving before the king stone cold. His majesty was not amused. The clever Frenchman in the kitchen came up with the perfect answer; he created soups that were intended to be served cold and chilled soups became the sensation of the court.

Surely the premier cold soup, vichyssoise, must have been one of those early creations. Mais non. The first bowl of vichyssoise ever served came out of New York's Ritz Carlton Hotel at the turn of the century. Its creator, Chef Louis Diat, may have drawn on his French heritage for inspiration, but that famous "French" dish, vichyssoise, is technically classified as an American soup!

APPLE VICHYSSOISE

Serves 6

¼ cup butter
1 cup finely chopped leeks, white part only
3 large tart apples, peeled and coarsely chopped
¼ teaspoon curry powder
2 medium-size potatoes, peeled and diced
4 cups Chicken Stock (see Index)
2 cups buttermilk
2 tablespoons finely chopped celery leaves

1. Melt the butter in a 4-quart soup pot. Add the leeks and saute them on low heat until limp. Stir in the apples, curry powder, and potatoes. Cook 5 minutes longer on medium heat.

2. Add the chicken stock, bring to a boil, lower heat, cover, and simmer until potatoes are tender (about 20 minutes). Cool slightly.

3. In a blender container, puree soup in small batches until smooth. Return to pot and stir in the buttermilk. Cover and chill until serving time.

4. Stir soup well before serving. Garnish with celery leaves.

25

BANANA COCONUT SOUP

Serves 6

2 tablespoons butter
1 large onion, finely chopped
2 cups Chicken Stock (see Index)
¾ cup shredded fresh coconut
2 medium-size ripe bananas,
   sliced into 1-inch pieces
3½ cups milk
6 small sprigs mint

1. Melt the butter in a 4-quart soup pot. Add the onion, cover with a piece of wax paper, and steam on low heat until the onion is transparent. Remove the wax paper. Add the stock and coconut, bring to a boil, lower heat, and simmer 5 minutes. Cool slightly.

2. Place banana pieces in a blender container. Puree the bananas while gradually pouring in the soup mixture. Blend until smooth.

3. Return mixture to the pot and stir in the milk. To serve hot, bring to a boil, lower heat, and simmer 5 minutes. Or chill without further cooking and serve cold.

4. Garnish each portion with a small mint sprig.

CASHEW, GRAPE, AND PEAR SOUP

Serves 6

2 tablespoons butter
1 Bermuda onion, coarsely
   chopped
3 pears, diced
1 teaspoon curry powder
4 cups Chicken Stock (see Index)
1 cup cottage cheese
1 cup milk
¾ cup raw cashews
1 cup seedless green grapes

1. Melt the butter in a 3-quart soup pot. Add the onion and saute until limp but not brown. Add pears to the pot and stir to coat with the butter and onion. Sprinkle the curry powder over the onions and pears and cook 1 minute. Add the stock, bring to a boil, lower heat, cover, and simmer 10 minutes. Cool slightly.

2. Process the cottage cheese and milk in a blender until smooth. Transfer to a large bowl. Puree the pear soup mixture in 2 batches in the blender. Add this puree to the cottage cheese mixture.

3. Work the soup mixture through a sieve into another large bowl. Chill until serving time.

4. Divide the cashews and grapes among 6 serving bowls. Ladle the chilled soup over the nuts and fruit.

Fruit for Cholesterol Control

Pectin is believed to be effective in lowering cholesterol counts in humans by as much as 20 percent. The amount required to do this is 10 to 15 grams daily—the amount in three to six whole apples. Bananas, cherries, grapes, oranges, peaches, pineapples, raspberries, and tomatoes are also good sources.

PLUM SOUP

Serves 6

1 pound Italian prune plums,
  stems removed
5 cups water
1 tablespoon cornstarch
2 tablespoons lemon juice
1 tablespoon grated orange rind
½ cup honey or to taste
Garnish
 2 cups plain yogurt
cinnamon

1. Wash plums, then place them in a 3-quart soup pot with the water. Bring to a boil, lower heat, cover, and simmer until tender (about 30 minutes).

2. Remove fruit from liquid with a slotted spoon. Discard pits and puree fruit through a food mill.

3. Combine cornstarch and lemon juice. Stir to form a smooth paste. Whisk paste into the cooking liquid. Add the orange rind. Return liquid to a boil while constantly stirring, and cook 5 minutes longer. Stir in the honey and the fruit puree.

4. Serve soup hot or cold. Spoon ⅓ cup yogurt on top of each portion and sprinkle lightly with cinnamon before serving.

TOMATO ORANGE SOUP

Serves 6

2 tablespoons butter
1 medium-size onion, coarsely
  chopped
1 garlic clove, minced
3 cups Chicken Stock (see Index)
6 medium-size tomatoes,
  quartered
1 celery stalk, cut into 1-inch
  pieces
1 tablespoon cornstarch
½ cup cold water
2 tablespoons grated orange rind
¼ teaspoon cardamom
1½ cups orange juice
Garnish
snippets of celery leaves
 1 cup plain yogurt

1. Melt the butter in a 5-quart soup pot. Add the onion and saute until transparent. Add the garlic and cook 1 minute longer. Add the chicken stock, tomatoes, and celery. Bring to a boil, lower heat, partially cover, and simmer gently 20 minutes. Press through a food mill or sieve; return to pot.

2. Mix the cornstarch with the water. Stir the cornstarch mixture, orange rind, and cardamom into the soup. Cook 5 minutes longer. Remove from heat and cool slightly.

3. Stir in the orange juice, cover, and chill until serving.

4. Garnish with celery leaves and dollops of yogurt.

FRESH FRUIT AND YOGURT SOUP

Serves 6

1 green, tart apple, cut into ½-inch cubes
2 pears, cut into ½-inch cubes
3 peaches, cut into ½-inch cubes
¼ cup lemon juice
1 cup strawberries, hulled and sliced
3 cups water
2 tablespoons honey
2 cups freshly squeezed orange juice (6 or 7 oranges)
2 tablespoons arrowroot
1 cup plain yogurt
½ teaspoon cardamom
6 sprigs mint or 6 whole strawberries

1. Sprinkle the apple, pears, and peaches with lemon juice to prevent discoloration. Add the strawberries.

2. In a 2-quart soup pot, mix water and honey together and bring mixture to a boil; add fruit and orange juice and reduce heat. Simmer 3 minutes.

3. Mix arrowroot with enough water to dilute into a thin paste and slowly add to soup. Simmer 3 minutes more. Remove from heat, cool, and add yogurt and cardamom.

4. Chill soup until ice-cold. As a garnish, freeze a small sprig of mint in an ice cube and float it on top of soup, or decorate with a sprig of mint or a whole strawberry.

Hot soup at table is very vulgar; it either leads to an unseemly mode of taking it, or keeps people waiting too long whilst it cools. Soup should be brought to table only moderately warm.

Charles Day, Hints of Etiquette, *1844*

INDIAN APPLE SOUP

Serves 6

2 tablespoons butter
2 medium onions, thinly sliced
1 tablespoon curry powder
4 cups Chicken Stock (see Index)
4 red, crisp apples, cut into ½-inch cubes
½ teaspoon cloves
½ teaspoon mace
white pepper to taste
2 cups light cream

Garnish
1 red apple, diced
3 tablespoons sliced or slivered almonds, toasted
2 tablespoons minced parsley or coriander leaves

1. Melt the butter in a 5-quart soup pot and add the sliced onions. Stir and sprinkle with curry powder. Saute on low heat 5 minutes, stirring occasionally.

2. Add stock to pot. Cover, bring to a boil, lower heat, and simmer 5 minutes. Add apples, cloves, mace, and pepper; cover and simmer 20 minutes.

3. Puree a few batches at a time in a blender. Let cool slightly, stir in cream, and chill.

4. Toss all garnish ingredients together.

5. Serve soup ice-cold. Pass garnish to be sprinkled over soup to taste.

PRUNE SOUP

Serves 6

1 orange
5 cups water
1 pound pitted prunes
1 apple, cored and quartered
¼ teaspoon cinnamon
¼ teaspoon cloves
1 cup plain yogurt

1. Squeeze the orange, reserving the juice. Cut the rind into julienne strips. Bring the water to a boil in a 3-quart soup pot and blanch the strips in the boiling water 1 minute. Remove the strips with a slotted spoon (reserve the water), and refresh them under cold running water. Dry them on a paper towel, and chill them in the refrigerator until ready for use.

2. Add the prunes and the apple to the boiling water. Lower the heat, cover, and simmer until tender (about 30 minutes). Add the cinnamon and cloves. Cool slightly. Puree in a food mill. Return puree to pot.

3. Stir the reserved juice and the yogurt into the soup. Chill.

4. Serve soup cold, sprinkled with the orange strips.

The Ann Ar Soup Bowl

On a crisp, cold day in Pennsylvania, snow is falling. Inside the warm Ann Ar Soup Bowl kitchen, David is juicing watermelon and squeezing oranges. Fruit soup in January? "Why not?" is David's response. "I looked through my cookbooks for fruit soup recipes; they were all cold. Finally I took a little from one, a little from another, and decided to try a warm version." Before making a few, final, late-afternoon calls to wholesalers, he pours the fruit juices into a pot, drops a small cheesecloth bag filled with "sweet" spices and herbs into the liquid, and turns the heat on simmer.

Hot fruit soup in January is not the only anomaly at the Ann Ar Soup Bowl. Here we find a gourmet, health-oriented restaurant lodged in a modest former carriage house. The shingle outside suggests that soup is the main fare, and yet creative sandwiches, attractive salads, homemade breads, and rich international desserts round out an impressive menu. Here also is a rather unique gathering of restaurant folk—people who all have a real flair for food.

Folks with a Flair

David Garcia, in the dual role of kitchen manager-head cook, orders the special ingredients and plans the menus that distinguish the Ann Ar Soup Bowl from traditional dining places. He also puts the finishing touches on the regularly served foods, creates new dishes, and guides budding cooks. This Mexican-American approaches his favorite pastime—making music—with some of the same movements he uses to shake a salad dressing or pound nuts. With a wide variety of Latin percussion instruments—gourds, moroccas, claves, and cabasas—he creates rhythms to accompany favorite records or the music of Latin friends who play professionally.

Susan Goldman, second cook, is a voice student. As a cook "on the road" for the folk singer Donovan and the rock group Yes she began to develop her vegetarian style. Two of her favorites (and ours) incorporate some of her "tricks":

David Garcia ladles a bowl of his special soup.

White Bean Soup Supreme and Chinese Hot and Sour Soup are both quick, simple, nonmeat preparations. What distinguishes them is the basic Garlic Broth on which I rely heavily. The finale-garnish in the bean soup is Herb Butter, one that changes its taste according to the season or my whims.

Bruce White, the salad man, is a small-magazine publisher, musician, poet, and lyricist. Carole Fredricks, the Ann Ar Soup Bowl's baker and dessert maker par excellence, a former theater major, dances and acts. The staff occasionally persuades her to leave her love affair with baking long enough to prepare Asian Fish Soup, "an unusual meal that people either love from the start or learn to love."

Two more vital members of this talented coterie are Anna Rodale, owner, and

Bruce White displays the raw materials for a perfect salad.

Ruth Kingsley, general manager. Mrs. Rodale is an art collector and publisher of a small newspaper. She conceived the idea for this high-quality, in-town restaurant. Ruth is a former high school art teacher. She so smoothly fuses the many different business elements that diners assume their comfort is achieved effortlessly. Ruth shares an early "behind the scenes" story:

> *We sponsored an ethnic soup contest to attract people and to make acquaintance with superior cooks and their recipes. With all good intentions, we planned the event for the day before our grand opening. In our 20-by-20-foot front room, we entertained 36 entrants, judges from the cooking school, and the press. We served refreshments, posed for pictures, and offered prizes to the winners. Meanwhile, in the kitchen, the hectic last-minute preparations were still going on. Basically we just worked right through until the doors opened the next day. We look back now and laugh and marvel at our accomplishment.*

The staff of the Ann Ar Soup Bowl in Allentown, Pennsylvania, is ready and willing to serve.

Sensational Soups

Three days after the snow, we return to lunch at the Soup Bowl. Other patrons are talking about soups for which they come here regularly. How is it, we wonder, that a certain group can so successfully exalt a particular food. Quality certainly plays its part. Fresh ingredients—not canned or frozen—and natural spring water go into these soups. This establishment uses organic products—meat, dairy, poultry, and produce—whenever they are available. During the summer most of these arrive from farms within a ten-mile radius. The richness of the staff is certainly the other major force behind the restaurant's magnetism. These creative, committed people enjoy doing a job artfully; they enjoy crafting and offering superb food.

GARLIC BROTH

Yields 6 to 7 cups

8 *large potatoes*
1 *bulb garlic*
2 *tablespoons olive oil*
1 *large onion, quartered*
2 *medium-size carrots, cut into large pieces*
1 *celery stalk, cut into large pieces*
8 *cups water*
few sprigs parsley
few sprigs thyme
few gratings nutmeg
1 *bay leaf*
pepper to taste
1 *to 2 tablespoons lemon juice*
dash hot pepper sauce (optional)

1. Wash potatoes thoroughly. Peel off skins and put them into a 4-quart soup pot. (Reserve potatoes for another use.)
2. Separate garlic cloves from bulb. Smash each with the flat of a large knife blade, then saute them 2 minutes in oil. (Do not be concerned with removing the skins.) Transfer garlic to soup pot.
3. Add onion, carrots, celery, water, parsley, thyme, nutmeg, bay leaf, and pepper to soup pot. Simmer about 1½ hours.
4. Strain vegetables from broth. Correct seasonings. Add lemon juice and hot pepper sauce, if used.

ASIAN FISH SOUP

Serves 6

1 *pound firm, lean fish fillets*
10 *cups Fish Stock (see Index)*
2 *bay leaves*
10 *peppercorns*
meat from 1 medium-size coconut, grated
3 *tablespoons butter*
2 *onions, finely chopped*
2 *garlic cloves, pressed*
5 *¼-inch-thick slices ginger root*
½ *teaspoon chili powder*
1 *tablespoon ground coriander seeds*
1 *teaspoon ground cumin*
1 *teaspoon pepper*
¼ *cup ground almonds*
2 *tablespoons flour*
2½ *cups cooked bulgur*
¾ *cup minced green pepper*

1. Cut fish into chunks. Put fish, stock, bay leaves, and peppercorns into an 8-quart soup pot and bring to a boil. Cover and simmer 30 minutes. Remove fish from pot and put it aside to cool. Continue to simmer stock, uncovered, until it is reduced to about 7 cups. Strain stock and discard flavorings. Add coconut.
2. Melt butter in skillet. Saute the onions and garlic until golden. Stir in spices and cook 5 minutes. Add the almonds and flour, and stir while cooking another minute. Gradually whisk in enough stock to form a thin paste. Bring to a boil and turn down to cook at low heat 2 minutes. Stir often. Add this roux to the soup pot.
3. Flake fish and add it to stock. Simmer, uncovered, 15 minutes longer.
4. Serve soup hot over bulgur. Garnish with a sprinkling of green pepper to add color.

CHINESE HOT AND SOUR SOUP

Serves 6

2 *ounces dried, black shiitake mushrooms*
2 *cups hot water*
2 *cups thinly sliced mushrooms*
1 *pound tofu*
3 *tablespoons corn oil*
3 *cups sliced and slivered Chinese cabbage*
1½ *tablespoons tamari soy sauce*
2 *tablespoons red wine vinegar*
1 *teaspoon pepper*
1 *teaspoon chili-pepper oil**
2 *cups Garlic Broth (see recipe in this section) or water*
2 *tablespoons cornstarch*
3 *tablespoons cold water*
1 *tablespoon dark sesame oil*
2 *eggs, beaten well*
4 *scallions, thinly sliced*

1. Soak the shiitake mushrooms in water until soft (about 20 minutes). Drain and reserve the liquid. Cut away the hard stems and slice thin.
2. Thinly slice the tofu and then cut into slivers.
3. Heat a wok or soup pot on high heat. Swirl in the oil and warm it. Stir in both types of mushrooms and toss quickly about 2 minutes.
4. Stir in the cabbage, tamari, vinegar, pepper, and chili-pepper oil.
5. Add the reserved liquid from the mushrooms, the broth, and the tofu.
6. Bring to a boil and simmer 3 minutes.
7. Mix the cornstarch with the water and sesame oil. Add to the mushroom-cabbage mixture and simmer until slightly thickened.
8. Drizzle in the beaten eggs while stirring.
9. Stir in the scallions.

*Available in stores stocking Chinese groceries and in specialty stores.

WHITE BEAN SOUP SUPREME WITH HERB BUTTER

Serves 6 to 8

2 *cups dried white beans, rinsed and drained*
6 *cups Garlic Broth (see recipe in this section)*
2 *medium-size onions, coarsely chopped*
2 *garlic cloves, minced*
3 *tablespoons oil or butter*
1 *bay leaf*
1 *teaspoon cayenne pepper*
2 *egg yolks, beaten*
1 *cup milk*
4 *to 6 tablespoons Herb Butter (see recipe below)*
6 *tablespoons lemon juice*
2 *tablespoons minced parsley*

1. Soak beans in broth in a 5-quart soup pot. Cover and place in the refrigerator overnight.
2. The next day, saute onions and garlic in oil until transparent. Add to beans and broth and bring to a boil. Add bay leaf and cayenne. Reduce heat and simmer until beans are tender (1 to 2 hours).
3. Drain beans. Return liquid to pot. Puree beans until smooth in a blender or food processor (use some bean liquid if necessary to create proper consistency). Pour puree into stock and put on heat to warm.
4. Add yolks to milk. Ladle several large spoonfuls of stock into yolk mixture. Pour mixture back into pot. Mix in herb butter and lemon juice, and gently warm only until butter melts in liquid. Adjust seasonings to taste. Garnish with parsley.

HERB BUTTER

Yields 1 cup

½ *pound butter, softened*
3 *garlic cloves, minced*
1 *scallion, minced, or 1 tablespoon minced chives*
1 *tablespoon minced parsley*
1 *teaspoon minced dillweed*

Blend all ingredients in a food processor, blender, or by hand just until all seasonings are evenly distributed.

FRUIT SOUP

Serves 6 to 8

flesh from 1 medium-size watermelon
 (seeds removed), juiced
juice of 10 oranges
 1 cinnamon stick, broken into several
 pieces
¼ teaspoon allspice
seeds from 4 cardamom pods
¼ cup coarsely chopped fresh or dried
 apricots*
¾ pound mixed fresh fruit (such as
 apples, bananas, pears, pineapple),
 cored, peeled, and chopped into
 ⅜-inch pieces
½ cup dark raisins
¼ cup golden raisins
½ pound fresh small berries (such as
 strawberries, blueberries,
 raspberries)
⅓ cup honey
⅓ cup lemon juice
Garnish
 8 thin fresh pineapple rings
¾ cup sour cream
freshly grated nutmeg

*Dried apricots will make a sweeter puree.

1. Bring fruit juice to a boil in a 4-quart soup pot. Turn heat to simmer and add seasonings tied in a small piece of cheesecloth. Continue heating liquid, covered, 45 minutes.

2. Meanwhile, place apricots in a small saucepan with just enough water to cover. Bring liquid to a boil, turn down to simmer, and cook until fruit is very soft (20 to 30 minutes). Cool slightly, then turn contents into a blender container and puree. Set aside.

3. Add fruit and raisins to simmering fruit juice during last 15 minutes of cooking time. Add berries during last 5 minutes.

4. Remove cheesecloth from fruit stock. Add honey, apricot puree, and lemon juice and stir well. Garnish individual portions with a pineapple ring, a dollop of sour cream, and a sprinkling of nutmeg.

Grain and Legume Soups

CHICK-PEA BLENDER SOUP

Serves 6 to 8

2 large onions, finely chopped
3 garlic cloves, minced
1 medium-size sweet green pepper, finely chopped
1 small hot green pepper, finely chopped (optional)
1 medium-size carrot, finely chopped
¼ cup minced coriander leaves
½ cup sesame oil
1 tablespoon ground cumin
1 teaspoon cayenne pepper
1 teaspoon dried thyme
4 cups well-cooked chick-peas
1 cup tahini
¾ cup lemon juice
about 5 cups chick-pea cooking water

Garnish
½ cup minced scallions
1 cup finely chopped tomatoes
1 cup finely chopped cucumbers
1½ cups Garlic Croutons (see Index)

1. Saute onions, garlic, peppers, carrot, and coriander in ¼ cup of the oil until vegetables are tender. Add cumin, cayenne, and thyme and saute 1 minute longer.

2. Incorporate sauteed vegetables into chick-peas. Toss tahini, lemon juice, and remaining oil through the mixture.

3. In small batches, blend chick-pea mixture with enough cooking water to create a soft ice-cream-like consistency.

4. Serve the soup either heated or slightly chilled. Pass bowls of each garnish at the table.

GARBANZO SOUP

Serves 6

1 cup dried chick-peas, rinsed and soaked overnight in water to cover
3 tablespoons olive oil
1 large onion, coarsely chopped
1 celery stalk, finely chopped
2 garlic cloves, minced
2 tomatoes, coarsely chopped
5 cups Chicken Stock (see Index)
½ small head cabbage, shredded
2 tablespoons finely chopped parsley

1. Drain the chick-peas, place them in a 3-quart soup pot, and cover with fresh water by 1 inch. Bring to a boil, lower heat, cover, and simmer 1 hour. Drain and set aside in another container.

2. Heat the oil in the same soup pot. Add the onion and celery and saute 5 minutes. Stir in the garlic and cook 1 minute longer. Stir in the tomatoes; cook 5 minutes. Add the chick-peas and stock. Bring to a boil, lower heat, cover, and simmer 30 minutes.

3. Add the cabbage and parsley to the soup and cook 15 minutes longer. Serve hot.

Mint——for That Elusive Magic

Mint was (perhaps still is) the aphrodisiac of choice among sophisticated Arabs and Frenchmen. The English thought it worked best to encourage basic lust when mixed with vinegar. The insatiable Queen of Sheba had a daily elixir d'amour *made of crushed mint blended with cabbage, carrot, and potato juices.*

FRESH HERBED GREEN PEA SOUP

Serves 6

4 cups shelled peas (about 4 pounds)
1 thin leek or 8 scallions, coarsely chopped
½ cup Chicken Stock (see Index)
1 tablespoon butter
¼ teaspoon white pepper
3 sprigs mint or ½ teaspoon dried
1 fresh basil leaf or ¼ teaspoon dried
3 sprigs marjoram or ½ teaspoon dried
2 sprigs thyme or ¼ teaspoon dried
4 cups milk, warmed
6 sprigs mint

1. Combine peas, leek, stock, butter, and pepper in a 5-quart soup pot. Stir and cook on medium heat 5 minutes until butter melts and peas soften slightly.

2. Add the fresh herbs, tied with string for easy removal (or sprinkle the dried herbs over the peas) and add 2 cups of the milk. Cook 2 minutes.

3. Remove any fresh herbs. Then puree in several small batches in a blender. Return to pot and add the rest of the milk. Heat over low heat. (Do not boil or soup will curdle.)

4. Add additional seasonings if necessary. Garnish each serving with a sprig of mint.

BREAD SOUP

Serves 6

8 cups Beef Stock (see Index)
2 scallions, finely sliced
6 slices day-old rye or whole wheat bread
3 eggs
1 tablespoon tamari soy sauce
1 tablespoon grated onions
6 tablespoons butter
½ cup olive oil
1 garlic clove
¼ cup minced parsley

1. Place the stock and scallions in a 4-quart soup pot. Bring to a boil, lower heat, and simmer gently while preparing the remaining ingredients.

2. Quarter each slice of bread. Break the eggs into a shallow bowl and add the tamari and onion. Beat with a fork until mixed.

3. Melt the butter with the oil in a large skillet. Add the garlic and cook until it just begins to sizzle. Remove the garlic. Dip the bread quarters into the egg mixture, drain slightly, and fry until golden. Turn once. (Depending on the size of your skillet, this will have to be done in 2 or 3 batches.)

4. Place half the bread pieces in a warmed soup tureen or in individual warmed bowls. Sprinkle with the parsley and ladle the hot stock over the bread. Serve the remaining bread on the side.

ITALIAN LIMA BEAN SOUP

Serves 6 to 8

7 cups Beef Stock (see Index)
1 medium-size potato, diced
1 pound Italian plum tomatoes, coarsely chopped
4 cups shelled lima beans (about 4 pounds)
½ pound green beans, cut into 1-inch pieces
1½ pounds unpeeled zucchini, quartered lengthwise and cut into ½-inch slices
½ teaspoon pepper
¼ teaspoon white pepper
⅓ cup small whole wheat elbow macaroni
2 garlic cloves
12 fresh basil leaves or 3 teaspoons dried
4 sprigs parsley
1 tablespoon ground walnuts
2 tablespoons olive oil
½ cup grated Parmesan cheese

1. Heat stock in a 5-quart soup pot. Add potato and tomatoes. Bring to a boil, lower heat, cover, and simmer 10 minutes.

2. Add lima beans and green beans to liquid. Cover and cook 10 minutes more.

3. Add zucchini, pepper, and macaroni to liquid. Cover and cook until macaroni is tender (about 10 minutes).

4. In a blender or food processor, blend garlic, basil, parsley, and walnuts together. Gradually add the oil. If using a blender, add ½ cup of clear soup from the pot to thin out the basil sauce and allow it to blend more easily. Add this sauce to the soup just before serving. Stir once and serve hot with Parmesan cheese sprinkled on top.

LIMA BEAN SOUP

Serves 6

2 cups dried lima beans, rinsed and soaked overnight in water to cover
6 cups Vegetable Stock (see Index) or water
3 tablespoons olive oil
1 large onion, coarsely chopped
1 cup coarsely chopped celery
2 garlic cloves, minced
1 large potato, diced
2 cups tomato juice
2 tablespoons minced parsley
2 tablespoons minced basil
1½ cups grated cheddar cheese

1. Drain lima beans. Place stock in a 4-quart soup pot and bring to a boil. Add lima beans, lower heat, cover, and simmer 1½ hours.

2. Heat the oil in a skillet. Add the onion and celery and saute until softened. Add the garlic and cook 1 minute longer. Transfer mixture to the soup pot.

3. Add the potato and tomato juice to the soup pot. Return to a boil, lower heat, cover, and simmer 25 minutes longer. Stir in the parsley and basil. Simmer 5 minutes.

4. Just before serving, stir in the cheese. Ladle into warm bowls.

PINTO BEAN AND SAUSAGE SOUP

Serves 6

1½ cups dried pinto beans, rinsed and soaked overnight in water to cover
1 tablespoon butter
3 cooked homemade sausages, uncured (about ¾ pound)
1 medium-size onion, finely chopped
2 celery stalks, finely chopped
1 garlic clove, minced
4 cups Beef Stock (see Index)
1 cup tomato juice
3 turnips, diced
2 carrots, diced
½ teaspoon dried oregano
2 tablespoons finely chopped parsley

1. Drain the beans and set aside.

2. Melt the butter in a small skillet. Add the sausages and saute until lightly browned on all sides. Remove from pan and set aside. Add the onion and celery and saute 3 minutes. Add the garlic, cook 1 minute longer, then transfer to a 3-quart soup pot.

3. Add the pinto beans, stock, and tomato juice. Bring to a boil, lower heat, cover, and simmer 1 hour and 15 minutes.

4. When the sausages are cool enough to handle, cut them into ⅜-inch slices, cover, and refrigerate.

5. Add the turnips, carrots, oregano, and parsley to the soup. Cook 30 minutes longer. Add the sausages and cook until heated through (about 5 minutes). Serve hot.

PINTO BEAN SOUP   For this recipe, see page 103

CAULIFLOWER AND TOMATO SALAD   For this recipe, see page 208

CREAM OF CAULIFLOWER-RICE SOUP

Serves 6

1 large cauliflower (about 2 pounds)
4½ cups Chicken Stock (see Index)
½ cup brown rice
white pepper to taste
2 cups milk
½ cup heavy cream
¼ teaspoon nutmeg
3 to 4 drops hot pepper sauce

1. Wash and carve out tough center core of cauliflower and trim outside leaves. Break and separate into small florets. Steam over boiling water 10 minutes or until tender. Reserve several very small pieces of cauliflower for garnish.

2. Heat stock to boiling in a 4-quart soup pot. Add rice, lower heat, and cook, covered, until rice is tender (about 30 minutes).

3. Add the cauliflower, pepper, and milk to the liquid. Simmer 5 minutes.

4. Puree pot contents in several small batches in a blender. Return to pot, add cream, stir, and simmer until hot (do not boil). Add nutmeg and hot pepper sauce. Garnish with cauliflower florets.

THREE-BEAN SOUP

Serves 6

⅓ cup dried lima beans
⅓ cup dried garbanzo beans
⅓ cup dried navy beans
3 cups water
¼ cup olive oil
½ pound boneless lamb shoulder, cut into ¾-inch cubes
1 tablespoon whole wheat flour
½ teaspoon ground cumin
⅛ teaspoon cinnamon
¼ teaspoon curry powder
1 large onion, minced
2 cloves garlic, minced
7 cups Beef Stock (see Index)
1 bay leaf
2 carrots, diced
3 tomatoes, peeled and diced
1 medium-size zucchini, diced

1. Rinse the lima, garbanzo, and navy beans and combine in a large mixing bowl. Add the water, soak overnight, and drain.

2. Heat the oil in a 4-quart soup pot. Dredge the meat with the flour, cumin, cinnamon, and curry powder. Saute on medium-high heat until browned on all sides. Add the onion and garlic and cook 1 minute longer. Add the stock and bay leaf. Add the drained beans. Bring to a boil, lower heat, cover, and simmer 2 hours. Remove bay leaf.

3. Add the carrots, tomatoes, and zucchini. Cook 30 minutes longer. Serve hot.

SCOTCH BROTH

Serves 6

2 pounds lamb shoulder with bone, cut into 2-inch pieces
11 cups water
1 bay leaf
¼ teaspoon thyme
½ cup barley
3 tablespoons butter
1 large onion, finely chopped
2 shallots, minced
3 carrots, minced
2 stalks celery, minced
1 small turnip, minced
¼ pound mushrooms, thinly sliced

Garnish

1 cup plain yogurt
2 tablespoons finely chopped parsley

1. Place the meat, water, bay leaf, and thyme in a 6-quart soup pot. Bring to a boil and lower heat. Partially cover and simmer 1 hour. Add barley. Partially cover again and simmer gently for another hour.

2. Use a slotted spoon to transfer the lamb to a plate. Remove the meat from the bones and dice it. Discard the bones and bay leaf. Return meat to the pot.

3. Melt the butter in a small saucepan. Add the onion, shallots, carrots, celery, turnip, and mushrooms. Cover with a buttered round of parchment and the lid. Steam over low heat about 5 minutes or until the vegetables are slightly limp. Add to the soup. Cook 30 minutes longer.

4. Garnish with yogurt dollops and parsley.

The Hopi and Their Time-Honored Foods

All I have is my planting stick and my corn.
HOPI GREAT SPIRIT

Present-day Hopi Indians follow many of the same traditions they were practicing 400 years ago when Spanish explorers found them living atop the mesas. In 1970, the tribe built the Hopi Cultural Center as a showcase for native arts, crafts, and foods and as a monument to all those Indians, past and present, who have honed a distinctive culture out of this grudging and stubborn northeastern Arizona desert.

The arrangement and architecture of the complex closely parallels that of the Hopi village. An inner courtyard is enclosed by gift shops, guest rooms, a lecture hall, a museum, and a restaurant. Most of the surrounding population is concentrated in communities on this and two other nearby mesas.

Ferrell and Dorothy Secakuku oversee the operation of the Cultural Center restaurant. For ten years, they have worked to make their business pursuits truly reflective of Indian life. In the bright dining room, colorful yucca baskets adorn the walls. Here Indian chefs prepare *Nok Qui Vi,* the ubiquitous Hopi Stew which tourists and Indians alike request. Handsomely attired in native costume, men and women serve traditional stews accompanied by baked chili peppers and *piki* bread, a paper-thin, translucent treat that can be experienced nowhere outside this area.

In late July, Dorothy, Ferrell, and their six girls return to Dorothy's home on First Mesa for Home Dance, the celebration of the arrival of the first ears of corn. Elaborately dressed Hopi priests from the Kachina Clan (the Rain Bearers) ceremoniously present stalks of corn, with little gifts attached, to small children to introduce   45 them to these "perfect spirit beings." These ancient surroundings and rituals inspire the customs and traditions the Secakukus bring to the restaurant.

Ancient Ways

Life on First Mesa has changed amazingly little in the last 400 years. Three windswept villages span the irregular surface 600 feet above the plateau. Sichomovi, the central one, is in the pueblo-style—small, flat-roof adobe buildings abutting one another and circling an inner quadrangle where the ceremonial dances take place. The typical home is a simple, three-room structure—living room, sleeping area, and kitchen. Most families use coal or wood stoves for cooking and heating the rooms.

Much food preparation goes on outside the tiny living spaces. Behind her house, Dorothy's mother bakes dough in beehive-shaped bread ovens. Other women station their flat *piki* stones over wood fires nearby. With their hands, they smear thin cornmeal batter across the hot surface and retrieve at last tissuelike blue sheets. Since most people have no refrigeration and not all families have accepted the "modern" icebox,

A Hopi elder examines the tribe's vital corn crop.

drying is an important part of routine chores. Children and women frequently sit in the courtyard or climb wooden ladders to work on the flat roofs where they shell beans and spread them to dry in the sun.

As arrangements for Home Dance come to a close, men gather in groups to talk in the courtyard, and children, munching on handfuls of parched corn, run along the outer mesa rim. Women, on the other hand, stay close to the kitchens where they lay out the traditional feast. On an ornately patterned woven cloth, small white "Indian" beans and butter-yellow corn kernels emerge from a large stew pot. Peanut-size red chili peppers and long curving green ones ring the base. Earth-colored baskets reveal blue and yellow sheets, squares, or tiny fingers of cornbread.

At the table in Dorothy's mother's house, corn is indeed the most pervasive food. "It is part of every celebration, and it is used in every ceremony," says Dorothy. "Some families put a taste of the blue cornmeal into a newborn's mouth and say, 'This corn is your life's strength. Eat this and grow strong and have a happy life.' "

Corn and Stew Combinations

Dorothy's mother crumbles *Huzusuki* (Hopi Finger Bread), a version of cornmeal bread, over the surface of a meat soup. Little blue cornmeal dumplings bob up and down in a hearty stew to which she adds fresh green corn right off the cob. Dried sweet corn kernels and beans are the primary ingredients in another large tureen. Lamb-base *Nok Qui Vi* (Hopi Stew), made with another corn mixture, *Pa-tsa-me* (Hominy), takes prominence in the center of the banquet table. "At every dance, at every occasion that has any significance to it, people will be serving this stew," says Dorothy.

Hopi women, like Dorothy and her girls, learn early in their training to choose from four different types of corn—red, white, blue, and sweet—for particular dishes. *Someviki,* for instance, small cornmeal soup accompaniments boiled in corn husks, traditionally demand blue cornmeal above all others. Blue corn is a special variety rarely found beyond the confines of the reservation. Ferrell and Dorothy, who require a more abundant source for the restaurant, make an appearance directly after local weddings. "Family and friends bring sacks of all kinds for the ceremony and for the food. We see if we can buy all the blue that remains," Ferrell remarks.

In September, Hopi bake their sweet corn harvest in outdoor "earth ovens." In pits approximately six feet deep and five feet across, Indian men lay the dampened ears over hot coals and corn husks and cover the opening. Twenty-four hours later, women and children arrive to husk and string the corn to dry. Over a millennium, this method has been an essential part of Hopi survival. Early on, they learned that the long steaming and further drying preserved this corn better than just leaving it to dry in the sun. Through long periods of drought, their stores kept them alive. Today, dry sweet corn provides that same insurance for Hopi people, and through centuries of experimentation, they now possess numerous soup and stew recipes that include its unique flavor.

Ash as Food

As far back as Dorothy can remember, her people have been using ash broths (ashes of certain plants diluted in water) in many corn mixtures. Hominy, for instance, which is served alone as a cereal or in stews, is white corn cooked with the addition of culinary ash, which causes the hull to drop off. The ash lightens the corn and imparts a distinctive flavor to the dish in which it is included. Many Hopi now realize that many of their instinctive inner guides that have created these timeless preparations bring them good health. Ash particularly high in calcium complements the already abundant mineral supply in corn. Such a bonus is important in a culture where people rely so heavily on one particular food.

Hopi Generosity

The Hopi are a peaceful people who have chosen to preserve their quiet

Dorothy Secakuku presents a meal from the Cultural Center restaurant.

traditions while a much more complex world has grown up around them. Fortunately, they have not closed off that modern society from experiencing their ancient customs. During vacation season, the hottest, driest months of the year, tourists pack the Cultural Center dining room and fill the guest lodgings. Some who are enroute to the magnificent canyons that are within a few hours drive stay only long enough to get a taste of this tranquil setting. Others set aside several weeks to immerse themselves in it. "I have seen it happen over and over," says Dorothy. "We provide few vestiges of contemporary life—no telephones, televisions, or recreation programs in the evenings. After these new guests tour the museum, visit the little shops, and sample Indian foods, they look around for something familiar to do. But faced with only a vast sea of flatland and towering rock, a view of the San Francisco peaks 100 miles away, and a pace unlike any that they know, they inevitably 'discover' us. They start finding little lizards and incredible flowers among the scrubby brush, and before long, they are climbing the mesa steppes to watch us dance, bake bread, and come together just as we have always done. No matter how foreign it is to them at first, or how far away, most come back."

MEAT SOUP WITH *HUZUSUKI*
Serves 4

4 *cups water*
1 *cup leftover* Huzusuki *(see recipe below)*
½ *cup meat drippings or chopped mutton, lamb, or beef*
salt to taste

1. Bring water to a rolling boil.
2. Crumble *huzusuki* into bite-size pieces and add to boiling water.
3. Add meat drippings and salt.
4. Simmer until soup thickens.

HUZUSUKI (HOPI FINGER BREAD)

2 *cups water*
¾ *cup blue cornmeal (see page 50 for sources), ground medium-fine*

1. Bring water to a boil; then reduce heat to low.
2. Gradually add cornmeal to boiling water. Stir constantly until all meal is mixed in. Break up lumps that form with a fork. You will have a very stiff mixture.
3. Spoon mixture out onto a plate and let set until firm.
4. Break off pieces and eat it with your fingers or serve it with roasted meats, soups, or stews. Many Hopi like to cut it into slices and eat it for breakfast.

GREEN CORN STEW WITH BLUE CORN DUMPLINGS
Serves 4 to 6

batter for Blue Corn Dumplings (see recipe below), prepared through step 2
2 cups ground mutton, lamb, or beef
1 tablespoon shortening
salt and pepper to taste
2 cups fresh green corn [immature sweet corn], cut from cob
1 cup summer squash, cubed
1 cup coarsely chopped onions
½ cup coarsely chopped peppers
4 cups water (about)
2 tablespoons water
2 tablespoons cornmeal

1. Brown meat in shortening and stir in salt and pepper. Add vegetables to meat and cover with water. Cover stew and simmer 15 minutes.
2. Stir water into cornmeal until smooth and add to stew. Stir well.
3. Proceed with steps 3 and 4 for making Blue Corn Dumplings. After 15 minutes uncover pot and serve stew with several dumplings in each bowl.

BLUE CORN DUMPLINGS
Serves 4 to 6

1 cup blue corn flour*
2 teaspoons baking powder
1 teaspoon salt
1 teaspoon shortening
⅓ to ½ cup milk

*Two sources for blue corn flour and blue cornmeal are: Bueno Food Products, 1224 Airway Drive, SW, Albuquerque, NM 87105, and Jake's Market, P.O. Box 3326, Espanola, NM 87533.

1. Mix dry ingredients thoroughly in a mixing bowl.
2. Cut in shortening and add enough milk to create a consistency that will just fall off the end of a spoon.
3. Drop by tablespoons on top of a soup or stew.
4. Cover kettle and steam dumplings 15 minutes. Liquid should be kept bubbling throughout the cooking process.

SWEET CORN AND BEANS
Serves 6

2 cups Indian beans*
6 cups water
1 cup coarsely cracked dried sweet corn
2 tablespoons meat drippings
1 tablespoon salt
8 to 16 Someviki (optional—see recipe in this section)

*If tepary, Indian beans, are not available in your area, pinto beans are an adequate substitute.

1. Combine the beans and water in a covered pot and simmer until the beans are partially cooked (about 1 hour). Add the cracked corn and continue to simmer until both corn and beans are done (about 1½ hours). Pour in more water as needed.
2. At the end of the cooking time, mix in the drippings and salt for flavor.
3. If you choose, float one or two *someviki* on top of each bowl or pass a basket of them separately.

SOMEVIKI

Serves 4 to 6

¼ *cup culinary ash**
2¾ *cups boiling water*
½ *cup finely ground blue cornmeal*
    (see page 50 for sources)
⅓ *cup sugar*
15 *corn husks, soaked in very hot*
    water 10 to 15 minutes

*1 tablespoon baking soda may be substituted.

1. Mix ash with ¾ cup of the water and set aside.
2. Combine cornmeal and sugar.
3. Add remaining water. Stir with a fork until the wet and dry ingredients are well blended.
4. Pour ½ cup or more ash water through a strainer into dough until the mixture is distinctively blue in color.
5. Distribute dough evenly on each corn husk and fold husk around dough (sides first and then ends). Secure with threads from corn husks or cotton string.
6. Drop rolls into a 4-quart pot of boiling water. Cover and simmer 20 to 25 minutes.
7. Drain off liquid and discard. Remove husks from *someviki* and serve them on top of beans, soups, or stews, or leave wrapped and pass a basket of them at the table.

HOMINY

Yields about 3 cups

1½ *cups large white corn kernels*
¼ *cup culinary ash**
10 *cups water*

*1 tablespoon baking soda may be substituted.

1. Combine the corn kernels, ash, and water in an enamel pot. Bring liquid to a boil, turn down the heat so that the mixture just gently bubbles, and allow it to continue in this way until the skins slip off the corn (2 to 3 hours). The kernels will turn a bright orange at first and will slowly lose color until they become yellow and double in size at the end.
2. When the corn is ready, drain it in a colander and rinse it under cold water until all trace of the ash is gone. Return corn to the pot, add water, and boil it until the kernels are soft but still firm and the corn is a beige color (about 30 minutes).
3. Use hominy in recipes for soups and stews or as a hot breakfast cereal. If any remains, divide it among several containers and store it in the freezer for later use.

HOPI STEW
Yields 8 to 10 servings

8 *cups water*
1 *pound mutton, lamb, or beef,*
cubed
3 *cups prepared Hominy (see recipe*
in this section)
1½ *tablespoons salt*
8 *to 10 Anaheim green chili peppers*

1. Place the water in a medium-size pot and bring it to a boil. Carefully add the meat to the boiling water, turn down the heat, and simmer the mixture until the meat is partially cooked (about 2 hours). Add more water as needed to prevent scorching.

2. Mix in the prepared hominy and continue cooking until both the meat and hominy are tender. Add salt at this point.

3. Serve stew in large bowls with a pepper on the side of each.

Hearty Soups

FLORENTINE EGG SOUP

Serves 6

5 cups Chicken Stock (see Index)
leaves from ½ pound spinach
6 eggs
6 tablespoons sunflower seeds
6 teaspoons minced parsley

1. Bring the stock to a boil in a 3-quart soup pot.

2. Cut the spinach into thin shreds and add it to the boiling stock. Immediately remove from heat and let stand while preparing eggs.

3. Lightly poach the eggs. Place one in each serving bowl. Sprinkle each egg with a tablespoon of sunflower seeds and a teaspoon of parsley. Ladle the hot soup over the eggs and serve immediately.

SUCCOTASH CHOWDER

Serves 6

¼ cup butter
1 cup coarsely chopped onions
1 garlic clove, minced
½ teaspoon nutmeg
2 cups shelled lima beans (about 2 pounds)
4 cups Chicken Stock (see Index)
3 cups corn (about 6 ears)
½ cup milk
3 tablespoons minced parsley

1. Melt the butter in a 5-quart soup pot. Add the onions and saute until transparent; add the garlic and nutmeg and saute 1 minute longer. Add the lima beans and stock. Bring to a boil, lower heat, partially cover, and simmer 20 minutes. Add 2 cups of the corn and cook until the vegetables are tender (about 10 minutes).

2. In a blender, puree the remaining corn with the milk. Stir the puree into the soup and simmer 10 minutes.

3. Garnish with minced parsley. Serve hot.

CALVES' LIVER DUMPLING SOUP

Serves 6

2 tablespoons butter
1 large onion, finely chopped
1 celery stalk, finely chopped
1 pound calves' liver
3 medium-size tomatoes, finely chopped
1 cup corn (about 2 ears)
5 cups Beef Stock (see Index)
1 cup tomato juice
2 slices whole wheat bread, torn into small pieces
1 egg, beaten
1 tablespoon minced onions
dash pepper
dash paprika
3 tablespoons finely chopped parsley

1. Melt the butter in a 3-quart soup pot. Add the onion and celery and saute until soft.

2. Grind or mince ¼ pound of the liver and set aside. Cut the remaining liver into ½-inch cubes and add to the hot pot. Saute and stir until meat is cooked through. Add the tomatoes, corn, stock, and tomato juice. Bring to a boil, lower heat, cover, and simmer 10 minutes.

3. In a small mixing bowl, combine the bread, egg, onions, pepper, paprika, and the reserved ground liver. Mix well and shape into ¾-inch balls. Add more bread if mixture seems too moist.

4. Drop balls into the hot soup and cook 10 minutes longer. Sprinkle with parsley and serve hot.

MEATBALL-POMEGRANATE SOUP

Serves 6

3 tablespoons butter
2 garlic cloves, minced
1 pound lean ground beef
1 tablespoon finely chopped mint
1 tablespoon finely chopped parsley
½ teaspoon ground cumin
⅛ teaspoon cinnamon
1 egg yolk, lightly beaten
1 onion, coarsely chopped
7 cups Beef Stock (see Index)
½ cup brown rice
1½ cups pomegranate juice*
1 cup firmly packed shredded spinach

*Some natural foods stores, supermarkets, and gourmet shops carry unsweetened pomegranate juice. (One brand is made by R. W. Knudsen.) If it is not on the shelves at a local shop, ask the merchant to order it for you.

1. To make the meatballs, melt 1 tablespoon of the butter in a skillet and saute the garlic until golden. In a large mixing bowl, combine the garlic with the beef, mint, parsley, cumin, cinnamon, and egg yolk. Mix well. Shape the mixture into small balls (about 1 inch in diameter). Melt the remaining butter in the skillet and saute the meatballs until lightly browned. Set the meatballs aside.

2. Saute the onion in the meatball drippings. Transfer the onion to a 6-quart soup pot and deglaze the skillet with some of the stock. Add the pan juices and the remaining beef stock to the onion. Bring the liquid to a boil and stir in the rice. Lower heat, cover, and simmer gently 40 minutes.

3. Add the meatballs, pomegranate juice, and spinach. Return broth to a boil, lower heat, and simmer, uncovered, an additional 5 minutes.

CHUNKY CALICO CHICKEN SOUP

Serves 6

3 tablespoons olive oil
1 large onion, finely chopped
2 celery stalks, finely chopped
2 garlic cloves, finely chopped
1 pound boneless chicken breast, skinned and cut into ¾-inch cubes
3 tomatoes, diced
1 medium-size potato, peeled and diced
5 cups Chicken Stock (see Index)
½ pound green beans, cut into 1-inch pieces
½ cup corn (1 ear)
1 medium-size zucchini, diced
1 small sweet red pepper, finely chopped
2 tablespoons finely chopped parsley

1. Heat the oil in a 3-quart soup pot. Add the onion and celery and saute 5 minutes on medium heat. Add the garlic and chicken and saute while stirring, 5 minutes longer. Add the tomatoes, potato, and stock and bring to a boil. Lower heat, cover, and simmer 15 minutes.

2. Add the green beans, cover, and cook 5 minutes longer.

3. Add the corn, zucchini, and pepper and cook an additional 5 minutes. Stir in the parsley. Serve hot.

EGGPLANT SOUP WITH VEAL BALLS

Serves 6

5 tablespoons butter
1 medium-size eggplant, peeled and diced
1 medium-size onion, finely chopped
2 garlic cloves, minced
2 large tomatoes, cut into ½-inch cubes
2 bay leaves
7 cups Beef Stock (see Index)
½ cup brown rice
½ pound ground veal
2 tablespoons finely chopped parsley
1 shallot, minced
pinch nutmeg
whole wheat flour
3 basil leaves, finely chopped

1. Melt the butter in a 3-quart soup pot. Add the eggplant and onion and cook on medium heat while stirring, until vegetables are soft. Stir in the garlic and tomatoes. Cook 5 minutes longer. Add the bay leaves and stock and bring to a boil. Add the rice, lower heat, cover, and simmer 30 minutes.

2. In a large mixing bowl, combine the veal, 1 tablespoon of the parsley, shallot, and nutmeg. Shape into small balls and roll in flour to coat. Drop balls into soup and cook 15 minutes longer.

3. Remove bay leaves. Serve hot, sprinkled with basil and the remaining parsley.

SOUTHERN BEAN AND RICE SOUP

Serves 6

1 cup dried pinto beans, rinsed and soaked overnight in water to cover
2 pounds short ribs
12 cups water
2 onions, quartered
1 carrot, halved
1 stalk celery, halved
1 bay leaf
6 peppercorns
¼ teaspoon thyme
2 tablespoons olive oil
1 medium-size onion, chopped
2 garlic cloves, minced
½ cup brown rice
1 cup tomato juice
1 tablespoon tamari soy sauce
2 parsnips, diced
¼ cup finely chopped parsley

1. Drain the pinto beans and set aside.
2. Place the short ribs in a 6-quart soup pot and add the water. Bring to a boil and lower heat to a simmer. Add the onions, carrot, celery, bay leaf, peppercorns, and thyme. Partially cover and simmer gently until meat is tender (about 2 hours). Strain soup into a 4-quart soup pot. Degrease the broth.
3. Remove the meat from the short ribs and trim off the fat. Slice the meat thinly and return it to the soup pot.
4. Add the beans to the soup pot. Bring to a boil, lower heat, cover, and simmer gently 1 hour.
5. Heat the oil in a skillet. Add the onion and saute until transparent. Add the garlic and rice. Cook, stirring constantly, on medium-high heat, until the rice is lightly browned (about 5 minutes). Transfer rice mixture to the soup pot. Add the tomato juice and tamari and return to a boil. Lower heat, cover, and simmer 20 minutes.
6. Add the parsnips and parsley. Cook 30 minutes longer. Serve hot.

MEATBALL SOUP

Serves 6

½ pound lean ground beef or lamb
1 small onion, minced
1 tablespoon finely chopped parsley
2 tablespoons butter
2 garlic cloves, minced
3 shallots, minced
4 small zucchini, diced
3 large tomatoes, peeled, seeded, and coarsely chopped
3 cups Beef Stock (see Index)
2 cups plain yogurt
2 egg yolks, lightly beaten
2 tablespoons minced dillweed
2 tablespoons minced chives

1. In a small mixing bowl, combine the ground meat, onion, and parsley. Shape the mixture into ½-inch balls.
2. Melt the butter in a medium-size skillet and saute the meatballs until they are browned on all sides. Transfer them to a warm plate and set aside.
3. Add the garlic and shallots to the pan and saute 2 minutes. Stir in the zucchini and tomatoes and cook 5 minutes. Transfer to a 3-quart soup pot. Add the stock, bring to a boil, lower heat, cover, and simmer 10 minutes.
4. In a small mixing bowl, beat together the yogurt, egg yolks, dillweed, and chives. Stir mixture into the soup. Just before serving, add the meatballs and heat soup through, but do not boil.

_____Serve Corn at Its Best_____

"Start the water to boil while you're picking the corn," says any gardener or farmer who has known the taste of corn only minutes from the field. If the alternative is fresh market corn, it should be kept in the coldest part of the refrigerator and not husked until immediately before cooking. Once the husks are removed, enzymes quickly change much of the sweet sugar to starch, causing loss of flavor. Corn is commonly overcooked; if heated to boiling temperatures for longer than two or three minutes, it will become tough and tasteless. Ideally, for the truest corn flavor, it should be served as fresh as possible and completely unheated. The raw kernels are a delicious salad ingredient or garnish for light summer soups.

WHOLE HARVEST VEGETABLE SOUP

Serves 6

6 cups Beef Stock (see Index)
2 carrots, coarsely chopped
2 medium-size onions, thinly sliced
1 leek (white part only), thickly sliced
1 celery stalk, thickly sliced
1 cup thinly sliced green peppers
½ cup corn (1 ear)
½ cup shelled lima beans (about ½ pound)
½ cup shelled peas (about ½ pound)
1 cup thickly sliced zucchini
½ cup thinly sliced turnips
2 tomatoes, coarsely chopped
1 garlic clove, crushed
2 teaspoons minced parsley
4 fresh basil leaves or 1 teaspoon dried
2 sprigs oregano or ½ teaspoon dried
½ teaspoon white pepper

1. In a 5-quart soup pot, heat the stock to boiling. Add all the vegetables and simmer 20 minutes on very low heat.

2. Add garlic, herbs, and pepper. Stir gently or vegetables will break during cooking. Cook until vegetables are tender (about 10 more minutes). Serve hot.

Firm vegetables like lima beans, carrots, celeriac, or mature peas, cooked and pureed, become substantial soup bases. Because they are full of starch and cellulose, the soups require none of the thickening agents used in other vegetable puree soups.

Veterans of the Chili Wars

Every man who cooks chili believes that his chili is infinitely superior to all others on earth.　　　　　H. ALLEN SMITH

No treaties get signed around here. No one waves laurel branches or white flags. These are long-standing wars that will never cease as long as the capsicum plant flourishes. Yes, these are the great Southwestern chili wars, the part of American history the school books leave out.

It all started back in August, 1967, when a writer/humorist, H. Allen Smith, published an article in *Holiday* audaciously titled "Nobody Knows More about Chili Than I Do." In his tongue-in-cheek bravado, he boastfully related his great prowess in these matters while taking to task all Texans who regard themselves as chili experts, bar none. To add insult to injury, Smith set down his iconoclastic recipe which includes the most odious of all procedures (at least to Texans)—cooking beans right along with the chili.

No sooner had the issue hit the newsstands than Texans were up in arms, especially the members of the Chili Appreciation Society International (CASI). Stalwarts founded the organization in 1959 to protect their chili from extreme adulterations (like beans). They had their honor to defend, and Smith was on the firing line. Partisans immediately dispatched a coercive message to Smith obliging him to bring his ammunition to Terlingua, Texas, on October 21 and be prepared to lock horns with a Lone Star contender.

Showdown at Sundown

In the 1800s, Terlingua was mercury capital of the world (population: 2,000). By 1967, it was a ghost town (population: 1), a small part of a huge ranch owned by famed sports-car builder, Carroll Shelby. Shelby agreed to offer this Mexican border spot for the heated showdown between Smith and CASI's chief cook, Wick Fowler, an Austin newspaperman. Reportedly their first meeting on the front porch of the decaying Chisos Oasis Saloon went like this:

> Fowler: *My chili has been known to open up 18 sinus cavities*
> *unknown to modern medicine.*
> Smith: *I'll cook you blue in the face, you big ox.*

Three blindfolded judges presided over the shenanigans. One voted for Fowler, one for Smith. The last fell to the microphone and announced that "my taste buds have been seared and singed, preventing any possibility of decision at this point in time." The Texans who designed the contest clearly as a one-time affair, solely to put Smith down, could not accept a draw. They demanded a rematch, same time, same place, the next year.

The press labeled the second Terlingua rivalry the "world's greatest nonevent." Spectators had decided to participate in style. Many arrived via stagecoach, parachute, motorcycle, and air balloon to watch Smith and Fowler out-simmer each other. Smith, however, was forced to withdraw because of a suspicious "allergy flare-up." Finding it nearly impossible to cancel the scheduled clash, Texans found another opponent, Woodruff DeSilva from California. Just as Scott Carpenter, the astronaut, was casting his ballot, a desperado brandishing a rifle grabbed the box and made off for one of the abandoned mine shafts. Once again, the battle was declared null and void, but at this point everyone present knew that these wars would go on annually—forever. There were differences here that would never be settled completely.

Step right up for a bowl of "red" that is a sure winner!

As the years passed, victors actually emerged from these contests. In 1970, Frank Tolbert, another Dallas newspaperman, announced the formation of the International Chili Society (ICS), a broader-based group than the Texas-oriented CASI. This only partly serious amalgamation of luminaries, business people, and ordinary "chili heads" were keenly aware that chili pride was spreading. (Places as far north as Springfield, Illinois, were calling themselves "Chili Capital of the World.") ICS members set themselves up to encourage chili competitions all over the globe, to establish standard rules for cooking and judging (even though they seldom agreed among themselves), and to assure fairness at all levels. Their most pleasurable responsibility, however, was to organize and preside over the outrageous annual World Championship Chili Cook-off.

In 1975 the ICS moved the event to the Tropico Gold Mine in Southern California's Mojave Desert to better accommodate the thousands of spectators who gathered to witness this outdoor extravaganza. Instead of the anticipated 10,000, 20,000 chili buffs packed the historic settlement where their usual carnival-style atmosphere prevailed—bluegrass music, jazz orchestra, parade, big-name judges. In the eight years since the original conflicts, the purpose of these gatherings still remained the same: the revelation of the "infinitely superior chili." The vitrolic confrontations, however, had turned to good-natured raillery.

Present-Day Skirmishes

Truett Erhard and Joe and Shirley Stewart epitomize this new breed of chili warrior. The three are both boon companions and opponents in all this spicy folderol. For example, Joe and Shirley won the ICS's 1979 World Championship Chili Cook-off (netting them a fat $15,000) with Joe's boss's recipe. Truett just happens to be his boss. Here is Shirley's version:

> *Truett won a regional contest in '78. That win got him into the World Championship. I was on his support team, and as I watched him cook his chili, I was convinced it was a terrific recipe. He didn't win, but Joe and I made him write everything down. We altered things a bit and in '79 won a regional contest with the recipe. The rest is history.*

Such generosity is pretty magnanimous, considering the high stakes. But Truett says, "Oh, I don't mind; I wouldn't have used the recipe again anyway. I never cook my chili exactly the same twice."

Prize-Winning Recipe

The 1979 World Championship Chili is essentially a thick meat-and-spice mixture, not a far departure from the first Texas chilies. Those were coarsely ground beef or other mature meats cooked slowly and for a long time in close fellowship with the

Shirley and Joe Stewart, 1979 champs, check out the competition.

pulp of chili peppers, crushed powder from wild marjoram, ground cumin seeds, and chopped garlic cloves. Judges frequently wonder how such a timeless formula still brings the Stewarts wide margins of success. "We've tasted other people's results from our recipe," responds Shirley. "They're not the same, and they're never as good. The secret is in the technique—how you do it—and in the timing—when you do it."

The prime ingredient in this valuable commodity is beef. The Stewarts purchase "coarse ground," known in chili country as "chili ground." To this they gingerly add the essential spice, chili pepper—both the pulp from boiled dried California Anaheim and Pasilla peppers and a fine Texas chili powder. "Judges are looking for good flavor, good aftertaste, good consistency, and good aroma. You can satisfy them on all these grounds, but if you insist on overspicing, it can make you lose points," reveals Joe. "Our chili has a nip, but no real bite."

Throughout the allotted cooking period at contests, Joe and Shirley are busy "feeding the pot." During the last half-hour, they bring the dry paste to the desired consistency. "Our way, we're not at the mercy of the altitude or how hot the fire is, or our deadline; we're not boiling something down in hopes that it will be just right at the allotted time."

All the Stewart's steps, in fact, are calculated in this way. They have appropriated jobs for themselves; Joe handles the tomatoes and Shirley deals with the peppers, for instance. They even time their movements with a watch. "We've tried making chili other ways, but this is the one that wins for us," they tell the crowds who watch them at their booth. "That's how we're going to win this year."

That's right. Joe and Shirley are going to take another shot at the championship, using the very same widely circulated and published recipe. Among their contenders will be two of their friends. "All of us will be making a basic meat-and-spice chili," says Joe. "We're all old cronies, so Shirley and I are rooting for everyone. We wish the other two the best of luck—at the numbers two and three slots." These prize-winning chili recipes appear as their authors wrote them. However, for those who find certain of their ingredients (like salt, MSG, and suet) inappropriate for their diets, we suggest eliminating them.

C. V. WOOD'S WORLD CHAMPIONSHIP CHILI, 1969, 1971

Yields 6 quarts

1 *3-pound stewing chicken, cut into pieces, and 1½ quarts water, or 4 or 5 10-ounce cans chicken broth*
4 *pounds flank steak*
5 *pounds thin center-cut pork chops*
6 *long green chilies, peeled*
2 *teaspoons sugar*
3 *teaspoons ground oregano*
3 *teaspoons ground cumin*
½ *teaspoon MSG (optional)*
3 *teaspoons pepper*
4 *teaspoons salt*
5 *tablespoons chili powder*
1 *teaspoon cilantro, also known as Chinese parsley**
1 *teaspoon thyme*
8 *ounces beer*
4 *15-ounce cans tomatoes*
¼ *cup celery, finely chopped*
2 *garlic cloves, finely chopped*
½ *pound beef suet or ½ cup cooking oil*
3 *medium onions, cut into ½-inch pieces*
2 *green peppers, cut into ⅜-inch pieces*
1 *pound Jack cheese, grated*
1 *lime*

*Available in stores stocking Mexican or Chinese groceries.

1. Combine chicken with water in a large pot and simmer 2 hours. Strain off broth and reserve chicken for other use or use canned chicken broth.
2. Trim all fat from flank steak and cut steak into ⅜-inch cubes. Trim all fat and bones from pork and cut pork into ¼-inch cubes.
3. Boil chilies 15 minutes or until tender. Remove seeds and cut the chilies into ¼-inch squares. Mix sugar, oregano, cumin, MSG (if used), pepper, salt, chili powder, cilantro, and thyme with beer until all lumps are dissolved. Add the tomatoes, celery, chilies, beer mixture, and garlic to the chicken broth.
4. Render suet to make 6 to 8 tablespoons oil or use oil. Pour about a third of the reserved suet or oil into a skillet, add pork, and brown. Do only half the total amount at a time. Add the pork to the broth mixture; cook slowly 30 minutes.
5. Brown beef in the remaining oil (about one-third of the total amount at a time). Add the beef to the pork mixture and cook slowly about 1 hour. Add onions and peppers. Simmer 2 to 3 hours until meat is broken down. Stir with a wooden spoon every 15 to 20 minutes.
6. Cool 1 hour and refrigerate 24 hours. Reheat chili before serving it. About 5 minutes before serving time, add grated cheese. Just before serving, add the juice of the lime and stir the mixture with a wooden spoon.

JOE AND SHIRLEY STEWART'S WORLD CHAMPIONSHIP CHILI, 1979

Serves 8

6 *dried chili pepper pods or 3 ounces
  ground chili pepper*
3 *pounds round steak, coarsely
  ground*
3 *pounds chuck steak, coarsely
  ground*
1 *cup vegetable oil or kidney suet*
pepper to taste
1 *3-ounce bottle chili powder*
6 *tablespoons ground cumin*
2 *tablespoons MSG*
6 *small garlic cloves, minced*
2 *medium onions, coarsely chopped*
1 *tablespoon dried oregano brewed in
  ½ cup beer (like tea)*
2 *tablespoons paprika*
2 *tablespoons cider vinegar*
3 *cups beef broth*
1 *4-ounce can diced green chili*
½ *14½-ounce can stewed tomatoes or
  to taste*
1 *teaspoon Tabasco sauce or to taste*
2 *tablespoons masa flour**

*Available in stores stocking Mexican gro-
ceries.

1. Remove stems and seeds from chili pepper pods, if used. Add pepper pods to boiling water and cook at low boil for 30 minutes. Drain. Save both water and pepper pods.
2. Brown meat in vegetable oil or kidney suet. Add black pepper to taste. Drain meat and add chili powder, cumin, MSG, garlic, and chopped onions. Cook 30 to 45 minutes. Use as little liquid as possible (add small amounts of water only as necessary). Stir often.
3. Remove skins from pepper pods, mash pulp, and add to meat mixture (or add ground chili pepper). Add strained oregano and beer mixture, paprika, vinegar, 2 cups beef broth, green chili, stewed tomatoes, and Tabasco sauce to meat mixture. Simmer 30 to 45 minutes. Stir often.
4. Dissolve masa flour into remaining beef broth; pour into chili. Simmer 30 minutes. Stir often.

PEDERNALES RIVER CHILI

Serves 12

4 *pounds chili meat, finely chopped*
1 *large onion, finely chopped*
2 *garlic cloves, minced*
1 *teaspoon dried oregano*
1 *teaspoon ground cumin seeds*
6 *teaspoons chili powder or to taste*
2 *16-ounce cans tomatoes, diced*
salt to taste
2 *cups hot water*

During their years in the White House, Mrs. Lyndon Johnson responded to requests for her husband's favorite chili recipe. At the time she said, "It has been almost as popular as the government pamphlet on the care and feeding of children."

1. Put the meat, onion, and garlic in a large skillet and sear until meat is lightly browned.
2. Add remaining ingredients, bring to a boil, lower heat, and simmer for 1 hour with the cover on the skillet.
3. Remove cover. Skim off any grease.

WOODRUFF DeSILVA'S WORLD CHAMPIONSHIP CHILI, 1968 (TIED)

Serves 8

5 *medium onions, coarsely chopped*
small amount cooking oil
salt and pepper to taste
4 *pounds chuck beef, coarse chili grind*
  or chopped into thumbnail-size
  pieces
5 *garlic cloves, minced*
4 *tablespoons dried oregano*
2 *teaspoons woodruff (an herb)*
1 *teaspoon ground cayenne pepper*
2 *tablespoons paprika*
scant tablespoon to full tablespoon chili
  powder
3 *tablespoons ground cumin*
scant teaspoon to full teaspoon chipenos
  (also known as chilipiquines),
  crushed*
4 *dashes Tabasco sauce*
3 *10-ounce cans tomato sauce*
1 *6-ounce can tomato paste*
water
4 *tablespoons flour or masa flour**

*Available in stores stocking Mexican groceries.

1. In a skillet, brown onions in oil. Season with salt and pepper. Place in chili pot. Brown beef in skillet. Add more oil as necessary. Add garlic and 1 tablespoon of the oregano. Add this mixture to the chili pot.

2. In a paper sack, shake together the woodruff, cayenne pepper, paprika, chili powder, cumin, the remaining 3 tablespoons oregano, and the chipenos. Add the blended spices to the chili pot with the Tabasco sauce, tomato sauce, and tomato paste. Add enough water to cover the meat and simmer at least 2 hours.

3. Cool the chili; refrigerate it overnight. Skim off the excess grease. Reheat the chili to the boiling point and stir in a paste made of the flour and a little water to thicken the mixture. Stir constantly to prevent sticking and scorching. Add water as necessary for the desired texture.

Lean-Meat Soups and Fish Soups

CHICKEN-SQUASH SOUP

Serves 6

5 cups Chicken Stock (see Index)
2 chicken breasts, skinned and boned
4 medium-size zucchini
4 medium-size yellow summer squash
¼ cup chopped parsley
2 tomatoes, peeled and cut into ½-inch cubes

1. Bring the stock to a boil in a 4-quart soup pot. Add the chicken breasts, lower heat, cover, and simmer until the meat is cooked through (about 20 minutes). Remove from heat.

2. With a slotted spoon, remove cooked chicken breasts from the stock. When cool enough to handle, cut meat into ½-inch cubes. Set aside.

3. Chop 1 zucchini and 1 yellow squash into ¼-inch cubes. Combine and measure out 1 cup and set aside. Toss any remaining chopped squash into the stock. Slice the remaining squash into ½-inch slices. Add to the stock. Return to a boil, lower heat, cover, and simmer 10 minutes. Remove from heat and cool slightly. Puree squash and stock in a blender. Return to pot. Add chicken and reheat.

4. Divide the parsley and tomatoes among 6 serving bowls. Sprinkle in the uncooked chopped squash. Ladle the chicken soup over top.

Chicken Soup and the Common Cold

Yes, hot chicken soup can help cure a cold, and the reason that it can, say doctors from Mount Sinai Medical Center in Miami, is that it reduces the amount of time that germ-laden mucus stays in contact with the nasal passages. (It makes your nose run!)

Concerning the precise mechanism responsible for this power of chicken soup, the researchers could not be specific. Partially due to its warmth, partially to its aroma, and partially to "some other mechanism related to taste," is all that Dr. Marvin Sackner, the director of Mount Sinai's Medical Services, could say.

HUNGARIAN FISH CHOWDER

Serves 6

¼ cup butter
1 large onion, coarsely chopped
3 celery stalks, coarsely chopped
3 garlic cloves, minced
1 medium-size leek, coarsely chopped
3 potatoes, peeled and diced
2 carrots, diced
4 large tomatoes, peeled and diced
1 teaspoon sweet Hungarian paprika
pinch saffron threads, crumbled
1 bay leaf
⅛ teaspoon cayenne pepper
5 cups Fish Stock (see Index)
3 pounds white fish fillets (such as cod, haddock, flounder)
2 tablespoons lemon juice
3 tablespoons minced parsley

1. Melt the butter in a 3-quart soup pot. Add the onion and celery and saute 5 minutes. Stir in the garlic and leek and cook 2 minutes longer. Stir in the potatoes, carrots, tomatoes, paprika, saffron, bay leaf, and cayenne. Pour the stock over all. Bring to a boil, lower heat, cover, and simmer 15 minutes.

2. Cut the fish into 2-inch pieces and sprinkle with lemon juice. Add to the soup pot, cover, and cook 10 minutes longer. Remove bay leaf and stir in the parsley. Ladle into heated bowls.

Use the Right Paprika for the Purpose

Paprika obtained from cone-shaped Hungarian capsicum is pungent, while an agreeably sweet, aromatic paprika almost without bite comes from the more rounded capsicum native to Spain. For a noticeable flavor and nip in soups and stews, choose the Hungarian type. Most people use the rich-colored Spanish powder to garnish salads and slaws. True spice merchants carry both types of paprika; supermarkets are more likely to stock only the milder, less intense version.

JAPANESE CHICKEN AND MUSHROOM SOUP

Serves 6

12 cups Chicken Stock (see Index)
2 chicken breasts, skinned, boned, and cut into thin, narrow slices
½ teaspoon pepper
½ teaspoon dry mustard
20 medium-size mushrooms, cut into ⅛-inch slices
2 cups cooked brown rice
4 scallions, thinly sliced on the diagonal
6 lemon rind strips

1. In a 5-quart soup pot, bring the stock to a boil. Add the chicken and spices and cook on medium heat 5 minutes. Add the mushrooms, then remove the pot from the heat.

2. Prepare the bowls for serving. Divide the rice among the bowls, sprinkle the scallions on top of the rice, and place a lemon rind strip in each bowl. Use a slotted spoon to transfer the chicken and mushrooms to the bowls. Ladle the stock over all.

MULLIGATAWNY SOUP

Serves 6

2½ pounds chicken, cut into pieces
8 cups water
3 tablespoons butter
1 large onion, coarsely chopped
2 garlic cloves, minced
2 celery stalks, cut into ¼-inch slices
1 tablespoon curry powder
½ teaspoon ground coriander seeds
½ teaspoon ground cumin
5 tablespoons cornstarch
⅔ cup tomato juice
1 tablespoon lemon juice
1 cooking apple, coarsely chopped
3 tablespoons minced parsley

1. In a 5-quart soup pot, simmer the chicken in the water 45 minutes. Remove cooked chicken and set aside; reduce stock to 6 cups by rapid boiling.

2. Melt the butter in a small skillet. Add the onion and saute until transparent. Add the garlic and celery and cook 1 minute longer. Add to the stock.

3. Combine the curry powder, coriander, cumin, and cornstarch in a small bowl. Stir in the tomato juice. Stir mixture into the simmering liquid. Add lemon juice and apple; cook 15 minutes.

4. Remove the meat from the chicken pieces and coarsely chop. Discard the skin and bones. Return chicken to the soup.

5. Serve hot, garnished with parsley.

In Southern India, where mulligatawny soup originated, the name means "pepper water." It began as a brew, made from black pepper and tamarind, that inhabitants frequently took as a remedy for indigestion.

BEEF SOUP WITH BEAN SPROUTS

Serves 6

1½ pounds lean beef, cut into ¾-inch cubes
2 tablespoons whole wheat flour
3 tablespoons sesame oil
2 leeks, thinly sliced
2 cups water
5 cups Beef Stock (see Index)
3 cups bean sprouts, rinsed
2 scallions, thinly sliced

1. Dredge the beef with the flour. Heat the oil in a skillet. Add beef and saute on medium-high heat until browned on all sides. Add leeks; cook and stir 2 minutes. Transfer to a 3-quart soup pot.

2. Scrape up all the brown particles in the skillet by deglazing the pot with the water. Add to the soup pot. Add the stock, bring to a boil, lower heat, cover, and simmer until the meat is tender (about 2 hours).

3. Just before serving, add bean sprouts and scallions to the simmering liquid. Return to a boil, remove from heat, and ladle into warm bowls.

Fish Soups and Chowders Champion

To own a whole fresh fish is to love it. Think of the myriad ways it
can be cooked—baked, charcoal grilled, steamed, poached. But before
you reach for the recipe book you must prepare it for the pot, and that
is a much less formidable undertaking than you might think.
THE COOKS' CATALOGUE

By age nineteen, Tom Ney had filleted at least four thousand pounds of fish.
"Over the years I must have filleted tens of thousands of pounds," he recalls of his
many years in the food business, particularly food from the sea.

Like so many east-coast college students, Tom spent summer holidays working at seaside resorts as a busboy, waiter, and chef's helper. A four-year stint in the U.S. Navy working on airplane communication and navigation systems did not dull his food interests. Living in an off-base residence with several other men, he voluntarily assumed the job of cook and relegated other household duties to those whose passion for cooking was less than his own. With such an edge he was able to schedule himself right out of clean-up operations.

Tom returned to civilian life as a student at the renowned Culinary Institute of America and with a summer job as a steamer cook at an ocean-front seafood restaurant. By July of that summer, the owners saw enough promise in this industrious young man to appoint him head chef after the former one hastily departed. Tom returned the next summer as head chef and manager. At times the work both exhausted and exasperated him. "Cooking came naturally, but managing people was a whole new ball game." Nonetheless, his experience was a crash course in all the necessary aspects of running a restaurant. During these summers along the coast Tom began to develop some of the chowders and steamed fish dishes that he has refined over the years. These have become mainstays in his food career.

In on the Ground Floor

After graduating from cooking school, Tom embarked on a ground-floor restaurant operation. With two partners, he created a charming chowder house from a dilapidated downtown building in Greenwich, Connecticut. They scavenged oak wainscoting from a crumbling mansion and bought large globe ceiling shades from the local school district's surplus supply. Long wooden pews flanked the walls, and antique wood chairs surrounded the tables. The kitchen, set apart from the dining area, was open to public view. The warm, comfortable atmosphere attracted a packed house from the first afternoon that the establishment opened for lunch. Thereafter, Tom's cooking guaranteed a steady stream of fish lovers for every meal.

Soup at Lewis Street Chowder House always transcended the ordinary. Tom humbly attributes this basic fact to the quality of his ingredients:

> *In the beginning I personally filleted every piece of fish that found its way into the cooking pots. Later, I had help, but the filleting process never went on outside of our doors. Therefore, I was certain, beyond doubt, of the freshest fish available. Besides, I got to keep what was left, including the heads—all of which make exceptional bases for soups.*

His steamed-fish-in-broth dishes—a perfect blend of olive oil, butter, leeks, onions, herbs, filleted fish, and shellfish—became the specialties of the house. "And I defy you to uncover a better white chowder recipe anywhere in New England," Tom declares. Recognizing that folks could easily make an entree with just one of his soups, Tom created meal-size portions (slightly larger than a bowl), accompanied by a mixed green salad and a homemade Roquefort cheese dressing.

Left, 1. *With a sharp knife, make an incision behind the gills. Cut behind the collarbone and remove the head.* Right, 2. *Make an incision 1 inch deep on one side of the dorsal fin, and continue cutting from nape to tail. Turn fish over and repeat procedure on other side.*

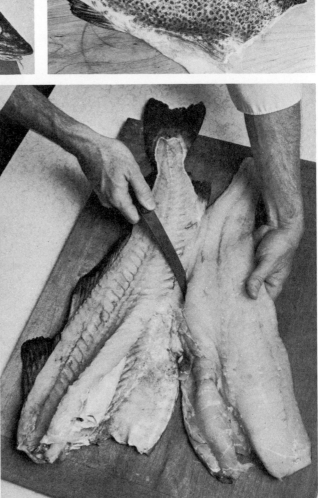

3. *Following the plane of the backbone, but not breaking the structure, shave the flesh from the rib cage. Peel back the fillet as you work.*

4. *Separate the top fillet from the bone structure, but leave the other half containing the whole backbone.*

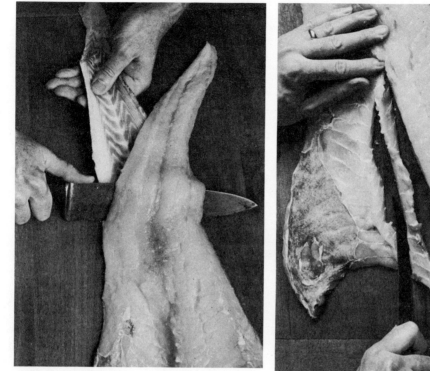 

5. Skin the fillet by moving a large knife blade in a sawing motion between the skin and the flesh (skin side down). Work with the blade at a slight angle to the skin and press it firmly against the skin. (I prefer a somewhat dull blade for this step.)

6. Remove the center line of lateral bones from the skinned flesh. Separate the thick section from the thin belly portion. (Use the former for Steamed Combo, the latter for New England Fish Chowder.)

Perform procedures 3, 5, and 6 on the opposite side of the fish, which still contains the whole backbone. Clean the carcass and fish head of remaining entrails and retain for making Fish Stock.

Cooking Class—Right Here

Today Tom Ney plays an indispensable role at Rodale Press where he is Director of Test Kitchens and Food Services. In the following pages he offers a cooking class with the flavor and smells of salt air and tall ships. In his own words he tells how he fillets cod at a fast clip. He demonstrates a flair for economy as he prepares a rich basic stock from commonly discarded fish heads and bones. He goes on to share the secrets which serve in part to produce his famous white chowder, and he very generously lists the proportions and describes the techniques that lead to a gourmet dish—steamed shellfish and cod in broth. Serve either of these substantial meals with a simple salad and the dressing that Tom created for the chowder house.

TOM'S FISH STOCK

Yields 3 cups

2 to 3 pounds lean fish carcass
8 cups water
4 lemon slices, ¼ inch thick
2 bay leaves
5 white or black peppercorns
2 sprigs parsley
¼ teaspoon dried thyme

1. In a 4-quart soup pot, cover the fish carcass with water. Add the remaining ingredients. Bring to a boil, lower heat, cover pot, and simmer 45 minutes.
2. Strain stock through triple layers of cheesecloth or filter paper. Bring strained stock to rolling boil and maintain boil to reduce stock to about 3 cups. Cool quickly and refrigerate in a closed container.

NEW ENGLAND FISH CHOWDER

Serves 6

1 medium-size onion, coarsely chopped
1 celery stalk, thinly sliced
1 large leek (white part only), thinly sliced
4 tablespoons olive oil
1 tablespoon mustard oil* (optional)
1 garlic clove, minced
1 large potato, cut into ½-inch cubes
3 cups Tom's Fish Stock (see recipe in this section)
1 cup Chicken Stock (see Index)
1 tablespoon minced parsley
½ teaspoon dried thyme
¼ teaspoon white pepper
2 bay leaves
1 teaspoon tamari soy sauce
1 tablespoon Prepared Mustard (see Index)
3 cups milk
1 cup light cream or heavy cream
1½ pounds cod or haddock fillets, cut into 1-inch cubes

*Available in stores stocking oriental groceries.

1. In a 5-quart soup pot, saute onion, celery, and leek in olive and mustard oils on medium heat until soft. Do not brown. Add garlic and potato. Continue to saute 1 to 2 minutes.
2. Add stocks, parsley, thyme, pepper, bay leaves, tamari, and mustard. Bring to a boil, lower heat, and simmer until potatoes are tender (15 to 20 minutes).
3. Warm milk and cream together in a separate pot. Do not boil.
4. Add fish chunks to the stock and vegetables and remove pot from the heat. Allow fish to steep in the hot stock 5 to 6 minutes. Add hot milk and cream mixture and serve.
Note: To prevent curdling, do not overheat chowder.

STEAMED COMBO

Serves 4

Broth

2 large leeks (white part only), thinly sliced
2 tablespoons olive oil
1 tablespoon unsalted butter
2 garlic cloves, minced
1½ cups freshly squeezed or natural white grape juice (for freshly squeezed, use 2½ to 3 pounds seeded white grapes)
2 tablespoons lemon juice
1 tablespoon lime juice
¼ teaspoon white pepper
2 bay leaves
¼ teaspoon dried thyme
1½ cups water

Combo

8 large mushrooms
8 ¾-inch-thick slices zucchini
1 large carrot, halved lengthwise and cut into 8 equal pieces
1 red or green sweet pepper, sliced into 8 equal strips
8 medium-size cauliflower florets
4 scallions, half green part cut off and discarded
1½ pounds cod or haddock fillet
16 medium-size shrimp, peeled, with tail intact
1 Alaskan King crab leg, cut into 12 equal pieces
1 5-ounce lobster tail, cut through shell into 4 equal sections

Garnish

8 fresh grapes
1 tablespoon minced parsley

1. In a 6-quart soup pot, saute leeks in the oil and butter over medium heat until soft. Do not brown. Add garlic and continue to saute 1 to 2 minutes. Add grape, lemon, and lime juices, white pepper, bay leaves, thyme, and water. Bring to a rolling boil and continue cooking, uncovered, 5 minutes.

2. Remove and reserve half the liquid from the soup pot. Set aside. Place the combo vegetables in groups in the soup pot with the remaining broth. Cover and steam the vegetables over high heat 7 to 8 minutes. Remove vegetables in groups to a large platter and place platter in a 250°F oven.

3. Pour reserved broth into pot. Place seafood in the pot in groups. Be sure to immerse the fillets in the broth on the bottom. Cover and steam the seafood 8 to 10 minutes.

4. Arrange equal portions of vegetables and seafood on 4 individual platters. Place a small cup of broth in the center of each platter for dipping vegetables and seafood. Garnish each platter with 2 grapes and chopped parsley.

LEWIS STREET ROQUEFORT CHEESE DRESSING

Yields 2⅓ to 2½ cups

½ cup sour cream
½ cup Mayonnaise (see Index)
½ cup plain yogurt
¼ cup buttermilk
½ teaspoon tamari soy sauce
¼ teaspoon cayenne pepper to taste
1 garlic clove, squeezed or mashed to pulp
¼ pound Roquefort cheese, crumbled

1. Combine sour cream, mayonnaise, yogurt, and buttermilk and blend thoroughly. Incorporate tamari, cayenne, and garlic pulp. Fold in cheese.
2. Store in closed container overnight in refrigerator or 2 hours at room temperature before serving.

GREEN BEAN ALMONDINE SALAD   For this recipe, see page 230

WALNUT VINAIGRETTE SALAD   For this recipe, see page 232
BROCCOLI AU GRATIN SOUP   For this recipe, see page 77

Vegetable Soups

BROCCOLI AU GRATIN SOUP

Serves 6 to 8

1½ pounds broccoli
4 cups Chicken Stock (see Index)
1 cup cottage cheese
1 teaspoon curry powder
2 cups milk
grated Parmesan cheese

1. Wash and trim the broccoli. Break it into florets and slice the thick stems into 1-inch pieces.
2. In a 5-quart soup pot, combine the broccoli and the stock. Bring to a boil, lower heat, cover, and simmer until broccoli is tender (about 20 minutes). Remove broccoli from soup base with a slotted spoon.
3. Puree broccoli and cottage cheese together in a blender until smooth. Return puree to the soup base.
4. Add curry powder and milk. Reheat and serve hot, sprinkled with Parmesan cheese.

CABBAGE BORSCHT

Serves 6 to 8

6 cups Beef Stock (see Index)
3 pounds lean short ribs
4 tomatoes, peeled and coarsely chopped
1 large onion, coarsely chopped
2 garlic cloves, crushed
2 pounds cabbage, shredded
¼ pound sauerkraut
3 tablespoons lemon juice
3 tablespoons honey
1 cup plain yogurt

1. Combine stock, short ribs, tomatoes, onion, and garlic in a 5-quart soup pot. Bring to a boil and skim off any foam that accumulates on the surface. Add cabbage and sauerkraut, lower heat, cover, and simmer 2 hours. Stir in the lemon juice and honey.
2. Serve hot, garnished with a dollop of yogurt.
Note: Provide separate plates for short ribs, as they are cumbersome in a bowl.

APPLE-SQUASH SOUP

Serves 6 to 8

1 pound butternut squash, seeded and diced
3 McIntosh apples, diced
1 medium-size onion, coarsely chopped
5 cups Chicken Stock (see Index)
¼ teaspoon dried rosemary
4 tablespoons butter
4 tablespoons whole wheat flour
1 cup buttermilk

1. Combine squash, apples, onion, stock, and rosemary in a 5-quart soup pot. Bring to a boil, lower heat, cover, and simmer 20 minutes. Cool slightly. Puree in small batches in a blender and return mixture to soup pot.

2. Melt butter in a small saucepan. Stir in flour and cook until bubbly. Remove from heat; gradually add the buttermilk. Return to heat and cook until smooth. Stir throughout the entire process.

3. Pour thickened liquid into pot. Bring soup to a boil; simmer and stir 2 minutes. Serve hot.

Stay Young with Rosemary

Just a sniff of rosemary now and then might be all you need to stay young. A sixteenth-century prescription says simply, "Make thee a box of the wood of rosemary and smell to it and it shall preserve thy youth."

PEA AND POD SOUP

Serves 6 to 8

¼ cup butter
1 cup coarsely chopped onions
1½ pounds fresh peas
1 large potato, diced
6 cups Chicken Stock (see Index)
6 Boston lettuce leaves, coarsely chopped
1 leek, sliced into ½-inch pieces
1 teaspoon honey

1. Melt the butter in a 3-quart soup pot. Add the onions and cook on low heat until transparent.

2. Shell the peas and set them aside. Slice the pods into 1-inch pieces. Add the sliced pods, the potato, and 4 cups of the stock to the pot with the onions. Bring to a boil, lower heat, cover, and simmer 25 minutes.

3. Cook the peas, lettuce, and leek in the remaining 2 cups stock until tender (about 15 minutes).

4. Puree both the pea pod and the pea bases through a food mill placed over a clean saucepan. Let cool.

5. Reheat before serving and then stir in the honey. Soup may be thinned with additional stock or milk, if desired.

"Pease" is Old English for the plural of "pea." So the "pease porridge" of the famous rhyme is nothing more or less than that old favorite, thick pea soup.

BEET MADRILENE

Serves 6 to 8

1 pound small beets, peeled and
  diced
1 medium-size onion, coarsely
  chopped
6 cups Beef Stock (see Index)
1 tablespoon lemon juice
1 teaspoon honey
2 tablespoons unflavored gelatin
½ cup tomato juice
Garnish
1 cup sour cream
chopped dillweed

1. Combine the beets, onion, and stock in a 5-quart soup pot. Bring to a boil, lower heat, cover, and simmer until beets are tender (15 to 20 minutes). Cool slightly. Stir in the lemon juice and honey. Puree in small batches in a blender or through a food mill.

2. Sprinkle gelatin over the tomato juice in a small, heat-resistant cup and let stand 5 minutes to soften. Place cup in a pan of hot water until gelatin is dissolved. Stir dissolved gelatin into the beet mixture.

3. Refrigerate 3 to 4 hours or until soup is softly set and ready to serve. Spoon soup into individual chilled bowls, top each serving with a dollop of sour cream, and sprinkle with dillweed.

RED CABBAGE SOUP

Serves 6 to 8

6 cups Beef Stock (see Index)
2 pounds red cabbage, shredded
3 cooking apples, diced
1 large onion, coarsely chopped
¼ cup cider vinegar
3 tablespoons honey
½ cup raisins
Garnish
1 cup plain yogurt
chopped parsley

1. In a 5-quart soup pot, combine the stock, cabbage, apples, and onion. Bring to a boil, lower heat, cover, and simmer 30 minutes.

2. Stir in the vinegar, honey, and raisins. Cook 10 minutes longer.

3. Serve hot, topped with a dollop of yogurt and sprinkled with chopped parsley.

CURRIED CARROT SOUP

Serves 6 to 8

3 tablespoons butter
1 large onion, coarsely chopped
1 pound carrots, sliced into
  ¾-inch chunks
5 cups Chicken Stock (see Index)
½ teaspoon grated lemon rind
2 teaspoons honey
1 tablespoon curry powder
1 cup plain yogurt

1. Melt the butter in a 5-quart soup pot and saute the onion until transparent. Add the carrots, stock, lemon rind, honey, and curry powder. Bring to a boil, lower heat, cover, and simmer until tender (about 25 minutes). Cool slightly.

2. Puree in small batches in a blender. Return to pot and reheat. Stir in yogurt just before serving.

SPRING ASPARAGUS SOUP

Serves 6 to 8

1 pound thin asparagus spears
6 cups Chicken Stock (see Index)
4 tablespoons butter
2 tablespoons whole wheat flour
1 teaspoon curry powder
1 cup plain yogurt
4 egg yolks, lightly beaten

1. Cut off asparagus tips and reserve them. Slice the spears into 2-inch pieces. Place them in a 4-quart soup pot with the stock. Bring to a boil, lower heat, cover, and simmer 15 minutes. Puree in a blender to break down any stringy or woody fibers.

2. Melt butter in another saucepan. Add flour and curry powder and cook until bubbly. Remove from heat and stir in puree. Return to heat and bring to a boil while constantly stirring; simmer 2 minutes. Add asparagus tips, lower heat, cover, and simmer until tips are tender (about 5 minutes).

3. In a small mixing bowl, whisk yogurt and egg yolks together. Stir into soup and heat through but do not allow to boil. Serve hot.

Increasingly popular, kohlrabi is a rich source of vitamin C. It is a cross between a turnip and cabbage but most resembles a turnip in appearance. Since its meat is sweet and has the wonderful crispness of raw cabbage stalk, it works well in salads as well as in soups. The young leaves are also an excellent addition to a bowl of tossed greens.

KOHLRABI SOUP

Serves 6 to 8

1 pound kohlrabi, peeled and diced
6 cups Beef Stock (see Index)
1 tablespoon butter
1 tablespoon cornstarch
1 teaspoon tamari soy sauce
2 tablespoons cold water
3 egg yolks, lightly beaten
3 scallions, thinly sliced

1. In a 3-quart soup pot, simmer the kohlrabi in the stock until tender (about 30 minutes). Remove the kohlrabi with a slotted spoon and mash it together with the butter. Return the puree to the stock.

2. Make a smooth paste by combining the cornstarch, tamari, and water in a small cup. Whisk paste into soup. Bring to a boil and simmer 5 minutes.

3. Remove soup from heat. Temper the egg yolks with a small amount of the hot soup and then stir the yolks into the remaining soup. Do not boil. Ladle into individual soup bowls and sprinkle with scallions.

SWEET PEPPER SOUP

Serves 6 to 8

6 large sweet red peppers,
  coarsely chopped
1 cup freshly grated coconut
½ cup tomato paste
pinch dried thyme
1 sprig parsley
2 teaspoons honey
3 cups Chicken Stock (see Index)
3 cups milk
nutmeg

1. In a 5-quart soup pot, combine the peppers, coconut, tomato paste, thyme, parsley, honey, and stock. Bring to a boil, lower heat, cover, and simmer 20 minutes. Cool slightly.

2. Puree soup mixture in small batches in a blender. Strain before returning to pot.

3. Stir in the milk and reheat before serving. Sprinkle each portion with nutmeg.

The Ranch House

Heaven is under our feet as well as over our heads.
HENRY D. THOREAU, *WALDEN*

Just at the edge of a Southern California town lies a beautiful, secluded garden encircled by stone walls, wild sunflowers, and an ivy-covered hillside. Here, tall, thick bamboo stalks tower over a pond where plump goldfish swim. On the terraced slope, a Japanese tea house and two handsome fountains appear amid high, straight oaks. Light green fern shoots and bright, colorful flowers blanket the earth. At one end, this grove opens onto a sunny area where paperlike tropical blossoms drape the surrounding walls. A walking path winds past a grassy lawn, a vegetable plot, and several flower and herb gardens. Narrow steps lead to a flagstone patio which provides a panoramic view of this lush restaurant courtyard.

At the Ranch House the same meticulous care lavished on the natural realm is also at work in the kitchen. Some of the vegetables come from these gardens; most of the herbs grow here. The bakery produces 100 exquisite loaves of bread every day.

Twenty-three years ago, however, this garden paradise was, according to owner Alan Hooker, "the driest, most decayed apple orchard you could possibly imagine."

Without constant irrigation in the summer, scorching temperatures, sometimes reaching 110°F, left a terrain unredeemable in most people's eyes.

One day in the mid fifties, Alan stood here in this valley just below the original miner's ranch house that he and his wife Helen had turned into a boarding house. The food they served there had gained such a formidable reputation that the Hookers were being urged to establish an actual restaurant—but where? Suddenly, as he gazed among the crooked boughs, Alan made the decision to build just where he was. Within the year, the orchard was cleared and an unpretentious ranch-house-style building was erected.

Bread from a Washing Machine

Right from the start Alan and Helen determined to maintain the standards of the boarding house on the hill. Home-baked bread and fresh garden fruits and vegetables, no matter what their cost in time, were essentials. When they could no longer hand-knead enough dough to meet the demand for their bread, Helen suggested converting their old wringer washing machine into a dough mixer. A machinist stopped the drain with a stainless steel plug and filled the bottom of the agitator with metal for easy cleaning; thereafter, the necessary number of loaves were in the ovens in no time.

Alan Hooker chooses the home-grown herbs that enhance Ranch House offerings.

Vegetables to be used in salads must pass inspection for texture and color.

A Special Chemistry at Work

As he had at the boarding house, Alan took charge of the kitchen. "Anything that concerns food, concerns Alan," Helen tells her guests. His love of food came from his father who learned special techniques and recipes from an ex-Waldorf chef. In the thirties, he worked as a baker and bakery manager. Even Alan's college chemistry background has been useful. It provides him with the discipline to work out recipes carefully, and many have become part of the Ranch House master list. Alan comments on his exactness:

> *I have the restaurant because I want to do certain things a certain way. In our kitchen, we use seven books containing 500 master recipes. I have developed them all, and each must be followed exactly. I taste everything, and if there's any variation I want to know what happened. Always my thumb is right on. After all, how can you run a restaurant unless you run a restaurant?*

Soup-Seasoning Blends

Until the Hookers decided to expand their menu for a wider audience, Alan served only vegetarian meals. Consequently, he learned to create appealing, varied soups without meat or fish foundations. To enhance the natural flavors in those early stocks, Alan turned to herbs, "the bulwark of my cooking knowledge." Over the years he has devised a number of particular herbal formulas. Those original ones have evolved into three major soup-seasoning blends, a delicate one for vegetable-base and cream soups (see Herb Blend for Soups in this section), a slightly stronger one for chicken-base soups, and one still stronger for beef and lamb broths.

When it comes to soups, Alan shares with his customers a partiality for the vegetable purees:

> *Many of these developed from my own natural frugality, my inability to throw out something good. One day I lightly steamed some asparagus spears. That water was so sweet and delicious that I thought, "I should do something with this." Well, it has become our famous Green Goddess Soup. Now we make all these purees—spinach, celery, watercress—from the tail end of numerous vegetables. You know, most of the flavor of the vegetables is close to the root, in the stalk, or in the stems.*

With the help of a powerful one-gallon commercial blender, the kitchen staff quickly puts together lightly steamed vegetables, liquid (milk or vegetable water), and fresh herbs to produce these creamy mixtures. No liaisons are ever added. "We like them just the way they are, and most are quite thick all by themselves," says Alan. Chopped, steamed vegetables and specific garnishes, like whipped sour cream, are the only additions. Careful attention to every detail produces smooth combinations that have lost none of nature's true colors or tastes.

Salad Herbs

Herbs quite naturally play an important role in Ranch House salads. Alan has formulated a general salad herb blend for green salads and dressings. Particular dressings, however, demand specific herbs. He makes a French dressing that contains lemon, lime, nutmeg, and apple geranium leaves. Ranch House Salad Dressing, Alan's herbal version of a standard French salad dressing, calls for lemon thyme. Most of these dressings start with the Ranch House's own special wine vinegar. It is an aged mixture of equal parts 5 percent apple cider vinegar and good, dry red wine seasoned with fresh tarragon and garlic.

Having survived so well for so long with a washing machine dough mixer, Alan is not immediately enchanted with "newfangled" kitchen equipment. One of his favorite salad-making tools, therefore, is a manually operated gricer, a freestanding grater to which several cones attach for varying textures. Alan has experimented with popular food processors, but his demand for preciseness always brings him back to this standard piece of equipment. Sturdy vegetables like carrots, beets, and turnips emerge in long thin threads, in shavings, or in a fine grind. They are never mushy. With the gricer,

The gricer is a favorite salad-making tool at the Ranch House. It can produce varying textures, such as threads, shavings, and fine grinds.

the Ranch House staff prepares efficiently one of its most popular summer courses, Raw Vegetable Salad Supreme. Children are enchanted with the beautiful colors and appreciate the uncomplicated, pure vegetable tastes.

Spectacular Fruit Salad

Travelers from colder climates are astonished by the abundance and variety of fruit in this vicinity. No refrigerated transport truck ever drops off cases of unripened produce at the Ranch House. Instead, local retired people, each of whom proudly raises one or two special crops, supply fully mature melons, citrus fruits, apples, peaches, and pears. ("Wednesday mornings, our kitchen door area looks like a farmers' market," Alan says jovially.) During particular seasons, some of the staff will scout the roadside stands for special delicacies. In May, they drive to Oxnard, just a few miles from the Pacific Ocean, where they buy big, luscious Sequoia strawberries, so perishable they never get marketed outside the region. Midsummer guests enjoy refreshing, chilled melon served with cottage cheese or colorful combination plates including smooth avocadoes, apricots, and cherries. The dressings are all carefully designed complements—exotic cardamom sauce, bright pomegranate topping, or a simple home-made mayonnaise flavored with lime and mint.

The Hookers' firm determination to do things the way they want them done has kept them very much an integral part of this Shangri-la. Their stamp is every-where—in the gardens, in all the recipes, in the atmosphere of the dining room and patios. Over the years, they have created a very special haven at which people from all over the world now stop on their way through this area. "I never want to lose the idea that it's a ranch house," says Alan. "That way we are not obliged to imitate the cuisines of other countries. This is not French food, or Italian, or German. It is our very own concept." Mulligatawny Soup at this restaurant will always be a la Hooker.

The following recipes are reprinted from *Vegetarian Gourmet Cookery,* copyright 1970, and *Herb Cookery,* copyright 1971, by Alan Hooker, with permission of the publisher 101 Productions, San Francisco.

FRENCH SORREL SOUP

Serves 8

The main thing is to have enough fresh sorrel so that its tartness is imparted to the soup. The addition of carrots gives a bit of sweetness, and this can be adjusted if one does not care to have a very tart soup. Carrots will sweeten it without adding sugar.

We do the whole soup in a kettle and then put it through the blender and strain it. At first, when the soup has just been made, it may seem to lack flavor, but letting it stand 24 hours will bring out all the hidden flavor. It should be put into a covered stainless steel pot or glass vessel and kept overnight in the refrigerator. Sometimes people ask what kind of cheese we put in it, probably because of the combination of tartness and sour cream used as a garnish. Cook in pressure cooker 10 minutes at 15 pounds:

    7 cups water
    1 large carrot, chopped fine
    2 stalks celery, cut fine
    ½ small cucumber, chopped fine
    1 medium onion, cut fine
    2 large leaves cabbage, chopped
    ½ teaspoon soup herbs [see Herb Blend for Soups in this section]
    5 vegetable cubes
    ¼ cup parsley, chopped

Cook 5 minutes in separate pot, slowly:

    6 large sorrel leaves and stems
    ¼ cup water

Combine all ingredients and put through blender and strain. Then add:

    1 tablespoon lemon juice

Chill 24 hours and serve with sour cream.

GREEN GODDESS SOUP
Serves 8

Cook until just done:

 1 *small bunch asparagus*
¼ *cup water*

Heat, but do not boil:

 4 *cups fresh green peas in*
¼ *cup water*

Liquefy the above and strain into:

1½ *quarts warm milk*

To which has been added:

 ¼ *teaspoon marjoram (4 sprigs)*
 2 *mint leaves*
pinch thyme (1 sprig)
1¼ *tablespoons herb salt [see Herb Salt in this section]*

Liquefy without straining and add to above:

1 *large avocado in*
1 *pint milk*

Heat and serve. Garnish with unsweetened whipped cream and parsley.

SOUR CREAM
GARNISH DRESSING

Put into mixer and whip until thoroughly mixed:

 1 *pint sour cream*
 8 *ounces Philadelphia cream cheese*
 2 *teaspoons herb salt [see Herb Salt in this section]*
⅓ *cup parsley French dressing [see Parsley French Dressing for Vegetables in this section]*
 3 *drops green coloring*

PARSLEY FRENCH DRESSING FOR VEGETABLES

Put in blender and liquefy for at least 2 minutes:

1½ *cups parsley tops*
4 *tablespoons vinegar, 5%*
4 *tablespoons water*
¾ *cup lemon juice*
2 *tablespoons sherry*
¼ *cup chives or 2 green onions with tops*
1 *teaspoon dry mustard*
½ *teaspoon salt*
1 *teaspoon salad herbs [see Herb Blend for Salads in this section]*
1 *teaspoon herb salt [see Herb Salt in this section]*
½ *teaspoon black pepper, fresh ground preferable*

Add and blend for 1 minute:

2 *tablespoons honey*
1 *cup peanut or other oil*

RANCH HOUSE SALAD DRESSING

Mix well together:

1 *cup wine vinegar*
½ *teaspoon dry mustard*
½ *teaspoon fresh-ground black pepper*

Grind together and mix in:

4 *sprigs basil*
4 *sprigs marjoram*
2 *sprigs tarragon*
2 *sprigs lemon thyme*
2 *sprigs rosemary*
1 *teaspoon Herb Salt [see Herb Salt in this section]*

(Use only fresh herbs; dry will not do.)
Add and mix in:

2 *cups olive oil*

Do not refrigerate.

HERB BLEND FOR SALADS

> *4 parts each: marjoram, basil, tarragon, parsley, chervil, celery, chives.*
> *1 part each: lemon thyme, summer savory, costmary.*

HERB BLEND FOR SOUPS

> *2 parts each: thyme or summer savory, parsley, chervil, basil, sweet marjoram, celery or lovage leaves.*
> *1 part each: sage, rosemary, dried ground lemon peel.*

HERB SALT

Blend your own! Start with:

> *1 teaspoon garlic salt*
> *2 teaspoons onion salt*
> *1 teaspoon dry parsley*

Next time, add to the above:

> *½ teaspoon basil*
> *½ teaspoon marjoram*

These two herbs are mild; you might like to add:

thyme or mint, a small pinch

(Careful, don't overdo it!) This way you will soon learn the strength of each herb and see for yourself what you like and how much of it to use. It can be great fun.

To release the flavors of the herbs you are going to add to a dish, grind them in the mortar with the salt or herb salt. This blends them before they go into the mixture. You can do this with dry or fresh herbs.

RAW VEGETABLE
SALAD SUPREME

In the spring when, if you have a garden, new carrots, beets, turnips, and the ever-present radishes are available, a colorful and very interesting salad can be made. Wash all vegetables well but do not peel them. Put them through the finest cone of a gricer to make long threads. If you do not have one, a grater will do if it can make the long threads. . . . First the turnips, then radishes, then carrots, and lastly the beets so you won't have to wash it between each using. On a plate which has been dressed with a bronze lettuce leaf, pile one mound each in a triangle, carrots, turnips, and beets. In the center place the radishes. They are a bit peppery and your taste will have to determine the amount. Pass a bowl of Sour Cream Garnish Dressing [see recipe in this section] that is slightly green from the addition of a few drops of coloring. This will bring many oohs and ahs from your guests.

Root-Vegetable Soups

ONION SOUP WITH CHEESE

Serves 6

10 tablespoons butter, melted
3½ pounds Bermuda onions, thinly sliced
1 teaspoon honey
1 tablespoon whole wheat flour
1 garlic clove, minced
7 cups Beef Stock (see Index)
½ bay leaf
¼ teaspoon pepper
6 slices stale bread (preferably whole grain French or sourdough)
1 tablespoon olive oil
¼ cup grated Gruyere cheese
¼ cup grated Parmesan cheese

1. Melt 8 tablespoons of the butter in a 4-quart soup pot. Add onions. Stir and cook over low heat until onions are transparent (about 20 minutes). Add honey. Increase the heat and continue cooking until onions are a rich, golden color (about 20 minutes more). Sprinkle with the flour, add the garlic, and stir for a few minutes.

2. Add stock, bay leaf, and pepper to onions. After liquid comes to a boil, lower heat, partially cover, and simmer 45 minutes longer.

3. Preheat the oven to 350°F. Place bread on a cookie sheet. Combine remaining butter and oil and pour over bread. Mix the two cheeses together and sprinkle bread carefully with ¼ cup of the cheese. Slip under the broiler a few minutes until cheese melts.

4. Pour the soup into an 8- or 10-cup ovenproof casserole, float the bread on top, and sprinkle the rest of the cheese over the bread. Bake in the oven for an additional 20 minutes or until a melted crust of cheese has formed on the top of the soup.

In France, the leek is called "the asparagus of the poor." It is a hardy winter vegetable that is unbeatable for soups. Historians report that Nero ate leek soup every day to maintain the clarity of his voice.

SPANISH LEEK AND POTATO SOUP

Serves 6

6 tablespoons butter
6 thin leeks (white part only), thinly sliced
1 large onion, minced
4 potatoes, diced
½ teaspoon saffron threads
6 cups boiling Chicken Stock (see Index)
pepper to taste
1 cup heavy cream
6 drops hot pepper sauce
6 tablespoons minced chives

1. Melt butter in a 5-quart soup pot. Add leeks and onion to butter and saute over low heat until wilted. Add potatoes and toss to coat with butter.

2. Soak saffron 10 minutes in 2 tablespoons of the stock. Add the remaining stock, saffron liquid, and pepper. Simmer 45 minutes. Let cool.

3. Puree in several small batches in a blender. Stir in heavy cream and pepper sauce. Serve hot, topped with minced chives.

Some large, raw potatoes have nearly as much vitamin C as an orange! To maximize that nutrient and others, cut potatoes into large chunks, not small pieces, and cook immediately after peeling and cutting. No soaking! Those that are cooked with their jackets on lose almost none of their nutrients. Good news for weight watchers: A cup of boiled potatoes contains only about 100 calories.

POTATO SOUP AU GRATIN

Serves 6 to 8

4 large potatoes, peeled and coarsely cubed
4 celery stalks, quartered
1 medium-size onion, quartered
2 cups Chicken Stock (see Index)
1 cup ricotta or cottage cheese
1 cup milk
3 scallions, thinly sliced

1. Place the potatoes, celery, and onion in a 5-quart soup pot. Pour in the stock and add enough cold water to completely cover the vegetables. Bring to a boil, lower heat, cover, and simmer 30 minutes.

2. Puree the ricotta cheese in a blender with the milk until it is smooth.

3. Drain the cooked vegetables and return their cooking liquid to the soup pot. Process the vegetables in the blender with the cheese-milk mixture until smooth. Add mixture to the soup pot and stir well. Soup may be thinned with additional milk, if desired. Reheat before serving.

4. Garnish each serving with a generous sprinkling of sliced scallions.

FENNEL SOUP

Serves 6

2 tablespoons butter
1 large onion, coarsely chopped
1 garlic clove, minced
1 large fennel bulb
2 medium-size potatoes, diced
5 cups Chicken Stock (see Index)
¼ teaspoon freshly ground pepper

1. Melt the butter in a 4-quart soup pot. Add the onion and saute until transparent (about 5 minutes). Add the garlic and cook 1 minute longer.

2. Snip off the feathery leaves from the fennel and set them aside for garnish. Coarsely chop the bulb and stalk into 1-inch pieces. Add the fennel, potatoes, and stock to the pot. Bring to a boil, reduce heat, cover, and simmer until the vegetables are tender (25 to 30 minutes). Cool slightly.

3. Puree soup in a blender until smooth. Return the pureed soup to the pot and reheat before serving. Stir in the pepper.

4. Garnish soup with the snipped fennel leaves.

MUSHROOM-PARSNIP SOUP

Serves 6 to 8

3 tablespoons butter
½ pound button mushrooms
½ cup finely chopped leeks, white part only
1 pound parsnips, thickly sliced
6 cups Chicken Stock (see Index)
pinch nutmeg

1. Melt the butter in a 5-quart soup pot. Set aside 2 or 3 mushroom caps for garnish; finely chop the remaining mushrooms and stems. Add the chopped mushrooms and leeks to the melted butter. Cover with wax paper and steam over low heat 10 minutes. (Wax paper takes on weeping effect—keeps moisture locked in.) Discard paper.

2. Stir in the sliced parsnips. Add the stock and nutmeg. Bring to a boil, lower heat, cover, and simmer gently 30 minutes.

3. Transfer the vegetable and stock mixture to a blender in small batches and puree it until smooth. Return pureed mixture to the pan and reheat before serving.

4. Thinly slice reserved mushroom caps and use as a garnish over the hot soup.

BEETS AND GREENS SOUP

Serves 6 to 8

5 tablespoons butter
1 cup finely chopped onions
1 cup finely chopped celery
2 garlic cloves, minced
3 cups grated beets (about 1½ pounds)
7 cups Beef Stock (see Index)
2 tablespoons cider vinegar
1 teaspoon dried dillweed
1 cup diced potatoes
2 cups loosely packed shredded beet greens
¼ cup finely chopped parsley
1 cup sour cream or yogurt

1. Melt the butter in a 5-quart soup pot; add the onions, celery, and garlic and saute 5 minutes. Add the beets, stock, vinegar, and dillweed and bring liquid to a boil. Lower heat and simmer 15 minutes.

2. Add the potatoes; simmer another 15 minutes. Add the beet greens and parsley; cook 10 minutes longer.

3. Garnish soup with dollops of sour cream.

DANDELION ROOT EGG DROP SOUP

Serves 6 to 8

7 cups Chicken Stock (see Index)
1 teaspoon tamari soy sauce
½ pound dandelion roots, shredded
1 tablespoon cornstarch
2 tablespoons cold water
2 eggs
1 teaspoon sesame oil
2 scallions, thinly sliced

1. Bring the stock and tamari to a boil in a 5-quart soup pot. Add the dandelion roots, lower heat, and simmer, uncovered, 15 minutes.

2. Dissolve the cornstarch in the cold water; add it in a gentle stream to the simmering soup. Cook and stir 2 minutes.

3. Beat the eggs with the oil. Turn off the heat and drizzle the beaten eggs into the soup. Gently stir while you pour, then stop stirring; the egg will float to the surface like a cloud.

4. Ladle the soup into bowls and garnish with scallions.

Note: Plan to use all of this soup at one meal. Reheating makes dandelion bitter.

CELERY ROOT (CELERIAC) SOUP

Serves 6

4 tablespoons butter
1 large onion, coarsely chopped
1 large leek, coarsely chopped
6 cups Chicken Stock (see Index)
5 cups peeled and diced celery root (about 2 pounds)
1 parsnip, peeled and diced
1 large potato, peeled and diced
1 cup plain yogurt
minced parsley or freshly grated nutmeg

1. Melt the butter in a 4-quart soup pot; add the onion and leek. Cover the pot and steam the vegetables 4 or 5 minutes until the leek is tender but not browned. Add the stock, celery root, parsnip, and potato. Bring to a boil, lower heat, cover, and simmer until vegetables are tender (about 45 minutes). Cool slightly.

2. Puree cooked ingredients in small batches in a blender. Return to pot and stir in the yogurt. Reheat to serving temperature but do not boil.

3. Garnish with parsley or a pinch of nutmeg.

A Veritable Feast at 10,000 Feet

I am one who eats his breakfast gazing at morning glories.
BASHO

Kathie Lamm and her daughter, Chamisa, are inveterate travelers. They have hiked through tropical Guatemalan forests and slept in caves along deserted Hawaiian beaches. When they touch base, home is in the Colorado Rockies where they live in a comfortable tepee nestled beneath towering, snowcapped mountains.

A late-winter letter triggered our trip to the Colorado high country. On a brown bag, Kathie had carefully printed a map and the essential details for entering into her isolated encampment, near the former mining town of Lenado. Born in Pennsylvania, 97 she sensed the need to prepare us for conditions we Easterners might not have expected:

> *In early May, the trail will probably still be snowbound. I'll leave*
> *skis leaning against a large woodpile in Lenado. The tepee is a mile*
> *farther on; the uphill walk should take you one and one-half hours.*
> *Bring warm clothes, and please carry up a jug of water.*

That spring we arrived at Lenado, parked the car at the woodpile, and hesitantly added to our baggage the skis that Kathie had left for us. (At that point, we could see no use for them.) Within minutes our walk took us from the gravelly trail to a path of crusted snow at least two feet deep. With skis strapped on, we continued our climb.

The afternoon was warm. Sweating under our burden of backpacks and the water jugs Kathie had asked us to carry, we at last perceived gray white smoke spiraling above the trees. Shouts echoing into the hills and a horse's whinny told us that we had reached our destination. Kathie and Chamisa were calling to us to slide down the incline that dropped from the road and come onto their claim.

Kathie is a handsome, robust woman with intense blue eyes. Equally vigorous, Chamisa, age seven, is a lovely dark-skinned child with blue black hair. Together they extended us a hearty welcome and immediately began sharing the life which they have fashioned in this rugged place.

Life at 10,000-Foot Elevations

The tepee is a 20-by-20-foot structure of heavy canvas supported by wood poles that Kathie cut. Look out from the entrance and you face one of the surrounding steep hills that leads to the magnificent peaks above. To one side of the clearing, split-wood posts fence in a spacious corral where Black Son, the family's horse, grazes. Behind the enclosure are two simple outhouses and a covered platform five feet high for keeping hay bundles dry and protecting tools.

Kathie's experience as a traveler and her skill as a mountaineer arm her with the kind of confidence and independence one needs for surviving this high-country life. Presently, she maintains herself and her family through several enterprises. For three weeks, starting in August before the road becomes impassable, she rises before dawn to cut down dead trees that stand on top of the mountain. In an old pick-up truck she hauls her load to Lenado where she stacks it until a buyer approaches.

Weaving is another occupation. Several years ago she and Chamisa traveled by bus from Mexico to Guatemala so that she could learn Indian weaving techniques from local craftswomen. Today Kathie imparts those experiences to university students who attend her all-encompassing classes in loom building, spinning, natural dying, and weaving.

Kathie and Chamisa Lamm relax in the sun beside their tepee home.

Weekdays during the winter, mother and daughter ski over the mountain toward Aspen. Within a half-mile, the two "park" their skis and walk the rest of the way to town where Chamisa attends a small private school. (Her mother finances part of the tuition through her woven murals that decorate some of the classroom walls.) Kathie's job as a part-time cook at a local hotel corresponds with Chamisa's school hours.

Mountain Shopping

The Lamm's small, rocky garden in the clearing supports only a few reliable crops that will come through the short growing season, but Kathie and Chamisa are resourceful "shoppers." Wherever and whenever Nature is willing to offer up her bounty, they are willing to receive it. In spring they scour the landscape for vegetable food. Young greens—watercress, miners lettuce, lamb's-quarters—newly emerging fern shoots, some varieties of flowers, and particular wild tubers and bulbs provide delectable treats. Occasionally, they find chamisa (after which her daughter is named), one of Kathie's favorite plants, both for eating and dying wool. In late summer, they hunt for special ingredients to crown their refreshing fruit salads. With no trouble they find gooseberries, currants, and Utah serviceberries or Juneberries. As fall approaches they set aside evenings for removing the nuts from pinon pine cones which offer them a nutritious food.

Staples arrive via truck or horse when the road is open. June to October, Kathie carts supplies of grain, flour, beans, and honey to hold the two of them through the snowy months. Most of these she stores in large, covered plastic trash containers. Some root vegetables, like onions and turnips, go into Peruvian-wool saddlebags (otherwise used during long camping trips on Black Son) that hang from a structural pole. All these measures keep food dry and out of reach of neighborly mice. When winter actually sets in, Kathie sometimes skis to the tepee with 25 to 30 pounds of fresh produce, olive oil, and cheeses in her backpack.

A Veritable Feast

For our first visit to their tepee, Kathie had planned a veritable feast for us ravenous hikers. Sitting cross-legged on the floor, we talked with her as she completed her preparations. Using a bottle, she rolled pieces of dough into thin corn tortillas. She fried these one by one in an oiled, black iron skillet on top of the woodstove. Occasionally she lifted a pot lid and ran a wooden spoon through thick bean soup. "I cook beans Mexican-style, that is, until they are very, very soft. Otherwise, they're just not right," she insisted.

Closer to dinner, she removed the cover from her cellar box, a 2½-foot-deep rectangular hole in the earth. "It cools food and prevents freezing. Before I constructed it, we used to protect oranges and grapefruits in the cold months by bundling them under our covers at night," she commented. From the opening she brought up salad ingredients, including fresh soybean sprouts and a large, white, tuberous vegetable, jicama. Finally, she grated creamy yellow cheese directly into a wooden bowl, poured a colorful sauce into a small crock, and set out a clear glass of sour cream. We feasted.

Waking to a Trickling Stream

The next morning, early risers—young rabbits and chipmunks scurrying through the low shrubs on the hill—woke us. Kathie was already seated on a stool near the warm stove as she quietly cut fruit and watched this outdoor pageant. "Do you hear that sound? That's the stream. It has unfrozen and just started to trickle down the mountain. That means good water for us."

Outside Chamisa had neatly arranged coconut-shell halves on a round spool table under a budding aspen. From the wooden bowl, she dipped fresh fruit—black bing cherries, fresh pineapple chunks, half-moon mango slices, and purple black grapes—into the shells and topped each with large scoops of cottage cheese. Magpies

Kathie reaches into her "cellar box" for the next meal's ingredients.

Chamisa helps with the cooking as her mother keeps an eye on the dish in progress.

picked burrs from Black Son's tail, and blue jays hopped from one tree to another as we ate breakfast and planned our departure. To our great pleasure, Kathie had conceived a way both to prolong the visit a little longer and for her to get a jump on dinner preparations.

"All along the roadsides at lower altitudes," she informed us, "the wild asparagus spears are just starting to poke up through the ground. We'll ski out with you to the car, and you can drop us at the first abundant source. Then we must say good-bye—but it will be only for a while."

Kathie's Veritable Feast for Ravenous Hikers

Cooking Schedule

1. At least 6 hours before dinner, start Pinto Bean Soup after soaking beans overnight.
2. Between 1 and 3 hours before soup is finished, prepare Colorado Picante Sauce.
3. During last 1½ hours that soup is cooking, make tortillas.
4. During last hour, set guests to work at grating cheese, making salad, and entertaining the cook.

Comments on the Ingredients

You will find most of the unfamiliar ingredients in the recipes—chili peppers, jicama, coriander—in Latin grocery stores, particularly Mexican ones. Occasionally the Spanish section in a supermarket will also carry them.

Many Indians make their own tortilla dough, and in the West and Southwest, people can buy it from tortillarias and roll and fry the cakes at home. Quaker puts out a masa harina, a truly acceptable meal that is parched corn treated with lime and then ground. It is sold in most Western supermarkets. If your retailer does not carry it, I would expect that he could order it for you. My recipe for Corn Tortillas explains how to use it.

Serving Suggestions

Get everyone started with a big dish of salad. Ladle soup into ceramic bowls. Cover the surface with a thick layer of cheese and spoon a large dollop of sour cream on top. Pass Colorado Picante Sauce as a condiment for both soup and salad. Offer baskets of warm tortillas for dipping into soup and scooping up the beans. Mmm.

SIMPLE SALAD
Serves 6

1 garlic clove
2 heads red-leaf lettuce, torn into bite-size pieces
1 small head endive, torn into bite-size pieces
2 handfuls very young dandelion greens, torn into bite-size pieces
½ medium-size jicama, coarsely grated
1 medium-size carrot, coarsely grated
1 handful soybean sprouts
1 medium-size onion, cut in half lengthwise and then into thin strips
olive oil
tamari soy sauce to taste
fresh oregano, minced, to taste

1. Rub garlic all over the surface of a wooden salad bowl and place lettuce, endive, and dandelion greens in it.
2. Gently top greens with jicama and carrot, and scatter sprouts and onion strips over all.
3. Immediately before serving, toss all ingredients with just enough oil to coat the leaves (about 3 tablespoons). Add tamari and oregano and toss once more.

PINTO BEAN SOUP

Serves 6 to 8

½ *pound dried pinto beans, rinsed and soaked overnight in water to cover*
2 *tablespoons olive oil*
10 *cups water*
2 *large onions, coarsely chopped*
½ *garlic bulb, cloves separated and minced*
1 *medium-size tomato, peeled and coarsely chopped*
leaves of 6 sprigs coriander, coarsely chopped
tamari soy sauce to taste
Garnish
1 *pound Monterey Jack cheese, grated*
2 *cups sour cream*

1. Drain the beans and discard the soaking water. Allow beans to drain well for at least 30 minutes.
2. Heat oil until smoking in a 5-quart iron soup pot. Stirring throughout, fry beans in the oil. After 5 minutes, turn off heat.
3. Add water to beans, bring liquid to a boil, cover pot, and allow beans to cook on very low heat for 6 hours.
4. During last 2 hours of cooking time, add onions and garlic to soup.
5. During last hour, add the tomato, coriander, and tamari.
6. Ladle into bowls and garnish with a sprinkling of cheese and a dollop of sour cream.

CORN TORTILLAS

Yields about 16 5-inch tortillas

2 *cups masa harina*
1⅓ *cups water*
corn oil

1. Put flour in a mixing bowl and add the liquid all at once. Mix together quickly just until ingredients are combined. Set the dough aside for 20 minutes.
2. Directly before you begin to roll your first tortilla, place an iron skillet (or Mexican comale if you have one) over a medium flame to heat it thoroughly.
3. Between two sheets of plastic (2 sides of produce bags), flatten a 2-inch ball of dough into a flat 5-inch cake ⅛ to ¼ inch thick.
4. Heat about 3 tablespoons oil in skillet for each tortilla. Cook each one until it just begins to dry out around the edges. Then, flip it over and cook it on the second side until it just begins to color. Flip it back to the first side and finish cooking it. The entire process should take about 2 minutes. Remove tortilla and wrap it in a thick cotton towel to stay warm and pliant.
5. Proceed in the same way with the rest of the dough.

COLORADO PICANTE SAUCE

Yields about 2 cups

> 1 medium-size onion, minced
> 3 medium-size sweet green peppers, minced
> 3 to 4 jalapeno peppers, seeded and minced
> ½ cup olive oil
> 4 fresh tomatoes, blanched 1 minute and finely chopped
> leaves of 6 sprigs coriander, finely chopped

Pica in Spanish means "hot," "sharp." Use this sauce, therefore, with discretion. The traditional Mexican sauces are made from all uncooked ingredients, but mine is a mixture of both cooked and raw.

Saute onion and peppers in oil until onions are transparent. Remove to a ceramic bowl or glass jar. Add tomatoes and coriander and cover for at least 1 hour and no more than 3 hours, after which sauce will lose its crispness.

Salad-Greens Soups

SWISS CHARD SOUP

Serves 6

1½ pounds Swiss chard
3 tablespoons butter
1 medium-size onion, coarsely chopped
4 medium-size carrots, scrubbed and coarsely sliced
6 cups Chicken Stock (see Index)
¼ teaspoon nutmeg
⅛ teaspoon white pepper

1. Remove the leaves from the ribs of chard. Chop the leaves and set them aside. Chop the ribs.

2. Melt butter in a 4-quart soup pot. Add the chopped chard ribs and the onion. Saute until the onion is transparent. Add the carrots and stock. Bring to a boil. Lower heat, cover, and simmer until the vegetables are tender (about 30 minutes). Cool slightly.

3. Puree vegetable-stock mixture in a blender or work it through a food mill. Return it to the soup pot. Add the nutmeg and pepper and reheat.

4. Just before serving, stir the chopped chard leaves into the simmering liquid. Ladle soup into a tureen or individual bowls.

Two for the Price of One

Chard—a member of the beet family—offers two different types of vegetables in one large leaf. Chard "greens"—either green or red in color—are attached to long, crispy stalks. The leafy part resembles spinach in taste; the stalks, after the leaves have been removed, suggest the texture and chewiness of celery. Both parts are delicious served raw or lightly steamed and work well as a side dish or as an ingredient for a soup or a salad.

KALE LENTIL SOUP

Serves 6

1 bay leaf
2 whole cloves
1 cup dried lentils
4 cups water
1 carrot, sliced into ¼-inch rounds
1 celery stalk, sliced into ¼-inch pieces
1 medium-size onion, minced
1 garlic clove
1½ cups Beef Stock (see Index)
1 cup tomato juice
½ pound kale, shredded

1. Tie the bay leaf and cloves in a cheesecloth sack. Place them in a 4-quart soup pot with the lentils and water. Cover and bring to a boil. Lower heat and simmer, partially covered, 1 hour.

2. Add the carrot, celery, onion, and garlic. Simmer another hour. Remove and discard sack containing bay leaf and cloves.

3. Add the stock and tomato juice. Bring soup to a boil. Stir in the kale and cook just until wilted (about 5 minutes longer).

4. Ladle hot soup into a tureen or individual bowls.

CARAWAY SOUP WITH SPINACH LEAVES

Serves 6

8 cups Beef Stock (see Index)
2 to 3 tablespoons caraway seeds or to taste
1 carrot, cut into 1-inch julienne strips
½ cup shelled peas (about ½ pound)
2 scallions, finely sliced
12 spinach leaves, finely shredded

1. Bring the stock and caraway seeds to a boil in a 4-quart soup pot. Simmer, uncovered, 15 minutes. Strain soup, discard the seeds, and return the broth to the pot.

2. Add the carrot and peas to the hot broth. Return to a boil, lower heat, and simmer 5 minutes. Remove from heat.

3. Place the scallions and spinach in a warmed tureen or divide them among 6 bowls. Ladle the soup on top and serve hot.

FRESH BASIL SOUP

Serves 6

3 tablespoons butter
2 large onions, finely chopped
3 garlic cloves, minced
6 cups Chicken Stock (see Index)
½ cup brown rice
1 cup tomato juice
3 medium-size tomatoes, diced
1 pound basil, chopped

1. Melt the butter in a 4-quart soup pot. Add the onions and saute until they are transparent (about 5 minutes). Add the garlic and cook 1 minute longer.

2. Add the stock and bring to a boil. Stir in the rice. Lower heat, cover, and simmer 35 minutes.

3. Add the tomato juice, tomatoes, and basil. Return soup to a boil, lower heat, and cook the liquid, uncovered, an additional 10 minutes.

4. Serve hot.

If you want to keep your stomach calm, get basil into your meal somehow. If basil is added to food as it cooks, according to some old herbals, the food becomes more digestible.

SORREL SOUP

Serves 6

6 cups Chicken Stock (see Index)
2 large potatoes, peeled and diced
leaves from 1 pound sorrel
1 teaspoon chopped chervil
Garnish
1 cup plain yogurt
2 tablespoons minced chives

1. Bring the stock to a boil in a 4-quart soup pot. Add the potatoes, lower heat, cover, and simmer until potatoes are tender (20 to 25 minutes).

2. Measure 1 cup of the sorrel, loosely packed, and cut it into shreds. Set the shredded sorrel aside.

3. Add the remaining sorrel to the soup and cook an additional 10 minutes. Cool slightly. Add the chervil.

4. Puree the soup in a blender until completely smooth. Return soup to the pot.

5. Just before serving, heat soup to a boil. Immediately remove from heat and stir in the reserved sorrel. Serve hot.

6. Combine yogurt and chives. Place a dollop over each portion of soup.

My own remedy is always to eat, just before I step into bed, a hot roasted onion, if I have a cold.
George Washington

ONION AND SPINACH SOUP

Serves 6

¼ cup butter
6 large onions, thinly sliced
2 large leeks, thinly sliced
5 garlic cloves, minced
⅛ teaspoon cayenne pepper
6 cups degreased Chicken Stock
  (see Index)
1 cup tightly packed spinach
  leaves
alfalfa sprouts

1. Melt the butter in a 4-quart soup pot. Add the onions, leeks, garlic, and cayenne and saute until transparent (about 5 minutes).

2. Add the stock, bring to a boil, lower heat, cover, and simmer 30 minutes. Add the spinach and cook 5 minutes longer. Remove from heat and cool slightly.

3. Puree the soup mixture in a blender until smooth.

4. Line a sieve with 2 layers of cheesecloth and place it over a clean pan. Press hard on the solids; strain the puree.

5. Reheat soup before serving. Sprinkle each portion with a few alfalfa sprouts.

ASPARAGUS AND ESCAROLE SOUP

Serves 6

2 tablespoons olive oil
1 pound thin asparagus, sliced
  diagonally into ¼-inch pieces
3 scallions, sliced diagonally into
  ⅛-inch pieces
3 cups loosely packed shredded
  escarole leaves
6 cups Chicken Stock (see Index)
1 tablespoon minced basil
1 teaspoon minced thyme
2 garlic cloves, minced
¼ teaspoon white pepper
2 tablespoons minced parsley

1. Heat the oil in a 4-quart soup pot. Add the asparagus and scallions and saute 3 minutes on moderate heat. Add the escarole and stock. Bring to a boil, lower heat, and simmer 5 minutes.

2. With a mortar and pestle, mash the basil, thyme, garlic, and pepper. Stir the garlic mixture into the soup and cook 5 minutes longer. Remove from heat. Stir in the parsley.

3. Serve hot.

ITALIAN SALAD SOUP

Serves 6

3 tablespoons butter
1 tablespoon olive oil
¾ cup coarsely chopped onion
4 garlic cloves, minced
6 cups loosely packed coarsely
  chopped romaine lettuce leaves
  or curly endive (about ¾
  pound)
6 tablespoons tomato paste
6 cups Chicken Stock (see Index)
¼ cup brown rice
¼ teaspoon dried basil
½ teaspoon dried oregano
⅛ teaspoon cayenne pepper
¼ teaspoon pepper
¼ cup grated Parmesan cheese

1. In a 4-quart soup pot, heat the butter and oil on medium heat. Add the onion, stir, and saute 3 minutes. Then add the garlic and stir an additional minute. Add the romaine; cook and stir another 3 minutes.

2. Add the tomato paste and 1 cup of the stock. Stir and add the rice, the remaining stock, the herbs, and pepper. Cover and simmer 30 minutes until rice is tender. Serve hot, sprinkled with Parmesan cheese.

BEET MADRILENE   For this recipe, see page 79

BRUSSELS SPROUTS SALAD   For this recipe, see page 241

WATERCRESS SOUP

Serves 6

1 large potato, peeled and diced
4 cups Chicken Stock (see Index)
leaves from 2 bunches watercress,
  coarsely chopped (about 2 cups)
1 large onion, coarsely chopped
1 garlic clove, minced
1 celery stalk, cut into 1-inch
  pieces
1 tablespoon honey
1 tablespoon cornstarch
2 tablespoons cold water
¾ cup light cream
¾ cup milk
1 tablespoon butter

1. Place the potato and stock in a 4-quart soup pot. Bring to a boil, lower heat, cover, and simmer 20 minutes.

2. Add the watercress, onion, garlic, celery, and honey. Cook an additional 10 minutes. Remove from heat and cool slightly.

3. Puree soup mixture in a blender until smooth. Return to pot. Make a paste with the cornstarch and water. Stir it into the pureed soup. Bring soup to a boil while constantly stirring and cook 1 minute. Stir in the cream, milk, and butter. Simmer and stir 5 minutes.

4. Serve soup hot.

FRESH PEA AND LETTUCE SOUP

Serves 6

2 tablespoons butter
2 celery stalks, cut into ½-inch
  slices
1 medium-size onion, coarsely
  chopped
1 garlic clove, minced
4½ cups Chicken Stock (see Index)
3 cups shelled peas (about 3
  pounds)
1 small head Boston lettuce,
  shredded
6 sprigs parsley

1. Melt the butter in a 4-quart soup pot. Add the celery and onion and saute until the vegetables are soft (about 5 minutes). Stir in the garlic and saute 1 minute.

2. Add 3 cups of the stock and 2 cups of the peas. Bring to a boil, reduce heat, cover, and simmer 20 minutes.

3. Add the lettuce and parsley and simmer 5 minutes longer. Cool soup slightly. Puree soup in a blender until smooth. Return soup to the pot.

4. Cook the remaining peas and stock in a 1-quart covered soup pot until tender (about 10 minutes). Stir this into the pureed soup. Mix well.

5. Reheat soup and serve hot.

The Old Reliance Hotel

We may live without poetry, music and art . . .
But civilized man cannot live without cooks.
EDWARD ROBERT BULWER-LYTTON, *LUCILE*

We started going to the Reliance Hotel about 12 years ago after we had heard of its reputation for sensational soups and sandwiches. In those days, ten of us would pile into a car and drive through the beautiful Pennsylvania farmlands toward Souderton, a small industrial town where this restaurant is located. Upon pulling into the dirt parking lot, the driver inevitably would comment on how easy it would be for the uninitiated to bypass this neglected old building.

Day or night, the public rooms of the Reliance (as it was familiarly called) offered enough diversity to please almost anyone. The barroom decor harkened back to more stately times. A handsome wooden bar with all the added adornments of mirrors and Romanesque columns dominated one wall. Across the room, five antique tables stood in front of shutter-covered windows. The adjoining room was dimly lit. Someone had obviously paid special attention to filtering out the revealing rays of sunlight and the everyday world. Oil paintings with ornate frames decorated the walls, and countless plastic flower garlands obscured a dark, upright piano miraculously wedged into the small area. Five more tiny tables left little space for waitresses or roaming children. A separate, rectangular-shaped room, reminiscent of so many church basements, ran parallel to the barroom. Only a pool table and several large banquet tables with chairs furnished it.

In those days the clientele mostly consisted of local working-class people. They came to relax and to eat and drink cheaply and well. Factory workers filled the barstools and chairs during weekday lunches. On weekends, farmers and their families gathered around the big tables while their children gave the pool table a workout. Young couples and other small groups huddled in the back room.

Over the years, we returned many times and never once left without a brief visit from the colorful owner and host. According to rumor, he did everything around the place, but somehow, in various guises (spattered chef's coat, immaculate serge suit), he always found time to chat with the customers: "Enjoying your meal? Soup hot? Nice to see you." One night we overheard him tell a couple, "I prepare a secret blend for the cheese in my onion soup. It's stringless, and I'll give you 50 bucks for every thread of cheese you get out of a bowl. No one else can make that statement."

In time, a mystique began to grow up around the Reliance operation. People became intrigued with the artistry that went into the cooking. They began to develop theories about the owner's background. "He's really an experienced chef who enjoys working out of his element"; "He must get his recipes by visiting the kitchens of fine restaurants on his vacations—but he never goes anywhere!"

Gradually, word spread far beyond the immediate area about this food aficionado who bought live turtles from local residents and stayed up all night turning them into unsurpassable soup. Eventually, the three rooms could no longer suitably contain the crowds who made the pilgrimage to enjoy the food and the atmosphere.

Little by little, the Reliance changed. The menu started to include more entrees and a wider selection of soups. Later a large canvas awning appeared above the entrance. One evening, after a long lapse between visits, we crossed the railroad tracks and found ourselves staring incredulously at an imposing hotel. Inside and out, the place had become a formal dining spot serving elegant gourmet meals.

Billboarding

Frank Novak has none of our yearning for the old place. Today, this restaurant owner is ready to settle back and enjoy the rewards of his hard work and ingenuity. Twenty-four years ago, he gave up a successful engineering career to try his hand at bringing to life "an old, broken-down hotel." In the beginning he ran the entire place with a staff of two. "It was all work—sometimes 24 hours a day. I cooked, tended bar, waited tables, cleaned bathrooms," he recalls. Even in those early days Frank realized that plain hard work was not enough to bring him the kind of success he wanted. He therefore turned to a talent he calls "billboarding":

> *Originally, my customers were a rough crew. They fought a lot, swore a lot, and spent very little money. I wanted a different crowd, and I knew that the best way to get it was to advertise—advertise myself. I made sure I found time to start dressing up. I'd walk around and talk to everyone. I'd find out who they were and what they liked or disliked about my place. After a while, new customers started to come*

Frank Novak confidently checks on his customers' satisfaction.

"The chefs follow my recipes. When the pot is ready, I taste the soup. If it needs something, I say so."

partially to see me. They'd say to me, "You look terrific tonight, Frank," and I'd tell 'em, "Oh, I'm billboarding; all these clothes go back to my undertaker on Monday."

Almost a quarter of a century of effort has gone into developing the food for which the Reliance has become famous. Frank's original clientele had no desire to be weaned from beer and pretzels to his simple, homecooked dinners. When business started to decline he looked for a new approach:

It was my last resort—sink or swim. I switched to cheaper food—less cost to me and the customer, less loss. First, I drew up an actual blueprint and recipe for a roll to serve with my sandwiches and soups. I carried it from baker to baker until I found one who could make something to suit me. Then I concentrated on a small list of soup and sandwich specialties. I started by reworking old favorites like my mother's German Dumpling Soup. I wanted good, reasonable food that was unlike anything anyone else had.

Today, Frank supervises the cooking performed by a full staff of professional chefs, but he insists on having the last word on the soups: "The chefs follow my recipes. When the pot is ready, I taste the soup. If it needs something, I say so. Sometimes, it's a half-cup of lemon juice that does it."

Those of us who have seen Frank through the transitions have a good deal of respect for his accomplishments. We are also thankful that he hasn't forgotten our loyalty. Primarily for the old regulars, the kitchen still turns out all the original standards. We occasionally stop for Snapper Soup and a sandwich. Customers call during the week to find out what day to come for Frank's Health Soup. Every Friday afternoon, a discriminating Frenchman arrives for "stringless" onion soup and a beer. One night we found Frank packing one of his sandwiches and a container of soup into a small Styrofoam ice chest. He told us, "Guy in the dining room wants to fly this to Seattle for his mother."

HEALTH SOUP
Serves 8 to 10

Stock

6 pounds stewing chicken
20 cups water
1 carrot, quartered
1 celery stalk, quartered
1 medium-size onion, quartered
1 bay leaf
6 peppercorns
2 teaspoons salt

Meatballs

½ pound ground round steak
½ cup bread crumbs
1 or 2 garlic cloves, minced
½ medium-size onion, minced
1 egg, beaten
2 tablespoons minced fresh parsley
2 tablespoons dried oregano

2 cups coarsely chopped escarole
2 cups coarsely chopped romaine lettuce
1 medium-size Spanish onion, finely chopped
2 garlic cloves, minced
1 celery stalk with leaves, finely chopped
1 tablespoon white pepper

1. Cook chicken in water with carrot, celery, onion, and seasonings until meat just leaves the bone (about 1 hour). Remove from heat and let stand 15 minutes. Remove the chicken from the pot and allow it to cool, then pick the meat from the bones. Dice the meat and put it aside. Return the bones to the pot and simmer the broth, covered, another 45 minutes.

2. Meanwhile, combine the meatball ingredients in a 2-quart bowl. Mix well with your fingers and then form into ½-inch balls. Put aside in the refrigerator.

3. Fill the sink with ice-cold, lightly salted water. Immerse the greens 1 minute. Drain greens in a colander and put aside.

4. Strain the soup stock. Add the onion, garlic, celery, and pepper and bring to a boil. With a slotted spoon, introduce meatballs to the liquid. Cook, uncovered, about 15 minutes. Test for doneness.

5. Add diced chicken to soup and warm thoroughly. During the last 3 minutes of cooking time, scatter the crisped greens over the top of the broth and steam lightly.

FRESH SNAPPER SOUP

Yields about 4 gallons

14-to-15-pound snapper turtle in the
    shell, gutted and cleaned
2 *garlic bulbs, cloves separated and
    finely minced*
olive oil
4 *gallons rich, dark beef stock*
½ *cup turtle spice**
2 *tablespoons pepper*
2 *tablespoons salt*
2 *cups butter*
5 *cups flour*
12 *hard-cooked eggs, finely diced*
1 *teaspoon cloves*
2 *cups sherry*

*Commercial turtle spice is available in
most fish markets. If you prefer to make
your own, blend together equal parts of
dried coriander leaves and thyme, cayenne pepper, garlic powder, crushed bay
leaves, and minced fresh parsley.

*Here is Frank's recipe using whole, fresh, snapper
turtle. Readers who discover a source for such aquatic life
will find these instructions indispensable. The large
quantity makes abundant company fare, and the soup
also freezes well in smaller batches to be taken out later
for a first course for special dinners.*

1. In an 8-gallon soup pot or canner, cook the turtle
in water to cover for approximately 1 hour. Remove
the turtle and discard the liquid.
2. Place the turtle on a large surface and with a knife
or other sharp instrument, separate the meat from the
shell. (If the turtle has been boiled long enough, the
meat should leave the shell easily.) Make sure you
remove the tender white meat from under the vertical
structure attached to the underside of the shell. At this
point, the flesh will still contain the bones.
3. Return the turtle meat to the large pot. Lightly
saute the garlic in the oil. Add it to the pot along with
the stock, turtle spice, pepper, and salt. Cook ingredients until deshelled meat is tender and easily falls
off the bones (1 to 1½ hours). Remove the carcass and
put the stock aside.
4. Remove all the flesh from the carcass. Return the
bones to the soup pot. Cover and cook them another
40 to 45 minutes.
5. Dice the turtle meat and lay it on a double layer
of cheesecloth. Pull up the sides to form a bag, tie with
string, and add to stock after bones have finished cooking. Allow the meat to marinate in the broth overnight
in a cold area (in the refrigerator or outdoors during
colder months).
6. The next morning, remove the cheesecloth bag and
put it aside. Strain the broth and discard the bones and
spices. Put the stock on the stove to begin cooking.
7. Melt the butter in a skillet. Add the flour and
quickly work it into the butter. Adjust heat to low and
allow the flour to achieve a blonde color (about 5
minutes). Stir constantly. Add several soup ladles of
broth to the skillet and, with a wire whisk, blend in
the liquid. Whisking continuously, add several more
ladles until the skillet is three-quarters full. Stirring
throughout, cook this mixture 15 minutes. Add the
liquified roux to the turtle stock.
8. Add the diced turtle meat, the eggs, and the cloves
to the stock. Pour in the sherry. Warm through. Adjust
seasonings to taste.

GERMAN DUMPLING SOUP
Yields about 4 quarts

Stock

    3 pounds shin beef with bones
    1 pound veal knuckles
    ½ pound giblets
    2 carrots, coarsely chopped
    2 leeks, coarsely chopped
    2 celery stalks, coarsely chopped
    2 large onions, quartered
    1 turnip, quartered
 12 to 16 cups water
    2 sprigs thyme
    2 sprigs rosemary
    2 sprigs parsley
    1 large bay leaf
    6 peppercorns

Dumplings

 16 cups water
    4 tablespoons minced parsley
    ½ cup finely ground sauteed chicken
       liver
 about 1½ cups whole wheat flour
 about 2 tablespoons milk or water
    4 eggs, beaten

Roux

    ⅓ cup whole wheat flour
    ⅓ cup butter

    ½ lemon, sliced in rings
    2 teaspoons white pepper
    ½ cup Chablis
    ¼ cup sherry

Stock

1. Chop the meat and bones into large pieces and spread them in a large roasting pan. Add the giblets, carrots, leeks, celery, onions, and turnip and let them all brown in a 400°F oven 35 minutes.

2. Put the browned ingredients into a 6-quart soup pot. Deglaze the roasting pan with a small amount of water and add it to the pot. Add the water, herbs, and peppercorns. Bring to a boil. Cover and cook gently 2½ hours.

3. Strain the stock. Discard the vegetables and seasonings. Skim all the fat from the top of the soup and put the broth back into the same pot. Remove the meat from the bones and chop it into ½-inch cubes. Return it to the soup pot. Cook 30 minutes longer.

Dumplings

1. Begin to boil water. Cut the parsley and chicken liver into the flour. Put 2 tablespoons of the mixture into a mixing bowl. Beat in enough milk to make a heavy paste (like putty) and continue to beat until the dough looks shiny. Add eggs and gradually beat in remaining flour until all of it has been incorporated. If mixture gets too thick, add more liquid. The resultant consistency should be that of pulling taffy.

2. Lay dough out on a floured board and cut or form it into tablespoon-size dumplings. Drop each into the boiling water with a slotted spoon and cover and cook about 20 minutes. Remove dumplings to a plate.

Roux

1. Roast the flour in a dry skillet until it changes to a deeper shade (about 2 minutes). Stir often. Melt the butter in a small saucepan and quickly work it into the flour in the skillet. Whisk several ladles of hot stock into this mixture. Cook at low heat 5 minutes. Spoon the roux into the stock during the last 30 minutes of cooking.

2. During the last 15 minutes of cooking time, add lemon rings, pepper, Chablis, sherry, and dumplings to soup. Warm thoroughly.

Sea-Vegetable Soups

FISH CHOWDER IN
KOMBU-POTATO STOCK

Serves 6 to 8

2 large onions, coarsely chopped
1 tablespoon oil
2 tablespoons butter
2 garlic cloves, minced
6 cups *Kombu*-Potato Stock (see recipe in this section)
1 cup Fish Stock (see Index)
2 large carrots, diced
1 parsnip, thinly sliced across the grain
1 medium-size turnip, diced
2 medium-size potatoes, diced
2 cups corn (about 4 ears)
2 cups fish fillet (such as blue fish, red snapper), cut into ½-inch cubes
2 teaspoons dillweed
½ teaspoon cayenne pepper
1 cup milk, scalded
Garnish
1 scallion, finely chopped
½ cup finely chopped parsley

1. Saute onions in oil until transparent. Then add butter and garlic and continue to saute until just warmed.

2. Pour both stocks into a 4-quart soup pot. Add all the other vegetables. Bring to a boil and simmer until vegetables are tender (about 20 minutes).

3. Add fish, dillweed, cayenne, and milk. Simmer, with lid on, 15 minutes. Garnish with scallion and parsley.

GIFTS FROM THE SEA

Our ocean waters supply us with numerous sea vegetables with unusual names like *nori, wakame, dulse,* and *hiziki.* They are inexpensive sources of delicious, highly nutritious foods. In addition, they are not contaminated with chemical sprays or additives, and they will not thrive in polluted waters.

Sea vegetables (seaweed or algae) absorb the minerals leached from the earth and returned to the sea. They offer high concentrations of calcium and iodine (so essential in controlling thyroid conditions). They also contain surprisingly large amounts of certain vitamins. Some *nori* seaweeds exceed green peppers in vitamin C by ten times, and both *nori* and *wakame* equal tomatoes in vitamin C content. *Dulse* contains significant amounts of B_{12}, the antianemia vitamin lacking in nonmeat diets. Even protein is available in sea vegetables. One freshwater variety, *chlorella,* is almost a complete food in itself. It contains about 50 percent protein, with all the essential amino acids (except the sulfur-containing ones), fats, carbohydrates, vitamins, and minerals needed to sustain life.

Foragers in all parts of the world who scour rocky coastlines reap fresh, edible algae. Most oriental groceries and some natural foods stores carry dried forms. These are easily freshened by dropping them into warm or cold water until they regain their original state. (See "Sea-Vegetable Soups" recipes for soaking times.) Once freshened, use them immediately or store them in the refrigerator, drained or in their soaking liquid, for no longer than seven days. Upon removal, pat dry the more substantial ones (like *kombu*) and drain the others. Always save the mineral-rich water for soups or gravies.

Certain seaweeds (like *wakame*) contain a thick midrib. For delicate dishes, trim away the center with a scissors or a knife, then chop, tear, or cut the seaweed into desired sizes. Some people prefer to saute seaweeds such as *hiziki* for a few minutes after soaking and before adding them to soups or other cooking. Such treatment brings about a more subtle overall taste.

Roasted and unroasted seaweed powders and flakes provide flavorful seasonings. To roast the plant, spread it on a baking sheet and roast it in a 350°F oven for several minutes, or hold it one to two inches from a hot flame for about one minute, (*Nori* will change from a dark color to a bright green.) Grind or crumble it, and store it like herbs in a dry spot. Commercial powders and flakes are available.

Use a sharp-bladed knife when paring or slicing vegetables to prevent bruising them. Both vitamins A and C are lost whenever vegetable tissues are bruised.

KOMBU-SOBA SOUP WITH *NORI*

Serves 6 to 8

1 12-ounce package *soba* noodles
7 4 × 6-inch sheets *nori*
6 cups *Kombu* Soup Stock (see recipe below)
2 large onions, coarsely chopped
2 garlic cloves, minced
2 tablespoons oil
2 scallions, minced

1. Prepare *soba* noodles according to package directions. Rinse noodles well under lukewarm water and put aside.

2. Toast sheets of *nori* in a dry skillet until they become bright green. Cut each sheet into ½-inch squares and put aside.

3. Bring the stock to a boil in a 4-quart soup pot. Saute onions and garlic in oil until they are transparent and add them to the liquid. Add *soba* noodles. Warm thoroughly, then garnish with *nori* squares and scallions.

Variation

Kombu-Watercress Soup: Eliminate noodles and add the chopped leaves from two bunches watercress with the onions and warm thoroughly at least 7 minutes.

KOMBU SOUP STOCK

Serves 6 to 8

1 3 × 12-inch piece *kombu*
7 cups water
1 large onion, quartered
1 large carrot, cut into large pieces
1 medium-size celery stalk, quartered horizontally
1 sprig parsley
1 sprig thyme
1 bay leaf
1 garlic clove, quartered
½ teaspoon cayenne pepper
2 tablespoons lemon juice
3 tablespoons tamari soy sauce

1. Soak *kombu* in ½ cup of the water 30 minutes. Drain and pour soaking water into a 4-quart soup pot. With kitchen shears, cut *kombu* horizontally into 1-inch strips and put into soup pot.

2. Add remaining water, onion, carrot, celery, parsley, thyme, bay leaf, garlic, and cayenne. Boil, uncovered, 10 minutes. Then cover pot and simmer 1 hour.

3. For a thicker stock, strain solids from liquid. Return stock to pot, discard bay leaf, and press solids through a sieve back into stock. For a clear stock, simply strain liquid and discard all solids. Add lemon juice and tamari to either.

Variations

Kombu-Fish Stock: Add 3 tablespoons Iriko (small dried fish sold in Japanese groceries and some natural foods stores) at step 2 and proceed with directions.

Kombu-Potato Stock: Add the peels from 7 well-scrubbed, brown-skin potatoes at step 2 and proceed with directions.

MILLET SEA-VEGETABLE SOUP

Serves 6 to 8

1 3½-ounce package *hiziki* or *wakame*
¾ cup millet
2 tablespoons sesame oil
1 cup coarsely grated burdock root*
3 garlic cloves, finely minced
1 large Spanish onion, thinly sliced in rings
2 medium-size carrots, finely chopped
10 cups Vegetable Stock (see Index)
2 tablespoons tamari soy sauce
3 tablespoons lemon juice
finely chopped parsley and chives

*Burdock is a wild plant whose root is edible. If you gather it yourself, dig the root before the plant produces its prickly brownish-purple seedpods. Burdock is sometimes available at large produce markets or on special order.

1. Cover seaweed with cold water and soak 3 minutes. Drain liquid into a bowl. Finely chop the seaweed. Set both aside.

2. In a 4-quart soup pot, saute the millet in the oil on medium heat 5 minutes. Stir often. Add the burdock, garlic, onion, carrots, and seaweed. Saute 7 minutes.

3. Pour the stock and seaweed soaking water into the pot. Bring to a boil and cook, covered, on medium-low heat 40 minutes. Add the tamari and lemon juice and stir. Garnish with a generous amount of parsley and chives.

MISO *WAKAME* SOUP

Serves 6 to 8

1 3½-ounce package *wakame*
2 medium-size onions, quartered and thinly sliced lengthwise
3 tablespoons sesame oil
3 garlic cloves, minced
3 stalks celery, thinly sliced on the diagonal
3 carrots, thinly sliced on the diagonal
2 cups finely chopped cabbage
8 cups Vegetable Stock (see Index)
¾ teaspoon cayenne pepper
½ teaspoon dried rosemary
3 tablespoons miso

Garnish
1 cup finely chopped scallions
½ cup thinly sliced radishes

1. Wash the *wakame* under cold, running water. Cover with fresh water and soak 10 minutes. Drain and reserve soaking water. Remove the center vein from seaweed (if necessary) and chop into ½-inch pieces. Set both aside.

2. In a 4-quart soup pot, saute the onions in the oil until transparent. Add the garlic, celery, and carrots and saute 2 minutes. Toss the cabbage and *wakame* into mixture until they are coated with oil.

3. Pour the stock over the vegetables. Add the pepper and rosemary. Bring to a boil and then simmer until all ingredients, including the *wakame*, are tender (about 30 minutes).

4. Dissolve miso in enough seaweed water to form a thin paste. Remove soup from heat and stir miso paste into it. Ladle soup into bowls and garnish each bowl with scallions and radishes.

Soups from Leftovers

BAKED BEAN SOUP
Serves 6

2 tablespoons olive oil
1 medium-size onion, finely
   chopped
1 garlic clove, minced
1 celery stalk, finely chopped
1 tablespoon whole wheat flour
2 cups leftover baked beans
2 cups water
1 cup Beef Stock (see Index)
1 cup tomato juice
3 tablespoons minced parsley

1. Heat the oil in a 3-quart soup pot. Add the onion, garlic, and celery and saute 3 minutes, stirring constantly. Stir in the flour.

2. Stir in the baked beans. Add the water, stock, and tomato juice. Bring to a boil, lower heat, cover, and simmer 30 minutes. Stir occasionally.

3. Puree bean mixture in a blender. If necessary, thin with additional water. Reheat before serving. Sprinkle with parsley.

BROCCOLI STEM SOUP
Serves 6

1 to 1½ pounds broccoli stems
2½ cups Chicken Stock (see Index)
1 cup cottage cheese
2 cups milk
⅛ teaspoon freshly grated nutmeg
2 tablespoons minced chives

1. Chop the broccoli stems into ½-inch slices and place them in a 3-quart soup pot. Add the stock and bring to a boil. Lower heat, cover, and simmer just until tender (10 to 15 minutes). Cool slightly.

2. Process the broccoli, stock, and cottage cheese in small batches in a blender until smooth. Stir in the milk and nutmeg. Cover and chill.

3. Stir soup before serving. Sprinkle with chives.

122

ASPARAGUS STALK SOUP

Serves 6

2 pounds asparagus
3 cups Chicken Stock (see Index)
2 cups milk
¼ teaspoon nutmeg
2 teaspoons finely chopped basil
2 teaspoons finely chopped fresh tarragon or ½ teaspoon dried
½ cup plain yogurt

1. Cut off 2 inches of the asparagus tips and reserve them for another use. Peel the stalks and place the peelings in a 3-quart soup pot. Cut the stalks into 1-inch lengths and place them in the pot with the peelings. Add the stock and bring it to a boil. Lower heat, cover, and simmer 30 minutes. Remove pot from heat and allow liquid to cool.

2. Puree mixture in a blender until smooth. Return it to the pot.

3. Stir the milk, nutmeg, basil, and tarragon into the soup pot. Return liquid to a gentle boil, lower heat, and allow to simmer 15 minutes. Stir occasionally to prevent sticking.

4. Place a spoonful of yogurt in each bowl and then ladle in the hot soup.

STUFFED LETTUCE SOUP

Serves 6

12 medium-size Boston lettuce leaves (the tougher outside leaves may be used*)
1 slice slightly stale whole wheat bread, cut into ½-inch cubes
1 egg, beaten
1 tablespoon grated onions
1 teaspoon tamari soy sauce
¾ pound leftover cold roast beef or lamb, ground or minced
3 tablespoons minced parsley
8 cups Beef Stock (see Index)

*The tougher outside leaves, actually the most nutritious part of the head, work well in this recipe.

1. Trim the stalk ends from the lettuce and pare down any thick ribs (if necessary). Wash the leaves very well. In a large covered pan, steam the lettuce over boiling water just until limp (about 45 seconds). Spread the leaves in a single layer on a clean dish towel to drain.

2. In a small mixing bowl, soak the bread with the egg, onions, and tamari. Stir with a fork to mix. Stir in the ground meat and 1 tablespoon of the parsley. Place a rounded tablespoon of the meat mixture in the center of each lettuce leaf. Fold the base of the leaf over the filling, fold in the sides, and roll up.

3. Arrange the small rolls, seam side down, in a single layer in a large skillet. Gently pour in the stock. Bring liquid to a boil, lower heat, and gently simmer until thoroughly heated (about 15 minutes). Place 2 rolls in each bowl, ladle in the stock, and sprinkle with the remaining parsley.

CHILLED BEET AND MASHED POTATO SOUP

Serves 6

1 cup sliced or diced cooked beets
2 tablespoons lemon juice
1 small onion, finely chopped
1 cup mashed potatoes
3 cups Beef Stock (see Index)
1 cup plain yogurt
3 basil leaves, finely chopped

1. Put the beets, lemon juice, onion, mashed potatoes, and ¼ cup of the stock into the container of an electric blender. Process until smooth. With motor running, gradually add remaining stock until ingredients are blended.

2. In a medium-size mixing bowl, whisk the yogurt until smooth. Gradually beat in the stock mixture. Cover and chill until serving time.

3. Stir soup before serving and sprinkle with basil. Serve chilled.

SALAD SOUP

Serves 6

3 to 4 cups leftover dressed salad, drained
1 cup tomato or carrot juice
3 cups Chicken Stock (see Index)
¼ cup chopped mixed vegetables (such as carrots, tomatoes, celery, green peppers)

Garnish

1 cup plain yogurt
2 tablespoons minced chives
2 tablespoons minced parsley

1. Process the salad with juice and stock in small batches in a blender. Cover and chill.

2. At serving time, stir the chopped vegetables into the soup. Top each portion with a dollop of yogurt. Combine the chives and parsley and sprinkle over the yogurt.

RICE TWICE SOUP

Serves 6

4 cups Beef Stock (see Index)
2 cups tomato juice
1 celery stalk, halved
1 tablespoon lemon juice
1 bay leaf
6 juniper berries
1 to 2 cups leftover cooked brown rice
2 tablespoons minced parsley
½ cup alfalfa sprouts

1. In a 3-quart soup pot combine the stock, tomato juice, celery, lemon juice, bay leaf, and juniper berries. Bring to a boil, lower heat, and simmer gently 5 minutes.

2. Remove celery, bay leaf, and juniper berries with a slotted spoon.

3. Break up any clumps of sticky rice so that the grains are separated. Stir the rice and parsley into the hot soup. Cook just until heated through.

4. Ladle soup into warm bowls and sprinkle with alfalfa sprouts.

FISH HEAD SOUP

Serves 6

¼ cup butter
1 large onion, coarsely chopped
1 cup coarsely chopped celery
2 large fish heads (cod, haddock, or bass—about 3 pounds), gills removed
1 bay leaf
3 sprigs thyme
10 cups water
1 pound potatoes, diced
1 pound tomatoes, peeled and coarsely chopped
minced parsley

1. Melt the butter in a 4-quart soup pot. Saute the onion and celery until limp (about 5 minutes).
2. Add the fish heads, bay leaf, thyme, and water. Bring to a boil, lower heat, cover, and simmer 1 hour.
3. Discard the bay leaf and thyme. Using a slotted spoon, transfer the fish heads to a cutting board. Add the potatoes and tomatoes to the stock.
4. Remove the fish meat from the bones and reserve it. Discard the bones and other waste.
5. Simmer until the potatoes are tender (about 20 minutes longer). Add the fish meat to the pot. Ladle into serving bowls and sprinkle with parsley.

ROAST OR STEAK BONE BROTH

Serves 6

2 to 3 pounds meaty leftover roast or steak bones
12 cups cold water
2 celery stalks, halved
2 carrots, halved
2 unpeeled onions, halved
2 whole cloves
3 garlic cloves, peeled
5 sprigs parsley
6 peppercorns
¼ teaspoon ground coriander seeds

1. Saw or chop the bones into small pieces.
2. Place bones and remaining ingredients in a 5-quart soup pot. Bring liquid to a boil, lower heat, and simmer, uncovered or partially covered, at least 6 hours. Skim foam from surface as necessary.
3. Rinse a clean dish towel in cold water and wring it out. Use towel to line a large strainer. Pour soup through strainer but do not wring cloth into the strained soup.
4. Serve liquid as a broth or use in any recipe calling for beef stock.

TURKEY GIBLET SOUP

Serves 6

giblets, wings, and neck of 1 turkey
6 cups water
5 peppercorns
1 large unpeeled onion, quartered
2 celery stalks, halved
1 carrot, quartered
½ cup brown rice
1 tablespoon butter
1 tablespoon whole wheat flour
2 tablespoons finely chopped
parsley
freshly grated nutmeg

1. Place the giblets, wings, and neck in a 4-quart soup pot with the water, peppercorns, onion, celery, and carrot. Bring to a boil, lower heat, and simmer very gently 1 hour.

2. Strain the soup into another 4-quart soup pot. Chop the giblets and add them to the soup. Remove any meat from the wings and neck and add it to the soup. Return to a boil and stir in the rice. Lower heat, cover, and simmer until rice is tender (about 30 minutes).

3. Blend the butter and flour and stir into the soup. Just before serving, add the parsley. Sprinkle each portion with nutmeg.

Vegetarian Soups

EGGPLANT SOUP AU GRATIN

Serves 6

3 tablespoons olive oil
1 large onion, finely chopped
2 celery stalks, thinly sliced
2 garlic cloves, finely chopped
2 medium-size eggplants, peeled and diced
½ teaspoon ground coriander seeds
½ teaspoon dried thyme
1 medium-size sweet red pepper, peeled and cut into ½-inch cubes
4 cups Vegetable Stock (see Index) or water
2 tablespoons minced coriander leaves
6 ¼-inch-thick tomato slices
1½ cups grated Swiss cheese

1. Heat the oil in a 3-quart soup pot. Add the onion and celery and saute until soft. Stir in the garlic and cook 1 minute longer. Stir in the eggplant, coriander seeds, and thyme. Saute 2 minutes. Add the pepper and stock. Bring to a boil, lower heat, cover, and simmer 30 minutes. Stir in the coriander leaves.

2. Ladle soup into oven-proof bowls or crocks. Top soup with the tomato slices and sprinkle the slices with the cheese. Place under a broiler until lightly browned and melted. Serve immediately.

Marigolds in the Soup Pot and Salad Bowl

Toss a few of the brilliant flower heads from your pot marigolds into the soup pot during the last 10 minutes of cooking time, or scatter some of the colorful petals over the top of a salad just before serving. They will add a unique dimension in flavor and appearance.

Other marigold varieties also have a culinary role: marsh marigolds (whose leaves must be cooked) and sweet-scented marigolds that produce tender young leaves which serve beautifully as salad greens.

AUTUMN VEGETABLE SOUP

Serves 6

8 cups Vegetable Stock (see Index)
½ cup brown rice
1 medium-size onion, minced
3 large tomatoes, peeled, seeded, and coarsely chopped
1 cup green beans, thinly sliced on the diagonal
1 turnip, cut into ½-inch cubes
1 sweet red pepper, diced
2 medium-size zucchini, diced
2 tablespoons vinegar
2 tablespoons minced parsley
2 tablespoons minced chives

1. Bring the stock to a boil in a 4-quart soup pot. Stir in the rice and onion. Lower heat, cover, and simmer 20 minutes.

2. Add the tomatoes, green beans, turnip, pepper, and zucchini. Mix well, cover, and simmer 30 minutes.

3. Just before serving, stir in the vinegar, parsley, and chives.

TOFU SOUP WITH CHRYSANTHEMUMS

Serves 6

1 pound tofu
3 tablespoons olive oil
1 large onion, coarsely chopped
1 cup coarsely chopped celery
6 medium-size tomatoes
4 cups Vegetable Stock (see Index) or water
1 cup milk
petals of 1 chrysanthemum, washed and drained

1. Rinse and drain the tofu. Arrange it on a folded tea towel in a shallow dish. Cover with another tea towel and place a heavy weight on top for 2 hours. (This will remove any excess moisture and compress the tofu.)

2. Heat the oil in a 3-quart soup pot. Add the onion and celery and saute until limp. Stir in the tomatoes and cook 5 minutes. Add the stock, bring to a boil, lower heat, cover, and simmer 30 minutes. Cool slightly.

3. Transfer mixture to a blender container and process until smooth. Strain the soup back into the pan. Stir in the milk.

4. Cut tofu into ¼-inch matchstick pieces. Divide among 6 soup bowls.

5. Reheat but do not boil soup. Ladle it into the soup bowls and sprinkle the surface with flower petals.

FRESH VEGETABLE TAMARI SOUP

Serves 8

6 cups Vegetable Stock (see Index)
⅓ cup minced onion
⅓ to ½ cup tamari soy sauce
1 tablespoon honey
⅓ lemon, cut into thin slices
1 tablespoon tomato paste
3 tomatoes, blanched, peeled, and coarsely chopped
½ cup olive oil
3 garlic cloves, minced
2 teaspoons minced ginger root
¼ cup minced parsley
½ teaspoon fresh thyme or ⅛ teaspoon dried
½ teaspoon fresh tarragon or ⅛ teaspoon dried
1 teaspoon fresh oregano or ½ teaspoon dried
2 tablespoons fresh dillweed or 1 tablespoon dried
⅛ cup thinly sliced carrots
1⅔ cups any substantial fresh vegetables (such as small pieces of broccoli and green beans)
⅓ cup thinly sliced celery hearts
½ medium-size Spanish onion, cut in half and then into thin slivers
⅛ cup thinly sliced scallions
⅔ cup thickly sliced mushrooms
½ cup finely shredded Chinese cabbage
½ cup sesame seeds, toasted

1. Pour the stock into a 4-quart soup pot. Add the onion, ⅓ cup tamari, honey, lemon slices, tomato paste, and tomatoes. Bring to a boil and then simmer on low heat.

2. Heat the oil in a skillet. Add the garlic, ginger root, and 2 tablespoons of the parsley and saute 1 minute. Add the herbs and saute another minute. Stir constantly to prevent scorching garlic or ginger root.

3. Begin adding the vegetables to garlic-ginger root saute. Start with harder ones like carrots and beans and finish with more delicate ones like scallions and mushrooms. Add more oil if necessary. After adding each group, spoon in about 1 tablespoon stock, cover pan, and allow vegetables to steam until they just start to soften. Do not overcook them.

4. Add steamed vegetables and remaining parsley to the soup pot. Continue to simmer 10 minutes. Add the cabbage and cook 1 minute longer. Add remaining tamari, if desired.

5. Garnish soup with sesame seeds.

_____ How to Store Ginger _____

A little ginger goes a long way, so a chunk weighing about 2 ounces can last a long time if properly stored. But even when kept in a refrigerator, ginger gets spongy and loses some of its pungency. A foolproof method is to freeze your supply until you need it for cooking. Then grate the needed quantity of ginger and put the rest back in the freezer for later use.

CABBAGE AND CAULIFLOWER CHEESE SOUP

Serves 6

¼ cup butter
1 large onion, finely chopped
1 small head cabbage, shredded
1 small head cauliflower, coarsely chopped
1 large potato, peeled and cut into ½-inch cubes
5 cups Vegetable Stock (see Index) or water
1 cup cottage cheese
¼ cup blue-veined cheese
1 cup milk
1 tablespoon caraway seeds

1. Melt the butter in a 3-quart soup pot. Add the onion and saute until transparent. Stir in the cabbage. Cover tightly and cook on medium-low heat. Shake the pan up and down vigorously from time to time. Cook until the cabbage is wilted (about 10 minutes).

2. Add the cauliflower, potato, and stock. Bring to a boil, lower heat, cover, and simmer 25 minutes. Remove from heat. Cool slightly.

3. Process both cheeses and the milk in a blender container until smooth. Slowly stir the cheese mixture into the slightly cooled soup.

4. Just before serving, heat but do not boil soup. Sprinkle with caraway seeds.

LAYERED MINESTRONE

Serves 6

6 tablespoons olive oil
3 large tomatoes, peeled and sliced
2 large onions, thinly sliced
2 garlic cloves, minced
3 medium-size zucchini, sliced ¼ inch thick
1 small head romaine lettuce, shredded
1 cup shelled peas (about 1 pound)
1 scallion, minced
2 tablespoons minced dillweed
1½ cups corn (about 3 ears)
½ cup minced parsley
¼ pound mushrooms, thinly sliced
3 large carrots, grated
2 tablespoons minced basil
grated Parmesan cheese

1. Grease a 3-quart soup pot with 1 tablespoon of the oil.

2. Place the tomatoes in the bottom of the pot. Top with the onions and garlic. Layer the vegetables in the following order: zucchini, lettuce, peas, scallion, dillweed, corn, parsley, mushrooms, and carrots. Sprinkle with the basil. Cover tightly and steam (without adding water) on medium-low heat until the bottom vegetables give off their juices (about 10 minutes).

3. Add the remaining oil and stir well. Recover and steam an additional 30 minutes. Stir often. (The vegetables will create their own liquid as they cook.)

4. Serve hot, sprinkled with cheese.

FRESH VEGETABLE MISO SOUP

Serves 8

½ cup olive or other oil
2 tablespoons arrowroot
12 cups Vegetable Stock (see Index) or water
3 nonsalted vegetable bouillon cubes (optional)
¼ cup minced parsley
½ cup ground almonds
1 bay leaf
½ cup thinly sliced carrots
1 tablespoon dried oregano
2 teaspoons dried thyme
¾ cup coarsely chopped onions
½ cup coarsely chopped celery
¾ cup thinly sliced mushrooms
1 cup thinly sliced bok choy or cabbage
½ cup mung bean sprouts
5 tablespoons miso

1. In a 5-quart soup pot, warm 5 tablespoons of the oil. Add arrowroot and stir until mixture is smooth. Add stock; bouillon cubes, if used; parsley; ground almonds; and bay leaf and set aside.

2. Put the remaining 3 tablespoons oil in a heavy skillet. Saute and steam the vegetables. Start by adding the carrots to the pan, toss them with the oil, add the herbs, and saute everything 2 minutes. Then, add several tablespoons stock, cover, and steam the mixture at low heat 5 minutes. Next, add onions and celery, recover, and steam another 5 minutes. Now add mushrooms and cook, uncovered, on low heat until the mushrooms are just limp.

3. Ladle the vegetables into the soup pot. Bring the liquid to a boil. Cover and cook on medium-low heat 15 minutes. Then add bok choy and sprouts. Recover and cook another 5 minutes.

4. Whisk miso in a small bowl with several tablespoons stock. At the end of the cooking time, remove the soup pot from the heat. Stir in the miso. Add more miso or more water if your taste indicates any adjustments.

Note: Do not boil this soup after you have added the miso or you will destroy all the "friendly" bacteria miso contains that help in digestion.

OKRA SOUP

Serves 6

4 cups Garlic Stock (see Index)
2 cups tomato juice
18 young okra, cut into ¼-inch slices
⅛ teaspoon cayenne pepper
Garnish
2 green onions, thinly sliced
2 tablespoons finely chopped celery leaves

1. Combine the stock and tomato juice in a 3-quart soup pot. Bring to a boil and add the okra and cayenne. Lower the heat, cover, and simmer 2 minutes.

2. Ladle soup into individual bowls and sprinkle each portion with green onions and celery leaves.

GREEK LENTIL SOUP

Serves 6

1 cup dried lentils, rinsed and
  soaked overnight in 9 cups
  water
1 large onion, coarsely chopped
2 garlic cloves, crushed
1 celery stalk with leaves, coarsely
  chopped
1 pound Italian plum tomatoes,
  coarsely chopped
1 bay leaf
4 sprigs parsley
3 sprigs oregano or ½ teaspoon
  dried
¼ cup olive oil
½ teaspoon pepper
leaves from ½ pound spinach or
  Swiss chard, shredded
2 tablespoons red wine vinegar

1. In a 5-quart soup pot, bring the lentils and their soaking water to a boil. Lower heat and add the onion, garlic, celery, and tomatoes. Cover and simmer 1½ hours.

2. Tie fresh herbs together with string for easy removal. Add herbs, oil, and pepper to lentils. Continue to simmer 1 hour more or until soup is very thick.

3. Remove fresh herbs from lentils. Add the spinach and puree mixture in a blender or food processor. Return to pot and reheat. Add vinegar just before serving. Serve hot.

SWEET AND SOUR CABBAGE AND TOMATO SOUP

Serves 6 to 8

13 cups coarsely shredded cabbage
  (about 2 pounds)
10 cups water
 2 large onions, coarsely chopped
 2 tablespoons butter
1¾ pounds Italian plum tomatoes,
  coarsely chopped
¼ cup lemon juice
 2 teaspoons mild honey
 3 eggs, beaten
¼ teaspoon white pepper
 1 cup sour cream

1. Place the cabbage and water in a 5-quart soup pot and let stand 20 minutes.

2. Saute onions in butter in an uncovered skillet on medium heat until they just begin to brown. Then stir ingredients, cover the pot, and set aside.

3. Add tomatoes to the cabbage. Bring to a boil (do not cover pot). Lower heat to medium and cook 1 hour. Stir occasionally.

4. Add the sauteed onions, lemon juice, and honey to the cabbage and cook 20 minutes more.

5. Remove cabbage from heat and gradually add about ½ cup of the hot soup liquid to the beaten eggs. Return egg mixture to pot, stir with a wooden spoon, and cook 10 minutes more on low heat. Add pepper.

6. Chill soup for several hours. Before serving, stir in sour cream. Serve ice-cold.

Note: This soup is even better the second day as flavors blend.

VEGETABLE CUSTARD SOUP

Serves 6

3 mushrooms, thinly sliced
2 scallions, thinly sliced on the diagonal
6 teaspoons grated Parmesan cheese
4 eggs, beaten
1 cup tomato juice
2 cups Vegetable Stock (see Index)

1. Divide the mushrooms and scallions among 6 custard cups. Sprinkle 1 teaspoon cheese into each cup.

2. In a medium-size mixing bowl, beat the eggs, tomato juice, and stock until combined. Divide the mixture among the custard cups.

3. Place the custard cups over hot water on a steaming rack in a pan. Water must not touch the bottom of the cups. To prevent any condensation from falling into the custards, place a pair of chopsticks on top of the cups and arrange a small towel or triple layer of cheesecloth over the sticks. Cover the pan and steam on medium-low heat 30 minutes.

4. Serve warm.

WHITE GAZPACHO

Serves 6

1 egg
2 tablespoons cider vinegar
⅔ cup olive oil
3 tablespoons lemon juice
2 garlic cloves, quartered
1 teaspoon minced tarragon
¼ teaspoon hot pepper sauce
5 slices day-old whole wheat bread
4 cups Vegetable Stock (see Index)
1 large green pepper, cut into thin strips
2 medium-size cucumbers, peeled and cut into ½-inch cubes
1 teaspoon honey
finely chopped cucumber and green pepper

1. Put the egg, vinegar, and ¼ cup of the oil into the container of a blender. Cover and process at blend. Immediately remove the feeder cap and add the remaining oil in a steady stream. Add the lemon juice, garlic, tarragon, and pepper sauce. Process until mixed.

2. Soak the bread in 1 cup of the stock. Add this to the blender container and process. With the motor still running, add the green pepper, cucumbers, and honey. Blend until smooth.

3. Place a strainer over a large mixing bowl and pour the contents of the blender into it. Strain the mixture while adding the remaining stock and forcing the solid pieces through the sieve with a wooden spoon. Discard any solids that will not pass through.

4. Cover the bowl and refrigerate until very cold. Serve soup cold, garnished with the chopped vegetables.

FRESH DOUBLE PEA SOUP

Serves 6

¼ cup olive oil
2 large onions, coarsely chopped
3 garlic cloves, minced
1½ pounds tomatoes, peeled, seeded, and chopped
1 bay leaf
1 cup shelled black-eyed peas (about 1 pound)
5 cups boiling water
1 cup shelled peas (about 1 pound)
2 celery stalks, diced
2 tablespoons finely chopped parsley
2 tablespoons finely chopped basil
grated Parmesan cheese

1. Heat the oil in a 3-quart soup pot. Add the onions and saute until transparent. Add the garlic and saute 1 minute longer. Stir in the tomatoes, bay leaf, and black-eyed peas. Pour in the boiling water, reduce heat, cover, and simmer 40 minutes.

2. Add the peas and celery; cover and cook 20 minutes longer.

3. Remove the bay leaf. Stir in the parsley and basil. Ladle soup into bowls and serve with Parmesan cheese on the side.

> "Et tu Bluto!" said Popeye as he
>   downed a bowl of the green infusion...
>   topped by a dollop of sour cream...
>   and on the side, a slice of black
>   Russian rye bread.
> made with:
> lots of spinach blended with water &
>   milk, and a mixture of onions-garlic-
>   wheat germ-flour-fried-in-butter
>   and some tomatoes
> seasoned with black pepper, cloves,
>   nutmeg & tamari.

The Rodale Press Soup Co-op

In the midst of a barren northern winter when so many sedentary office workers are feeling sluggish, a group of Rodale Press writers, editors, and researchers maintain a high level of physical activity—at lunch hour. In preference to unwinding over a sit-down luncheon, they bike, exercise, run, and jog. A nourishing meal, of course, is also important to their good conditioning. Before or after these jaunts they enjoy bowls of steaming, homemade soup.

These nine fresh-air devotees make up the Rodale Soup Co-op. With the common desire for a quick, hearty, vegetarian meal, they have joined together to make it a reality. On each of a cycle of nine work days, a different member brings soup for everyone. There is a simple directive: These are to be nonmeat soups with dairy products permitted. Ingredients on which the group frequently relies are grains, vegetables, vegetable stocks, dairy products, tofu, tahini, a vast array of spices and herbs, and, occasionally, fruits like apples, dates, and raisins.

How It Works

Amy Rowland works in the book division. She starts preparing her Pistou Soup several days ahead of time. One evening she soaks kidney beans; on the next she cooks them. The following night, she cooks potatoes, fresh green beans, and carrots with the beans. The next day she arrives at work with a shiny caldron which she stores in the refrigerator. (The Press provides a compact kitchen area for its employees.) Shortly before noon the next day, Amy begins warming this elaborate but, actually, rather effortless creation. On the counter she places a card which lists basic ingredients. Intermittently throughout the lunch hour, members fill their own ceramic mugs and bowls. Some people carry the soup to their desks, but most choose to remain standing about the stove where talk often revolves around food and recipes. After 1:00 P.M., Amy rinses an empty pot. Already Takla Gardey is asking Mary Jurinko from the *Organic Gardening* magazine staff what she's planning for Monday.

No Laughing Matter

Co-op members rely heavily on this substantial fare. Early one morning they noticed a piece of paper replacing the familiar soup pot atop the burners. The memo read:

RODALE PRESS MEMO

To: Date:

From:

Subject:

Sorry folks — no soup — the cook is out to lunch   Joe

Poor Joe had forgotten to check the schedule. Throughout the day his memo picked up good-humored scribblings like "fink," "bad move," and "boo." On another occasion, a member brought a rather minimal amount because unexpected guests at home had fairly well depleted her larder of basic ingredients. Nonetheless the group rallied. Out of the fridge came a cup of leftover yogurt, half of a lemon, and a pint of homemade tomato juice. They also retrieved a few sprigs of mint still growing outside the door. Into the soup it all went.

Cooks from All Walks

Jane Kinderlehrer and Carol Hopkins, directly involved in writing about food, have the advantage of consulting numerous recipes, although neither follows any slavishly. Jane has created an interesting vegetarian version of a standard Jewish borscht, and Carol has reworked conventional Mexican chili recipes into Spicy Mexican Lentil Soup. Members whose fields take them into other areas, such as solar energy and horticulture, also demonstrate a flexible cooking ability. Tom Wolfe uniquely combines spices to produce a Curried Black Bean Soup which comes from his Argentine heritage; Rosanne McGinn turns an ordinary corn chowder into an elegant soup laced with cheddar cheese, cream, and the interesting addition of cumin.

One of the most original achievements has been Marian Wolbers's Turnip Egg Drop Soup. "I wait until turnips are at their absolute sweetest before undertaking this one." Subtle tastes, such as garlic-flavored broccoli and a dash of homemade pickle juice combined with the delightfully sweet turnip stock, produce unusual results.

The soup co-op assembles for a tasting.

Joe Carter waits impatiently as Takla Gardey applies the all-important finishing touch.

The co-op is starting to gather a following as employees from other parts of the building detect particularly interesting aromas. Next month's schedule will include several new faces. You, too, can savor these tastes and smells by recreating some of the same recipes. The contributors, Amy, Jane, Carol, Tom, Rosanne, and Marian consider them only departure points for your own creativity. We, however, find that some are hard to improve upon.

Jane Kinderlehrer serves up a bowl of goodness.

CORN CHOWDER
WITH CHEESE

Serves 4 to 6

1 *large potato, peeled and cut into*
   ½-inch cubes
1 *bay leaf*
¼ *teaspoon dried sage*
1 *teaspoon cumin seeds*
2½ *cups water*
1 *onion, finely chopped*
3 *tablespoons butter, melted*
3 *tablespoons whole wheat flour*
1 *cup heavy cream, scalded*
2 *cups corn (about 2 ears)*
1 *tablespoon minced chives*
1 *tablespoon minced parsley*
1 *teaspoon nutmeg*
pepper to taste
1½ *cups grated sharp cheddar cheese*
4 *tablespoons lemon juice*

1. In a 4-quart soup pot, boil the potato, bay leaf, sage, and cumin seeds in water until potato is tender (about 15 minutes).
2. Saute the onion in the butter until transparent. Add the flour and mix well. Stirring with a whisk, add the cream. Cook on low heat 1 minute. Combine this sauce with the potatoes and at least 2 cups of their water.
3. Add the corn, herbs, and remaining seasonings. Simmer soup about 10 minutes. Stir in the cheese and the lemon juice and mix well. Heat until all the cheese is melted.

PISTOU
(FRENCH PROVENCAL
VEGETABLE SOUP)

Serves 6

½ *pound red kidney beans, rinsed and*
   soaked overnight in water to cover
4 *large carrots, diced*
2 *medium-size potatoes, diced*
2 *leeks, thinly sliced*
½ *pound green beans, snapped into*
   ½-inch pieces
3 *garlic cloves, crushed*
⅛ *teaspoon pepper*
¼ *cup finely chopped basil*
½ *cup olive oil*
1 *cup very thin artichoke flour*
   noodles
¼ *cup tomato puree or 1 fresh tomato,*
   peeled and finely chopped
½ *cup soft bread crumbs*
¼ *cup grated Parmesan cheese*

1. In an 8-quart soup pot, bring the beans and soaking water to a boil and cook until beans are tender (about 1 hour).
2. Put all the vegetables into the pot with the garlic and pepper, and add enough water to fill the pot. Bring to a boil and simmer until the vegetables are cooked but still a little crisp.
3. About half an hour before serving time, soak the basil in oil. Set this mixture aside so the flavors blend.
4. About 15 minutes before serving, reheat the soup to boiling. Add noodles and tomato puree. Cook, uncovered, at a slow boil until noodles are tender.
5. About 10 minutes before serving, add the oil and basil mixture, bread crumbs, and cheese. Pass a small bowl of cheese at the table.

SPICY MEXICAN LENTIL SOUP

Serves 8

8 *cups Vegetable Stock (see Index)*
2 *cups dried lentils*
2 *large onions, coarsely chopped*
¼ *to ½ cup molasses*
¼ *cup tamari soy sauce*
1 *bay leaf*
¾ *cup dried currants*
¼ *cup cider vinegar*
2 *to 3 tablespoons hot paprika*
½ *cup oil*
1 *teaspoon dried basil*
1 *teaspoon dried oregano*
½ *teaspoon dried thyme*
½ *cup minced parsley*
¼ *cup minced coriander leaves*
2 *tablespoons ground cumin*
½ *teaspoon cardamom*
6 *garlic cloves, minced*
3 *medium-size carrots, thinly sliced on the diagonal*
1 *medium-size green pepper, thinly sliced in strips*
3 *celery stalks, finely chopped*
½ *pound mushrooms, quartered*
3 *pounds tomatoes, peeled and coarsely chopped*
6 *ounces tomato paste*
3 *thin lemon rings*
3 *tablespoons miso*

1. Pour 3 cups of the stock into a 5-quart soup pot. Add the lentils, ½ cup of the onions, molasses, tamari, and bay leaf. Bring to a boil. Cover and cook on low heat 20 minutes.

2. Soak the currants in vinegar. Put aside.

3. In a skillet, warm the paprika in the oil. Add remaining herbs, spices, and garlic and saute 2 minutes. Spoon mixture into lentils and liquid, leaving oil in skillet.

4. In the same skillet, saute remaining onions, carrots, pepper, celery, and mushrooms in oil until they are just tender-crisp. Spoon into lentil mixture.

5. Pour remaining stock, tomatoes, and tomato paste into soup pot. Add the lemon rings, currants, and vinegar. Bring to a boil. Turn heat to low, cover, and cook 1 hour. Remove lid and cook, uncovered, another hour.

6. After you have removed soup from the burner, mix miso with just enough water to form a thin paste and stir mixture into the soup.

TURNIP EGG DROP SOUP

Serves 4 to 6

5 *medium-size turnips*
1½ *cups green beans, sliced crosswise*
into 1-inch pieces
2 *cups water*
1 *large beet, boiled in water to cover*
3 *garlic cloves, crushed*
3 *tablespoons butter*
1½ *cups broccoli, coarsely chopped*
2 *teaspoons dried basil*
1 *tablespoon olive oil*
3 *tablespoons tamari soy sauce*
1 to 2 *tablespoons cider vinegar*
1 *tablespoon sweet gherkin pickle*
juice
2 *eggs, beaten*

1. Wash the turnips well. Cut away any brown spots but leave the skins intact. Place them in a 4-quart soup pot with water to cover and boil them 15 minutes.
2. In a 1-quart saucepan, boil the beans in the water 8 to 10 minutes.
3. Drain the beet, reserving the liquid. Refrigerate the beet for another use.
4. Remove the hot turnips from their broth with a fork. Drain them on paper towels and place them on a wooden chopping block. When they have cooled a bit, slice them in half and then cut them evenly into ½-inch slices. Return these to the turnip broth and add the reserved beet liquid and the green beans with their liquid. Cover and simmer 15 minutes.
5. In a wok, fry the garlic in butter. Just as the garlic begins to brown, add the broccoli, basil, oil, and 1 tablespoon of the tamari. Saute 5 to 8 minutes. Turn the broccoli often with a wooden spoon.
6. Place the broccoli mixture in the simmering broth and add the remainder of the tamari, vinegar, and pickle juice. Bring the soup to a high bubbling point and then, in a thin stream, slowly pour in the eggs. Once they have congealed, remove the soup from the heat and serve immediately.

CURRIED BLACK
BEAN SOUP

Serves 6

2 *cups dried black beans, rinsed and*
   soaked overnight in 5 cups water
3 *cups water*
4 *medium-size onions, coarsely*
   chopped
5 *garlic cloves, minced*
2 *tablespoons oil*
2 *medium-size green peppers, coarsely*
   chopped
3 *tablespoons lemon juice*
2 *teaspoons curry powder*
2 *bay leaves*
⅛ *teaspoon cayenne pepper*
1 *teaspoon ground cumin*
½ *teaspoon chili powder*
¼ *teaspoon ginger*
¼ *teaspoon cloves*
¼ *cup minced parsley*
1 *cup raisins or finely chopped apples*
1 *pound tofu, cut into ½-inch cubes*
3 *tablespoons tamari soy sauce*

Garnish

1 *cup finely chopped peanuts*
½ *cup grated coconut*

1. In a 4-quart soup pot, bring the beans, soaking water, and additional water to a boil, then cover and simmer until beans are soft but still formed (about 1 hour).

2. In a skillet, saute the onions and garlic in oil 2 minutes. Add the peppers, lemon juice, spices, and parsley and saute 2 minutes longer. Spoon this mixture into beans. Adjust seasonings to your taste. Bring beans to a boil. Cover and simmer 1 to 1½ hours.

3. Five minutes before serving, add the raisins, tofu, and tamari and warm soup thoroughly. Garnish with the peanuts and coconut.

Variation

Black Bean Chili: Cook bean mixture, uncovered, 1 additional hour. Serve over brown rice.

HERBED TOMATO YOGURT SOUP
HOLIDAY TURKEY WALNUT SALAD

For this recipe, see page 147
For this recipe, see page 225

GREEN PASTA SALAD   For this recipe, see page 167

VEGETARIAN BORSCHT

Serves 8

8 *medium-size beets with leaves (2 bunches)*
1 *onion*
8 *cups boiling water*
1 *teaspoon kelp*
2 *eggs*
¼ *cup lemon juice*
2 *tablespoons honey or to taste*
sour cream or yogurt (if soup to be served cold)
8 *small boiled potatoes (if soup to be served hot)*

1. Cut the tops off about 2 inches above the beets and reserve them. Be sure to do this before you scrub them.

2. Carefully scrub the beets and place them in a 5-quart soup pot. Cover them with cold water and cook until fork-tender (about 15 minutes). The size of the beets will determine the cooking time.

2. Meantime, wash the beet leaves vey carefully and finely chop them. (I use my wooden chopping bowl.) Be sure to include the stems. They have good nutrients that shouldn't be wasted. Put these tops aside.

3. When the beets are tender, remove them from the liquid with a slotted spoon. Slip off their skins and then grate the beets. Grate the onion into the beets and add both to the liquid in the soup pot.

4. Add the chopped beet tops and boiling water to the soup pot. Add kelp and bring again to a boil; then reduce heat and simmer 5 minutes.

5. Beat the eggs and add the lemon juice and honey. Stir a little of the hot liquid from the borscht into the egg mixture. Mix it up quickly so the eggs don't cook. Pour the borscht quickly from one pot to another several times; this is my mother's trick for making it light and frothy.

6. When you serve the soup cold, add a dollop of sour cream or yogurt. When you serve it hot, add a boiled potato.

Yogurt Soups

CELERY YOGURT SOUP

Serves 6

2 cups plain yogurt
3 cups tomato juice
3 tablespoons lemon juice
1 tablespoon olive oil
1 cup finely minced celery
1 shallot, finely minced

Garnish
¼ cup finely chopped celery leaves
1 tablespoon minced chives

1. In a large mixing bowl, whisk together the yogurt, tomato juice, lemon juice, and oil. When smooth, stir in the celery and shallot. Cover and chill until very cold.

2. Serve in individual bowls and sprinkle each with celery leaves and chives just before serving.

YOGURT EATERS HAVE LOWER CHOLESTEROL LEVELS

In 1978, a team of doctors from Harbor/UCLA General Hospital in California supplemented the diets of 54 volunteers with yogurt to see if it would cut their serum cholesterol levels. The 24 men and 30 women, aged 21 to 55, ate three eight-ounce containers of the unflavored variety every day—and within a week their cholesterol counts dropped by as much as 10 percent. Yogurt's calcium hydroxymethyl gluterate and casein (a milk protein) seem to have the ability to keep cholesterol from forming by neutralizing the body's production of an enzyme crucial to cholesterol's makeup. Yogurt is rich in the B-complex vitamins, has a higher percentage of vitamins A and D, and is especially rich in protein.

HERBED TOMATO YOGURT SOUP

Serves 6

2½ pounds tomatoes, seeded and coarsely chopped
2 garlic cloves, minced
1 small onion, coarsely chopped
1 celery stalk, sliced into ¼-inch pieces
1 tablespoon olive oil
1 sprig thyme
1 sprig basil
1 sprig parsley
2 cups plain yogurt
1 lemon
1 cup plain yogurt

1. In a blender, puree the tomatoes, garlic, onion, celery, oil, thyme, basil, and parsley.

2. Whisk the yogurt in a large mixing bowl until smooth. Whisk in the tomato puree.

3. Avoiding the white pith, peel the rind from the lemon. Cut it into julienne strips. Blanch the lemon strips in a small amount of boiling water 1 minute, then refresh the strips in cold water. Drain the strips and wrap them in a paper towel. Refrigerate until serving time.

4. Squeeze the juice from the lemon and stir it into the soup. Cover the bowl and refrigerate until very cold.

5. Garnish each serving with a dollop of yogurt and top with a few lemon strips.

ROOT VEGETABLE YOGURT SOUP

Serves 6

2 tablespoons butter
1 small onion, finely chopped
2 cups Chicken Stock (see Index)
3 parsnips, diced
3 young turnips, diced
1 cup carrot juice
2 cups plain yogurt
2 egg yolks, lightly beaten
2 tablespoons finely chopped parsley or chervil

1. Melt the butter in a 3-quart soup pot. Add the onion and saute until transparent. Add the stock, parsnips, and turnips. Bring to a boil, lower heat, cover, and simmer just until tender (about 7 minutes).

2. Combine the carrot juice, yogurt, and egg yolks. Beat until thoroughly blended. Pour mixture into the pot containing the stock and vegetables.

3. Cook on medium heat just until mixture begins to simmer. Stir constantly. Lower heat and simmer gently 2 minutes. Do not allow to boil. Remove from heat.

4. Serve soup hot or chilled, sprinkled with parsley.

When you take any antibiotic prescription, take yogurt, too. Antibiotics destroy all bacteria—good and bad—but yogurt fortifies the good kind (the intestinal flora we need for digestion) so it can survive the attack.

YOGURT CUSTARD SOUP

Serves 6

2 tablespoons butter
1 cup spinach
¼ cup minced parsley
5 cups Beef Stock (see Index)
2 tablespoons minced dillweed
2 tablespoons chopped chives
1 cup plain yogurt
1 cup milk
4 eggs
¼ cup freshly grated Parmesan cheese

1. Generously butter a 9 × 9-inch baking dish. Preheat the oven to 350°F.

2. Melt butter in a large skillet. Add spinach and parsley and sprinkle with ¼ cup of the stock. Cover tightly and steam until the greens are wilted (about 5 minutes). Shake the pan occasionally. Transfer greens to the container of a blender. Add the dillweed, chives, yogurt, milk, and eggs. Process until blended. Blend in the cheese.

3. Turn the mixture into the buttered baking dish. Place the dish in a larger pan and set it in the oven. Add boiling water to the larger pan almost to the rim. Bake, uncovered, 45 minutes. Remove from oven and cool to room temperature. Cover with plastic wrap and chill until serving time.

4. Turn out custard and cut it into ½-inch cubes. Divide the cubes among 6 soup plates. Bring the stock to a boil in a 3-quart soup pot and ladle it over the custard cubes. Serve immediately.

ZUCCHINI SOUP, INDIAN STYLE

Serves 6

5 medium-size zucchini
1 large onion, diced
1 teaspoon ground cumin
½ teaspoon curry powder
½ cup grated fresh coconut
2 cups Chicken Stock (see Index)
½ cup milk
2 cups plain yogurt
grated fresh coconut

1. In a steamer set over boiling water, cover and steam 2 whole zucchini until tender (about 10 minutes). Set them aside to cool.

2. Dice the remaining 3 zucchini and place them in a 3-quart soup pot with the onion, cumin, and curry powder. Stir to coat evenly. Add the coconut and stock. Bring to a boil, lower heat, and simmer, uncovered, 20 minutes. Remove from heat and cool slightly.

3. Puree mixture in a blender. Add milk and fold in yogurt until it is well distributed. Chill soup thoroughly.

4. Dice the steamed zucchini and divide it among the soup bowls. Ladle the chilled soup over the zucchini and garnish each portion with grated coconut.

CHOICE-OF-VEGETABLE YOGURT SOUP

Serves 6

2 tablespoons butter
1 small onion, finely chopped
3 cups Chicken Stock (see Index)
2 cups chopped vegetables (such as broccoli, cauliflower, carrots, turnips, rutabaga, green beans)
1 tablespoon minced parsley
2 cups plain yogurt
2 egg yolks, lightly beaten
2 tablespoons chopped chives

1. Melt butter in a 3-quart soup pot. Add the onion and saute until transparent. Add the stock and vegetables and bring to a boil. Lower heat, cover, and simmer until tender (10 to 15 minutes). Remove from heat. Stir in parsley and allow to cool slightly.
2. Puree vegetable and stock mixture in two batches in a blender until smooth.
3. In a mixing bowl, whisk the yogurt and egg yolks together until thoroughly combined. Gradually stir in the pureed soup.
4. Return mixture to the pot and cook on medium heat just until mixture begins to simmer. Do not allow to boil. Stir the mixture occasionally. Simmer gently 2 minutes. Serve hot or chilled, sprinkled with chopped chives.

COLD MISO YOGURT SOUP

Serves 6

2 tablespoons miso paste, diluted with 2 tablespoons lukewarm water
2 tablespoons dark sesame oil or raw olive oil
¾ teaspoons grated lemon rind
3 tablespoons finely grated onions
3 tablespoons minced parsley
1 teaspoon minced dillweed
4 cups plain yogurt

Garnish
6 small radish roses
minced chives

Whisk together miso paste, oil, lemon rind, onions, parsley, and dillweed. Fold in yogurt. Chill for 30 minutes. Divide soup among 6 chilled bowls. Garnish each bowl with a radish rose and a sprinkling of chives.

Note: Dark sesame oil imparts a strong, nutty flavor; raw olive oil provides a distinctive olive taste. One is quite different from the other.

CURRIED TOMATO SOUP

Serves 6

2 cups plain yogurt
4 cups tomato juice
2 tablespoons lemon juice
1 tablespoon olive oil
2 tablespoons finely grated onions
2 teaspoons curry powder
2 tomatoes, diced
Garnish
2 tablespoons chopped chives
2 tablespoons minced parsley

1. In a large mixing bowl, whisk the yogurt until smooth. Gradually beat in the tomato juice, lemon juice, oil, onions, and curry powder. Taste for seasoning and add more curry powder, if desired.

2. Stir in the tomatoes. Cover with plastic wrap and chill until very cold.

3. Combine the chives and parsley. Ladle the soup into individual bowls and garnish each portion with the combined herbs.

WALNUT YOGURT SOUP

Serves 6

2 tablespoons butter
½ cup coarsely chopped walnuts
2 small cucumbers, coarsely chopped*
2 garlic cloves, minced
1 tablespoon lemon juice
1 cup degreased Beef Stock or Chicken Stock (see Index)
3 cups plain yogurt
mint leaves

*If the skin is bitter, peel the cucumbers.

1. Melt the butter in a small skillet. Add the nuts and saute on medium-low heat 2 minutes. Remove from heat and set aside.

2. Place the cucumbers, garlic, lemon juice, and ½ cup of the stock in the container of a blender. Process 10 seconds. Add the walnuts and remaining stock. Turn machine on and off 3 times. Transfer to a bowl and whisk in the yogurt until thoroughly blended. Cover and chill at least 2 hours.

3. Serve in chilled bowls and garnish with mint leaves.

YOGURT BARLEY SOUP

Serves 6

2 tablespoons butter
1 small onion, finely chopped
2 shallots, finely chopped
⅓ cup barley
3 cups Beef Stock (see Index)
3 cups plain yogurt
2 tablespoons finely chopped dillweed
3 medium-size mushrooms, finely chopped

1. Melt the butter in a 3-quart soup pot. Add the onion and shallots and saute until transparent (about 3 minutes). Add the barley and stock and bring to a boil. Lower heat, cover, and simmer until barley is tender (about 1 hour). Cool to room temperature, then chill until cold.

2. Whisk in the yogurt and dillweed until thoroughly blended.

3. Serve in chilled bowls and sprinkle each portion with chopped mushrooms.

HERB POT SOUP

Serves 6

3 cups Chicken Stock (see Index)
1 cup shelled peas (about 1 pound)
1 cup corn (about 2 ears)
2 tablespoons butter
1 tablespoon whole wheat flour
½ cup milk
2 shallots, finely minced
1 tablespoon minced chives
1 tablespoon finely chopped chervil
2 tablespoons finely chopped parsley
1 cup plain yogurt
2 egg yolks

1. Place the stock and peas in a 3-quart soup pot. Bring to a boil, lower heat, cover, and simmer until peas are almost tender (about 10 minutes). Add the corn and cook 5 minutes longer. Remove from heat.

2. Melt the butter in a small saucepan, add the flour, and stir until blended. Remove from heat. Stir in the milk. Return to heat and cook on low heat until thickened. Add about ½ cup stock to thin the sauce; then stir the sauce into the remaining stock. Add the shallots, chives, chervil, and parsley.

3. Beat the yogurt and egg yolks together until smooth. Stir into the stock mixture. Reheat just to the simmering point. Do not boil. Serve hot.

PART·TWO
Salads

The Cool, Spontaneous
Joy of Salads

It's hard to go wrong in making a salad. The few "rules" connected with producing this course are very flexible. A salad is one area of meal preparation that encourages experimentation, originality, even daring, regardless of experience. Sometimes the cook is inclined toward stark simplicity—robust spinach leaves moistened with slightly vinegared olive oil; at other times it's a massive salad of summer fruits studded with walnuts and draped with a dressing of homemade mayonnaise tinted pink with the juice of raspberries. Either way, the cook is assured of an enthusiastic reception. Most people like salads—any kind.

Clever cooks have been taking advantage of this near-universal appeal for generations. What an opportunity to use leftovers! What a way to stretch the meal to cover a couple of unexpected guests! What a chance to cut back on meat and other expensive ingredients in a meal!

A summertime salad is virtually free to anyone with room to grow a row of leaf lettuce. A cook with one or two leftover boiled potatoes has only to invest a bit of mayonnaise and herb seasonings to make an always-welcome potato salad. The glamorous chef's salad, which has become a ritualized combination that restaurants list on their menus, comes from the humblest origins: The thrifty chef sliced up bits of cold chicken or other roasted meat (whatever was left from yesterday's meal), tossed it with some cheese and plenty of greens, then moistened it with a simple dressing. A meal made from a meal! It always tastes delicious and is always more filling than you thought it would be. In the Middle East, salads are based on the rice that figures so prominently in the traditional meals of that culture. Cold, leftover rice is mixed with bits of meat and vegetables, herbs and spices, and tossed in oil and lemon juice to make a delectable, low-cost main dish.

No one can say exactly what must go into the standard salad dishes, for there are no hard and fast requirements. You can start out with the rice or potatoes or leftover meats and improvise. Whatever the combination you come up with, it can't be wrong. For the cook who craves guidance there are plenty of recipes, but few of them are ever exactly the same.

There are, however, some classic ways of doing things in the world of salad making. These are basic methods arrived at over generations of experience. Anyone who wants the best for his or her salad can profit from these tips.

The Salad Ingredients

1. The cool, crisp look of salad is a major factor in its appeal, so try to keep ingredients, bowls, and plates chilled up to the very moment the salad is served. (If you can't spare the refrigerator space, put the salad bowl in a larger bowl filled with ice.) Very fine restaurants even serve a chilled fork for eating the salad.
2. Wash all fruits and vegetables thoroughly before using. Avoid peeling them whenever possible, so you can retain the concentrated nutrients the skins often hold. If necessary, use a vegetable brush to get them clean. Wipe the fruits or vegetables with a paper towel. If they are not to be used immediately, put each type in its own plastic bag and refrigerate.
3. In preparing salad greens, use only the best looking and freshest; reserve the rest to be used in soup stock. Wash the greens under cold water, but don't soak them. Tear the greens into smaller pieces; never cut them with a knife, for the cut edges will wilt and discolor quickly. Drain by tossing them lightly in a clean kitchen towel, laying them on paper towels, or swinging them in a salad basket. The reason for this concern about drying the salad leaves thoroughly is that oil-based salad dressing coats the dry leaves evenly, but runs right off the wet ones.
4. If you don't plan to use the prepared greens immediately, store them in a plastic bag in the refrigerator. (Parsley and watercress do best in a covered jar in the refrigerator.) Place a paper towel in the bag with the greens to absorb any moisture left after draining.
5. If you plan to include cucumber slices or cut tomatoes in your salad, add them just before tossing, or their juice will not only wilt the greens, but also water down the dressing.
6. Unless you intend to toss them immediately with an acid fruit or a salad dressing, brush peeled apples, avocados, bananas, peaches, and pears with pineapple juice or citrus fruit juice to keep them from browning.
7. Don't assemble the salad until just before serving, for the weight of heavier fruits and vegetables tends to crush tender greens. Then toss it at the table whenever possible, so that the dressing is in contact with the greens for only a little time. Once contact is made, the greens begin to wilt. To minimize this problem, when the dressing and greens must wait in the bowl together, some people pour the dressing in the bottom of the bowl and cover it with two or three of the sturdiest leaves of the salad greens, thus keeping most of the greens and dressing apart until the appropriate time.

RIPE? MATURE? READY?

Most of us can tell when a peach or a plum or a strawberry is ripe just by looking at it or touching it. But not all fruits reveal themselves so easily. When the edible part of a fruit is hidden from view it's easy to make an unfortunate choice. We've all cut into a golden honeydew melon that turns out to be hard inside and barely as sweet as a cucumber; we've sliced into watermelons whose flesh was just pink and not the fiery red pulp that promises sweetness and flavor. And what about those avocados with the too-firm, all-green interiors!

Some people seem to be able to pick out the perfectly ripe fruit every time. It may be due partly to luck and guess work, but most of the credit goes to knowing how to check for ripeness. Anyone can learn the basics, and it's the kind of knowledge that can keep you from wasting money and being disappointed. Listed below are some of the most deceptive fruits and directions on how to see through them.

AVOCADOS

To test for ripeness, simply press the fruit gently between your palms; if it yields readily, it's ripe.

MELONS

Cantaloupes and watermelons achieve full flavor and sweetness when ripened on the vine. The clue: The "button" at the stem end is smooth and indented where it parted easily from the vine. Ripe cantaloupes also have a coarse netting over green-tinged, light yellow skin; the best watermelon colors are fresh green or gray with a yellow underside. Casabas can be light green dappled with gold or butter yellow. Ripe honeydews are creamy yellow and you can feel a "nap" on them. Only Persian melons stay green under the brown gray netting when ripe.

Whatever the melon, if it's ripe it will "give" to gentle pressure at the stem end, and (except for watermelon and casaba) it will have a fruity fragrance. Don't depend on the "thump test": a dull and muffled sound when a melon is slapped with the palm that is supposed to say "ripe and juicy." Dry, immature melons can produce precisely the same sound when slapped!

PEARS

Hard and juiceless pears turn succulent and sweet if you know what to wait for. Ripe Bartlett pears are deep red or golden yellow, depending on the variety. Comice and Anjou may be green when ripe, and Boscs are ready to eat when their jackets are cinnamon flecked with gold. All pears, when ripe, yield to a gentle thumb-and-finger pressure.

PINEAPPLES

Select a plump pineapple with a fresh, green crown and a body on the firm side. Sound is a reliable guide when testing a pineapple for ripeness. Snap the side with thumb and forefinger; if you hear a dull thud, buy that one—if not, look further. A sweet, fruity smell, with no hint of fermentation, is another good indication that the pineapple you are considering is ready. Eat it as soon as possible. If you must keep it, put the pineapple in a plastic bag and refrigerate it.

The Dressing

The classic salad dressing is simplicity itself: three parts oil, one part vinegar or lemon juice, seasonings to taste. Any salad will respond to that basic combination. However, there are innumerable variations, some of which have become classics in their own right—Vinaigrette, Russian, Italian, and French, to name a few. We offer recipes for these and many more in this book. Experiment with your own combinations. It's easy. See the accompanying box, "French Dressing—Plus."

Make the salad dressing early—aging improves it. The longer the ingredients are together, the better the flavor. If you have a favorite, make a batch that will last a few days. Just shake well before serving, and pour.

When making up your own dressing concoction, suit yourself, but start by going light on such assertive flavorings as oregano, curry powder, and cayenne, a little heavier on marjoram and red pepper; you can let yourself go on fresh basil, thyme, dill seed, and celery seed. Keep in mind that the flavors of dried herbs and spices are concentrated, so half as much goes just as far as fresh herbs and spices.

FRENCH DRESSING—PLUS

BASIC FRENCH DRESSING

Yields 1 cup

¾ cup oil
¼ cup lemon juice or cider vinegar
¼ teaspoon dry mustard
¼ teaspoon freshly ground pepper

Combine all ingredients in a screw-top jar, cover tightly, and shake to blend well. Store in refrigerator. Shake well before using.

Variations

Creamy French: Add ¼ cup sour cream to basic recipe and shake well.

Curried French: Add ¼ teaspoon curry to basic recipe and shake well.

Fruit French: Substitute orange or pineapple juice for the lemon juice or vinegar.

Garlic French: Add 1 garlic clove (halved) and allow at least 12 hours for flavor to be absorbed by dressing. Remove garlic and shake well.

Honey French: Use lemon juice, not vinegar, plus ¼ cup honey and ¼ teaspoon grated lemon peel.

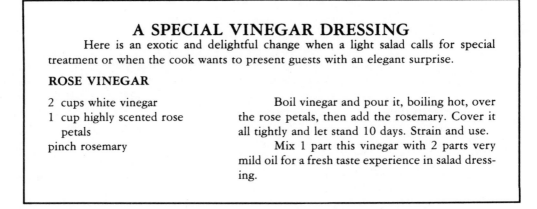

A SPECIAL VINEGAR DRESSING

Here is an exotic and delightful change when a light salad calls for special treatment or when the cook wants to present guests with an elegant surprise.

ROSE VINEGAR

2 cups white vinegar
1 cup highly scented rose
   petals
pinch rosemary

Boil vinegar and pour it, boiling hot, over the rose petals, then add the rosemary. Cover it all tightly and let stand 10 days. Strain and use.

Mix 1 part this vinegar with 2 parts very mild oil for a fresh taste experience in salad dressing.

The Salad Bowl

Some people hold their salad bowl sacred. They pamper it as they would a valued family heirloom. It's true—a well-seasoned salad bowl does bring an added dimension to a salad. So, if you have a choice, the best is an imported bowl made from olive wood, but walnut, mahogany, or maple bowls are also desirable.

The seasoning comes with use. You'll see a patina develop on the interior surface. Some of the flavor of the garlic, oil, vinegar, and spices simply stays with the bowl to permeate all of the salads made in it in the future. The garlic is literally rubbed into the wood by cutting a clove of garlic and running it over the inner surface of the bowl before starting the salad. After the salad is tossed and served, the oil and vinegar seep into the wood, too. Purists preserve this presence by refusing to wash the bowl; they just wipe it dry with paper towels. If this seems extreme to you, a light rinsing with lukewarm water will clean the bowl well enough, while leaving behind much of the good flavor and aroma. Never soak a wooden salad bowl, and don't use soap. Wipe the bowl dry as soon as it's rinsed, or it might warp or crack as it dries.

Remember, these salad bowl tips are for the specialists who insist on the best equipment. Most people do quite well with a ceramic salad bowl or a glass one. The seasoned bowl might make the difference between "excellent" and "superb" in the quality rating of a salad, but what's wrong with "excellent"?

Try to keep salad possibilities in mind as you shop for foods and do your regular kitchen chores. For example, in the summer when you do cook a hot meal, prepare for a day when you won't feel like standing over a hot stove by making extras for use in salads. Make double rice or beans, or enough chicken or fish to round out a main-course salad dish.

When thinning seedlings in your garden, think of baby greens as prime salad ingredients. Carrot ferns, young beet leaves, broccoli leaves, young cauliflower

GARLIC-INTENSITY CONTROL

Salad too garlicky or not garlicky enough? It's not only how much garlic you use, but how you use it that governs the bulb's effect on the finished product. To exercise more control, test each of these methods and vary them to suit the occasion.

The method familiar to most salad makers (for medium to strong taste) is to split a garlic clove and rub the exposed surface over the inside of the bowl before adding the greens or dressing.

Another approach, one that brings a subtler flavoring, is to rub a dry crust of bread or *chapon*, as it is called in France, on all sides with the cut portion of a split clove. Then combine the *chapon* in the bowl with the greens, add the dressing, and toss the ingredients. Remove the bread before serving the salad.

For a more intense garlic flavor, place 2 or 3 crushed cloves in the bottom of the salad bowl, add the dressing, and allow the flavors to meld about 10 minutes. Before tossing the dressing with the greens, remove the cloves.

leaves—all are precious salad gems. When the season doesn't allow for those, consider adding the tender green shoots of sprouts to the bowl. Nurturing rye, wheat, mung, or alfalfa sprouts throughout the year is simple, and they do add a touch of spring that can't be obtained in December in any other way.

Bakers who routinely add seeds to their breads and cakes are likely to forget what a nice touch sesame, caraway, or poppy seeds can add to a salad in terms of both flavor and crunch. The same is true of nuts; walnuts, almonds, and peanuts can't do anything but good for a salad!

TO HAVE YOUR SALAD WITH OPTIMUM NUTRITION. . .

1. Choose vine-ripened tomatoes; they have twice as much vitamin C as greenhouse tomatoes. When ripening green tomatoes in your kitchen, place them in a shaded place in the room to help them hold their nutrients. Left on a hot sill in the sun, they won't turn bright red; refrigerated, they get soft and watery while ripening and are apt to decay. Overripe tomatoes lose significant vitamin C.
2. Use bright orange, mature carrots, because they have several times more vitamin A than do the pale, young carrots.
3. For the best in calcium, iron, and vitamin A, include the well-formed, outer green leaves of lettuce heads. When there is a choice, opt for leaf lettuce over pale green iceberg lettuce for the higher vitamin A level it offers.
4. Keep all greens refrigerated in a crisper or a plastic bag. They hold nutrients best when stored at near-freezing temperatures with high humidity.
5. Red bell peppers (the ripe ones) have much more vitamin A than the green (unripe) ones.

SALAD OILS GUIDE

Name	Flavor	Suitability for Salads	Fatty Acids Saturated	Polyunsaturated	Offered for Sale in Supermarkets
Safflower Oil	Minimal	Unsuitable (unless blended with olive or aromatic nut oils)	Very low (has lowest ratio)	Very high	Yes
Corn Oil	Light	Suitable	Low	High	Yes
Sunflower Oil	Mild	Suitable (especially for raw vegetable salads)	Low	Very high	Yes
Olive Oil	Fruity, rich, delicate	Suitable	Low	High	Yes
Sesame Oil	Nutty	Suitable	Low	High	No
Peanut Oil	Mild	Suitable	Slightly higher than corn or olive	Slightly lower than corn oil	Yes
Soy Oil	Mild, to slight beany flavor	Suitable	Low	About the same as corn oil	Only a blend with other oils
Coconut Oil	Slightly soapy	Unsuitable	Very high	Low	No
Almond Oil	Mildly sweet, little distinctive nut flavor	Suitable	Low	High	No
Apricot Kernel Oil	Fresh green taste, no hint of apricot	Suitable	Low	High	No
Hazelnut Oil	Toasted nut	Suitable	Low	High	No
Walnut Oil	Nutty	Suitable	Low	High	No
Cottonseed Oil	Mild, unpleasant	Unsuitable	Slightly higher than peanut oil	High	Only as a blend with other oils
Grape Seed Oil	Distinctive, slight hint of olives	Suitable	Low	High	No
Avocado Oil	Light, slightly nutty, and sharp	Suitable	Low	High	No

Relative Cost	Can Be Interchanged with Other Oils	Comments
Average	Yes	Recommended for those who must watch cholesterol levels. Very high in essential nutrients. Texture unpleasant, greasy in salad dressings.
Average	Yes	Most popular, versatile oil.
Average	Yes	Suitable for salad dressings; less so for cooking.
Above average	Yes	Pleasant, but definite flavor. Popular for salad dressings.
Average	Yes	Brown sesame oil is highly flavored and best added to other oils for salad dressings. The lighter sesame oil can be used full strength.
Average	Yes	Huilor peanut oil, imported from France, is preferred for salads.
—	Yes	Best-tasting varieties are found in oriental shops.
—	No	Traditionally, coconut oil has been an industrial oil. Edible application is primarily "filled milk" products, such as coffee whiteners.
Above average	No	Use only for special effect.
Above average	No	High in vitamin E.
Extravagant	No	Use only for special effect.
Extravagant	No	Use only for special effect.
—	No	Heavily processed.
Extravagant	No	A blend of grape seed oil with olive oil, half and half, is desirable for salads.
Very extravagant	No	Like apricot kernel and almond, experts consider it primarily a novelty.

— Indicates information not available

THE SIGNS OF TOP-QUALITY SALAD VEGETABLES

Beets should be firm, round, and deep red, with a slender main root. If the beets aren't round, or if they have scaly areas on the surface, don't buy them—they'll be tough and strong tasting. Wilted or decayed greens offer another clue to undesirability.

Cabbage heads should be firm and heavy. Whether it's a red or a green cabbage, the leaves should have a healthy texture and characteristic color, free of spots or brown marks. If the leaves have worm holes, look out for more damage inside the head.

Carrots should be a rich orange, smooth and well formed. The green tops must look fresh and if the roots aren't firm and free of decay, don't buy.

Cauliflower is white and creamy at its best, and the head is firm and tightly packed. If you see discolorations or specks, they might mean insect damage, the growth of mold, or the start of decay.

Cucumbers have a good green color and a firm feel when they are in prime condition. Avoid the ones that are large in diameter, have a dull color, or show shriveled ends, for they're sure to be tough and bitter.

Lettuce is bright colored and crisp looking, or it's second-rate. Any sign of browning around the edges of the leaves or on the midribs means the lettuce has passed its prime. Iceberg heads which are very hard or near white are old, and if the heads are of an irregular shape, don't buy.

Mushrooms can be snow-white or, in the Western states, cream colored or brown, but the best of them are always firm and free of marks or cuts. The caps of button mushrooms are tightly closed when fresh, and the color of the group is uniform.

Onions tell a lot about their quality in their necks. Avoid those with wet or very soft necks, or necks that are very thick; necks should be small. The best onions are dry and free of fresh sprouts.

Peppers have a characteristic dark green color and firm walls when they're fresh and ready to eat. If the pepper is light for its size and has flimsy sides, avoid it. Don't buy peppers that are soft or have cuts, punctures, or decay spots on their surfaces.

Tomatoes are only fully ripe when they have that rich red (sometimes yellow) color. Tomatoes that are not quite there will mature at home nicely, provided they have a firm texture and a color ranging from pink to light red. Don't bother with tomatoes that are overripe or bruised or those with growth cracks.

When to serve a salad? At some tables, diners sit down to a crisp bowl of greens or an antipasto as a first course. Fancy restaurants serve the salad after the fish course to refresh the palate in preparation for the main event. Sometimes the salad is served and eaten with the main course; sometimes it is served separately following the main course. Every one of these services is perfectly acceptable. The chef decides.

Dieters often opt for eating a large salad first, hoping to fill up on low-calorie greens so they'll be less tempted to overindulge on the courses that follow. Mothers, anxious to get some nutrition-rich greens into the kids, serve a salad first to catch

FLOWERS IN YOUR SALAD

In the days when knighthood was in flower, so were the salads. Ever since medieval times Europeans and then Americans have added the petals of roses, violets, geraniums, nasturtiums, marigolds, or chrysanthemums to their salads. The blossoms add unexpected color and unusual flavor to the most ordinary of garden greens. If this idea is new to you and you want to try it, start with nasturtium petals—they are the most universally enjoyed.

Be sure that the flowers you pick for your salad are unsprayed. Gather them in the early morning, for they are said to be best just when the dew on them is evaporating. Then wrap them loosely in damp paper towels and refrigerate them until it's time to assemble the salad. Use them as you would any other ingredient intended to bolster the basic greens.

appetites at their peak. Salads can serve as an elegant and leisurely bridge between clearing after the main course and serving dessert. Of course, a salad can also be a meal in itself.

Any time is the right time to serve a salad.

To remove the effects produced by an excess of wine, etc., drink a wineglassful of olive oil. It will prevent hurtful fumes from rising. It will have the same effect if taken before the debauch.

Nineteenth-Century Medicine Manual

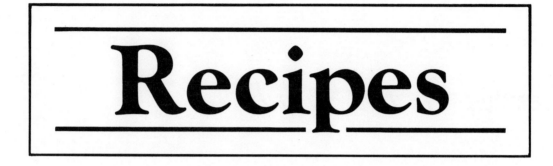

Recipes

Cooked-Grain Salads

Parsley. If there be nothing new under the sun, there are, at any rate, different uses found for the same thing, for this pretty aromatic herb was used in ancient times, as we learn from mythological narrative, to adorn the head of a hero, no less than Hercules: and now—was ever fall so great?—we moderns use it in connection with the head of—a calf. According to Homer's Iliad, warriors fed their chariot steeds on parsley, and Pliny acquaints us with the fact that, as a symbol of mourning, it was admitted to furnish the funeral tables of the Romans.

Mrs. Beeton, The Book of Household Management, *1861*

INDIAN RICE SALAD

Serves 6

2⅔ cups Chicken Stock (see Index)
1 cup brown rice
3 scallions, thinly sliced on the diagonal
½ cup sliced almonds
⅓ cup golden raisins
1 teaspoon curry powder
¼ cup Mayonnaise (see Index)
1 Golden Delicious apple, cut into ½-inch cubes

1. Bring the stock to a boil in a medium-size saucepan. Stir in the rice, cover tightly, lower the heat, and simmer gently until the stock is absorbed (45 to 50 minutes). Cool to room temperature and then chill in the refrigerator.

2. Stir the scallions, almonds, and raisins into the cold rice.

3. In a small cup, whisk the curry powder into the mayonnaise, then fold the mayonnaise mixture into the rice salad. Just before serving, mix in the apple.

Note: If desired, 1 to 1½ cups chopped cooked chicken may be stirred into this salad.

BULGUR PILAF SALAD

Serves 6

1½ cups bulgur
3 cups boiling water
3 scallions, sliced on the diagonal
1 garlic clove, minced
½ green pepper, slivered
¼ cup finely chopped parsley

Dressing

3 tablespoons olive oil
1 tablespoon lemon juice
⅛ teaspoon pepper
pinch dried thyme
pinch nutmeg

1. Place bulgur in a large mixing bowl. Pour the boiling water over the bulgur (do not rinse) and soak 1 hour or longer. Stir occasionally. Then chill mixture in the refrigerator.

2. Stir the scallions, garlic, green pepper, and parsley into the cold bulgur.

3. In a small cup, whisk together the dressing ingredients. Pour over the bulgur salad and toss to coat.

There is a saying that a clove of garlic planted beneath a rose bush upsets the plant so much that in utter defense it increases its scent.

GREEN PASTA SALAD

Serves 6

½ pound spinach spaghetti
½ cup Mayonnaise (see Index)
1 garlic clove, minced
2 tablespoons rice wine vinegar
1 teaspoon curry powder
5 asparagus spears
2 medium-size zucchini
¼ pound snow peas
¼ pound mushrooms, sliced ¼ inch thick
1 pint cherry tomatoes, halved
¼ cup minced parsley
¼ cup minced basil

1. Break the spaghetti strands into thirds. Cook the spaghetti in a large quantity of boiling water until tender (about 8 minutes). Drain and set aside.

2. Whisk together in a small bowl the mayonnaise, garlic, vinegar, and curry powder. Add this to the cooked spaghetti and gently mix.

3. Scrape the asparagus and cut each spear on the diagonal into 1-inch pieces. Steam these pieces in a small amount of boiling water 5 minutes. Drain and stir into the spaghetti.

4. Cut the zucchini in half lengthwise. Slice each half crosswise into ¼-inch pieces. Stir these into the spaghetti.

5. Cut the snow peas on the diagonal into ¾-inch slices. Stir these into the spaghetti.

6. Stir in the mushrooms and tomatoes.

7. Combine the parsley and basil. Shower the salad with the combined herbs but do not toss.

8. Salad can be served now or covered and refrigerated. If chilled, let it return nearly to room temperature for best flavor.

MILLET SALAD

Serves 6

¾ cup millet
1½ cups boiling Chicken Stock
(see Index)
2 small ribs fennel, thinly sliced
1 tablespoon minced fennel tops
1 tablespoon minced parsley
3 radishes, thinly sliced
Dressing
3 tablespoons walnut or sesame
oil
1 tablespoon rice wine vinegar

1. Simmer the millet, covered, in the boiling stock until the liquid is absorbed (15 to 20 minutes). Fluff millet with a fork and allow to cool.

2. In a large mixing bowl, combine the millet with the fennel, fennel tops, parsley, and radishes.

3. Beat the oil and vinegar together in a cup. Pour the mixture over the salad and toss lightly. Cover and chill until serving time.

Rice Around the World

There are more than 7,000 known varieties of rice around the world. Most brown rice is straw colored, but there are also some that are red, brown, purple, black, and variegated.

MOLDED BROWN RICE AND VEGETABLE SALAD

Serves 6

2 teaspoons unflavored gelatin
¾ cup cold degreased Chicken
Stock (see Index)
½ cup Mayonnaise (see Index)
3 cups cooked brown rice
⅔ cup diced green peppers
½ cup minced celery
½ cup coarsely chopped radishes
2 tablespoons chopped parsley
1 tablespoon chopped basil
1 teaspoon chopped tarragon

1. In a small saucepan, sprinkle the gelatin over the stock and let stand 5 minutes to soften. Place the pan over low heat until the gelatin is dissolved. Cool to room temperature. Stir in the mayonnaise.

2. In a large mixing bowl, combine the remaining ingredients. Stir in the gelatin mixture.

3. Lightly oil a 6-cup gelatin mold and turn the rice mixture into it. Cover and chill until set (about 6 hours).

4. Unmold the salad by running a thin, wet knife around the edge to loosen it. Place a serving plate over the top of the mold and invert the mold and plate together. Give a gentle sideways shake to loosen the mold, then remove it.

The Latin name for rice is oryza, *from which many words for it have developed:* rijst, *in Dutch;* riz, *in French;* reis, *in German;* ris, *in Swedish and Danish;* riso, *in Italian; and* arroz, *in Spanish.*

Get More Nutrients into Meatless Salads

Boost the nutritional value of a no-meat salad by including as many parts as possible—roots, leaves, and fruit—from a variety of plants. Put beets, celery, parsnips, or other root vegetables in with leafy greens, and try to add one or more of the fruit vegetables, such as cucumbers, peppers, peas, beans, and tomatoes. Sprouts and toasted wheat germ can add even more food value, plus a welcome flavor and texture.

RED CABBAGE AND RYE SALAD

Serves 6

2½ cups Beef Stock, Veal Stock,
   or Chicken Stock (see Index)
 1 cup whole rye grain
 2 tablespoons caraway seeds
 1 tablespoon oil
⅔ cup sesame oil
¼ cup cider vinegar
¼ teaspoon dry mustard
 1 teaspoon grated onions
 2 tart apples, diced
 1 small head red cabbage,
   shredded
¼ cup minced basil
 2 tablespoons chopped parsley

1. Bring stock to a boil in a 2-quart soup pot. Add the rye, caraway seeds, and oil. Lower heat, cover, and simmer very gently until all the liquid is absorbed (about 25 minutes). Toss to separate grains, then cool.

2. In a large bowl, mix sesame oil, vinegar, mustard, and onions. Stir in the apples, cabbage, basil, and parsley.

3. Add caraway-rye mixture to the cabbage mixture. Toss to mix. Cover and chill until serving time.

SAFFRON BROWN RICE SALAD

Serves 6

 2 tablespoons sesame oil
½ onion, coarsely chopped
 1 cup brown rice
¼ teaspoon crushed saffron threads
⅛ teaspoon ground cumin
 3 cups Chicken Stock (see Index)
½ green pepper, finely chopped
 2 tablespoons chopped parsley
 1 garlic clove, minced
 1 cucumber, scored and diced
Vinaigrette Dressing (see Index)
Garnish
 2 tomatoes, cut into wedges
 1 bunch watercress

1. Heat the oil in a saucepan, add the onion, and saute until transparent. Add the rice, saffron, cumin, and stock and bring to a boil. Lower heat, cover, and simmer until the liquid is absorbed and the rice is tender (about 45 minutes). Allow to cool.

2. Add the pepper, parsley, garlic, and cucumber to the cooled rice. Toss with dressing and chill until serving time.

3. Garnish salad with tomato wedges and watercress.

WILD RICE SALAD

Serves 6

- ¾ cup wild rice
- 3 cups boiling water
- ½ pound snow peas
- ¼ pound mushrooms, thinly sliced
- 1 scallion, sliced on the diagonal
- 2 tablespoons finely chopped parsley

Dressing

- 2 tablespoons walnut or sesame oil
- 2 tablespoons rice wine vinegar
- ⅛ teaspoon pepper
- pinch nutmeg
- ½ teaspoon tamari soy sauce

1. Stir the rice into a pan filled with the boiling water. Lower heat, cover, and simmer gently 1 hour. Spread the rice in a strainer to cool and dry.

2. Blanch snow peas in boiling water for 30 seconds. Drain and cool.

3. In a large mixing bowl, combine the rice, snow peas, mushrooms, scallion, and parsley. Cover and chill.

4. Combine the dressing ingredients in a small screw-top jar. Cover and shake to mix. Toss dressing with rice salad before serving.

BUCKWHEAT SALAD

Serves 6 to 8

- 1 cup buckwheat groats
- 1 egg, lightly beaten
- 2 cups boiling degreased Chicken Stock (see Index)
- ½ cup minced parsley
- ½ cup minced dillweed
- ⅓ cup finely chopped green peppers
- ⅓ cup finely chopped scallions

Dressing

- 2 tablespoons rice wine vinegar
- 2 teaspoons French-Style Mustard (see Index)
- 1 garlic clove, minced
- 1 tablespoon lemon juice
- 6 tablespoons sesame oil

- 2 tomatoes, cut into wedges

1. In a saucepan, combine the groats with the egg and cook on moderate heat. Stir until the grains separate. Add the stock, lower the heat, cover, and simmer until tender (about 20 minutes). Stir with a fork to separate the grains. Cool. Stir in the parsley, dillweed, green peppers, and scallions.

2. In a bowl, beat the vinegar, mustard, garlic, and lemon juice with a wire whisk. Add the oil in a stream and whisk until combined. Stir dressing into the groat salad. Chill before serving.

3. Garnish with tomato wedges.

Famous for Good Food

Beautiful soup, so rich and green,
Waiting in a hot tureen!
Who for such dainties would not stoop
Soup of the evening, beautiful soup.
        LEWIS CARROLL, *ALICE'S ADVENTURES IN WONDERLAND*

Cindy Dinsmore is a performer who plays to four audiences. One audience fills the chairs of the restaurant where she holds a part-time job. Two others come as entertainers and as spectators to a coffeehouse-club where she lives and works. The last is a single-person audience, Dave Fry, her partner at the Godfrey Daniels Coffeehouse in Bethlehem, Pennsylvania.

Recently Cindy received a Bachelor of Arts degree—four years overdue according to conventional standards. Her talent has kept her too busy to cram a full schedule of courses into her life, let alone think about what to do with a degree in social relations and fine arts. Cindy's widespread fame comes from her cooking abilities. She is the reigning queen of highly innovative, nutritious soups, salads, and desserts for more people than one can fairly estimate.

One morning while Cindy put the finishing touches on a weekly coffeehouse cleaning, we came to talk to her. She is a strong, energetic woman who speaks enthusiastically about her pursuits, as you can see from the following interview:

Cindy Dinsmore: Let me paint a typical week right before I graduated. I spent nine hours in the classroom, cooked two nights at a restaurant, and put in four to five days on Godfrey Daniels duties—cleaning, shopping, cooking, and running and closing up the coffeehouse.

Rodale Press: You devote a major portion of your energies to this spot. How did it all come about?

CD: Five years ago the only place in this area to hear folk music was in bars. People under 21 couldn't go there, and others who desired a more conducive environment just wouldn't go. So we rented a jelly-covered doughnut shop, scraped the sticky stuff

"Artists and audiences continually tell us that coming here is like stopping in at home."

off the floors, decorated, and opened up several months later. Now our small club is nationally—even internationally—known. I think that's due to the atmosphere of the place. Something that has developed as an extension of Dave and me has made this place unique to performers and spectators.

RP: Can you define the appeal of the atmosphere you create?

CD: We book a particular style of performer/performance and provide comfortable surroundings—two major elements. Artists and audiences continually tell us that coming here is like stopping in at home. The food at Godfreys is at least the other 50 percent of its success. You know how good food can heighten relationships.

RP: Did you set out to make Godfreys a good place to eat?

CD: No, it just happened. Soon after we opened, we started to offer performers the option of sleeping upstairs in our apartment after a show. They were so appreciative of that feature, plus the bowl of warm soup I occasionally served to them, that I began to enjoy preparing a specific meal for their arrival. It became policy. Soon after that, I started carrying the extras downstairs to share with the audience. They loved it! Now I regularly prepare for both.

RP: How do you manage to cook in such quantity and with such variety when you are already so busy?

CD: I have a system. I sit down and figure out what I want to do. I think about the steps necessary to get to that point. By the time I get to cooking, I'm completely ready for it. I order most of my food from the cooperative store two blocks down the street and carry it home when it arrives. I buy whole wheat flour, herbal teas, honey, grains, beans, and cheese in quantity. I pick up produce on the day that I'll be using it. I like being this close to my basic materials.

RP: You must cut some corners to save time.

CD: Yes. The freezer is a big help. Some foods actually improve in flavor when you freeze them. Bean and pea soups are the classic examples; their flavors meld. One afternoon a week, I'll cook four-gallon quantities of chili, stew, or bean soup. Then I'll freeze it in portions suitable for various needs—a meal for 8 musicians, soup for 50 club patrons, or dinner for Dave and me. I never freeze vegetable soups because

Cindy Dinsmore loads the blender as she gets started on one of her original soups.

mine are not the conventional kind. They are lightly steamed vegetables in an herb-flavored nonmeat stock. My aim is to produce a delicate dish that does not lose that last-minute quality.

Soups and Salads

RP: Besides homemade desserts, soups and salads are the other foods that really move here. Have you figured out why?

CD: They're both convenient to eat. People who congregate around the counter aren't just eating; they're socializing—discussing the music, complimenting the performer. Five courses just wouldn't work here. In addition, many performers prefer to eat lightly before a show. A nutritious bowl of soup and a salad suit most of them just fine.

It turns out that most of our clientele and the artists are vegetarians. I prefer cooking nonmeat dishes, so there's really no conflict. People who eat meat seem perfectly satisfied with what we serve. I make a spicy Three-Bean Chili with tofu which I serve with rice. It's a high-protein meal and, according to rumor, rather tasty. U. Utah Phillips, the "Golden Voice of the Great Southwest," likes to make jokes in his act about the vegetarian food here. But between sets he gobbles down bowls of the chili.

RP: Which soups are the favorites?

CD: You've got to remember that I offer *my* favorites, and the patrons can choose from them. My favorite soup in the whole world is plain, old, satisfying split pea soup.

"Audience appreciation is the stuff that really fuels me. On occasion, some first-time Godfrey performers have walked in the door and said, 'Okay, where's that wonderful food I've been hearing about?'"

That's a really popular one in the club. Another that pleases everyone is Creamy Spinach Soup—a warmed puree including yogurt, tofu, and herbs. It has a beautiful light-green color, and it is nourishing, delicious, and inexpensive to make. What more can anyone ask of a food? I'm ready to eat it twice a day for as long as it lasts.

RP: If you don't use meat, what serves as the base for these hearty soups?

CD: Good, rich, vegetable stock and bean and grain waters. I save all the clean, organic parings and vegetable scraps from my food preparation, and I pop them into a large plastic bag in the freezer until I have enough to cook in water. Occasionally I add a particular vegetable, like red beets or garlic, for a certain color or a definite taste. I freeze any surplus stock in small batches.

RP: Are cold soups popular?

CD: In the winter, no. In the warmer months, customers start requesting fruit soup, tangy gazpacho, or Cascadilla, a nice cucumber-tomato-yogurt blend.

RP: You don't offer many green salads on the daily menu.

CD: I prefer to serve bean and grain salads in the club because they have a good "keeping quality." Then I don't have to worry if they don't sell in the first hour. Our Bean and Rice Salad is especially popular in the summer when people are looking for a cold meal that combines taste with adequate nutritional value. I do make elaborate green salads that include avocados, cheese, and nuts for ourselves and the performers.

RP: What is the one thing above all else that keeps you going?

CD: Audience appreciation is the stuff that really fuels me. On occasion, some first-time Godfrey performers walk in the door and say, "Okay, where's that wonderful food I've been hearing about?" Some groups actually schedule an extra day here so they can share a dinner with us.

One of my nicest experiences concerns my stove. Eight months after we got started, I was still cooking and baking on an apartment-size, four-burner stove. The oven only had one temperature, a constant 450°F. For the club's first anniversary, regulars surprised me with an efficient, double-oven gas range.

Look, Godfrey Daniels is famous in this circuit for good food and that makes me feel good!

BEAN AND RICE SALAD

Serves 6 to 8

1 *cup cooked, chilled kidney beans*
1 *cup cooked, chilled chick-peas*
½ *cup cooked, chilled brown rice*
½ *cup pignolias (pine nuts)*
½ *small head cabbage, finely chopped*
1 *large carrot, finely chopped*
½ *cup radishes, finely chopped*
3 *scallions, thinly sliced*
1 *medium-size green pepper, finely chopped*
1 *bunch parsley, minced*
½ *cucumber, finely chopped and drained*
1 *celery stalk, finely chopped*
1 *teaspoon dried basil*
½ *teaspoon pepper*
dash cayenne pepper
2 *tablespoons tamari soy sauce*
2 *tablespoons vinegar*
2 *tablespoons safflower oil*
tomato wedges

1. Toss the beans, peas, rice, and pignolias together with the cut vegetables.
2. Blend the spices with the tamari, vinegar, and oil. Pour over bean-rice mixture. Mix thoroughly. Adjust seasonings to taste. Chill. Garnish with tomato wedges.

CASCADILLA

Serves 4 to 6

2 *scallions, finely chopped*
1 *large cucumber, finely chopped*
1 *medium-size carrot, finely chopped*
1 *medium-size green pepper, finely chopped*
1 *small onion, finely chopped*
1 *stalk celery, finely chopped*
4 *radishes, finely chopped*
1 *garlic clove, minced*
4 *cups thick tomato juice*
2 *teaspoons honey*
1 *cup plain yogurt*
salt and pepper to taste
1 *teaspoon minced dillweed*
½ *cup minced parsley*
Garnish
1 *cup sour cream or plain yogurt*
4 to 6 *sprigs mint*

1. Put half of the chopped vegetables in the blender with the tomato juice. Puree. Pour into a large serving bowl.
2. Stir in the yogurt, seasonings, and remaining vegetables. Chill about 1 hour before serving. Garnish each serving with a dollop of either sour cream or yogurt and a sprig of mint.

THREE-BEAN CHILI
Serves 6 to 8

1 *cup dried kidney beans, rinsed*
   and soaked overnight in water to
   cover
¾ *cup dried soy beans, rinsed and*
   soaked overnight in water to cover
¾ *cup dried pinto beans, rinsed and*
   soaked overnight in water to cover
2 *medium-size potatoes, quartered*
1 *medium-size yam, quartered*
½ *pound tofu, cut into ½-inch cubes*
½ *cup safflower oil*
1 *garlic bulb, cloves separated and*
   minced
1 *medium-size onion, coarsely*
   chopped
1 *celery stalk, coarsely chopped*
1 *carrot, coarsely chopped*
1 *green pepper, coarsely chopped*
¼ *pound mushrooms, coarsely*
   chopped
4 *teaspoons chili powder*
3 *teaspoons ground cumin*
1½ *teaspoons dried basil*
1 *bay leaf*
¼ *teaspoon ground cayenne pepper or*
   to taste
6 *ounces tomato paste*
3 *pounds tomatoes, steamed for 1*
   minute, skinned, and coarsely
   chopped
¼ *cup tamari soy sauce*
1 *tablespoon molasses*

1. Drain the beans and put each variety in a separate 3-quart soup pot. Add water to each pot to cover the beans (at least 3 cups) and cook until tender (kidney beans for about 1½ hours, soybeans about 3 hours, and pinto beans about 2½ hours).

2. Steam the potatoes and yam in a small amount of water until a fork can pierce them with some resistance. Drain the liquid into the bean pot. Put these vegetables aside.

3. Saute tofu in medium-hot oil until the pieces are crunchy on all sides. Drain on paper towels and set aside.

4. Saute the vegetables in a heavy-bottom 5-quart soup pot. Begin with the garlic and onions; add the celery, carrot, and green pepper. Saute and stir frequently until tender. Add the mushrooms and the reserved potato and yam. Next, add all the spices and cook a few more minutes. Add the tomato paste, tomatoes, tamari, and molasses. Fold in the sauteed tofu. Add the beans and simmer on very low heat, uncovered, at least 30 minutes, to allow flavors to blend.

PAPAYA-VEGETABLE SALAD   For this recipe, see page 250

CHUNKY CALICO CHICKEN SOUP   For this recipe, see page 55

CREAMY SPINACH SOUP
WITH TOFU

Serves 4

leaves from 1 pound spinach
¼ to ½ cup vegetable stock or water
1 bunch parsley, finely chopped
2 carrots, quartered horizontally
1 large potato, cut into chunks
1 medium-size onion, quartered
2 garlic cloves, coarsely chopped
½ pound tofu, cut into large chunks
1 cup plain yogurt
1 teaspoon pepper
dash cayenne pepper
1 teaspoon basil
½ to 1 teaspoon vegetable salt
⅓ cup whole wheat pastry flour
⅓ cup butter
pinch dried thyme
few gratings fresh nutmeg
1 cup scalded milk

1. Wash the spinach well. In a small amount of the stock, steam it until tender. (Save the steaming liquid.)
2. Chop the parsley and puree it in the blender with the spinach and steaming water. Pour puree into a large mixing bowl.
3. In a 3-quart soup pot, barely cover the carrots, potato, onion, and garlic with the remaining stock and steam until tender. Puree vegetables in several batches in the blender, adding a chunk of tofu to each batch. Stir the pureed vegetables and tofu into the spinach mixture. Stir in the yogurt.
3. Make a roux by melting the butter in a heavy skillet. Quickly whisk in the flour. Add the spices and cook 2 more minutes. Slowly add the milk. Stir constantly throughout the procedure. Simmer mixture about 5 minutes.
4. Combine the two mixtures in a 3-quart soup pot and heat through. Do not boil.

Fish Salads

BLUEFISH AND GREEN BEAN SALAD

Serves 6

1 pound green beans, tips removed
¾ cup Garlic Vinaigrette (see Index)
1 pound small new potatoes
2 pounds bluefish fillets
1 pint cherry tomatoes
¼ cup minced chives
3 tablespoons minced parsley
2 scallions, thinly sliced on the diagonal
3 hard-cooked eggs

1. Steam the green beans in a small amount of boiling water until tender (about 5 minutes). Drain and immediately toss them with 2 tablespoons of the dressing.

2. Boil the potatoes in water to cover until tender (about 25 minutes). Drain and cool.

3. Poach the fish in ½ inch boiling water in a covered skillet until it flakes easily when tested with a fork (10 to 15 minutes). Uncover and allow it to cool.

4. Assemble salad at least 2 hours before serving. Slice or quarter the potatoes and place them in a large bowl. Add the green beans and ¼ cup more of the dressing. Toss to coat. Flake the fish and gently toss it with the potatoes and beans. Stir in the cherry tomatoes. Sprinkle the salad with the herbs and scallions. Cover with plastic wrap and chill until serving.

5. Quarter the eggs and use them to garnish the salad. Serve remaining dressing on the side.

Chives provide a milder and more delicate flavor than most other varieties of onion. They are easy to grow from seed or by division of clumps. The more they are cut, the better they flourish. During the flowering period, masses of mauve or purple flower heads appear, a beautiful decoration for the herb garden.

SEAFOOD SLAW

Serves 6

1 cup tuna, drained and flaked
1 tablespoon minced parsley
1 tablespoon finely chopped onions
½ cup Mayonnaise (see Index)
2 tablespoons lemon juice
½ cup finely chopped celery
3 cups shredded cabbage
2 cups shredded carrots

1. In a mixing bowl, combine the tuna, parsley, onions, mayonnaise, and lemon juice by beating together with a fork.

2. In a salad bowl, combine the celery, cabbage, and carrots. Add the tuna mixture. Toss to coat. Cover and chill until serving time.

Excellent instructions for cleaning squid are available free if you send a self-addressed, stamped, business-size envelope to: Cooperative Extension Service, Virginia Polytechnic Institute and State University, Blacksburg, VA 24061. Request Food Science and Technology Notes: Squid—An Underutilized Species, *by Sharon R. Turner and Chieko E. Hebard.*

SQUID SALAD

Serves 6

3 pounds squid, cleaned
3 celery stalks, cut into ¼-inch slices
2 sweet red peppers, cut into julienne strips
2 medium-size carrots, shredded
Dressing
juice of 1 lemon
3 tablespoons rice wine vinegar
1 garlic clove, minced
2-inch piece ginger, grated
1 tablespoon tamari soy sauce
½ cup sesame oil

3 tablespoons minced chives

1. Cut squid body into ½-inch rings. Chop legs into ½-inch lengths. Drop into boiling water in a 3-quart soup pot, cover, and cook until white and tender (about 5 minutes). Do not overcook. Drain well and let cool.

2. In a large bowl, toss together the celery, peppers, and carrots.

3. In a cup, whisk together the lemon juice, vinegar, garlic, ginger, and tamari. Beat in the oil.

4. Toss the cooled squid in half the dressing. Pour the remaining dressing over the vegetables and toss. Arrange the squid on top of the vegetable bed. Sprinkle with chives. Serve at room temperature or chilled.

Note: Well-stocked fish markets usually carry fresh squid in season and stock frozen, cleaned squid year-round in their freezer cases. Upon request, most merchants are willing to clean the fresh kind for you.

TOFU TUNA SALAD

Serves 6

2 eggs
1 tablespoon French-Style
   Mustard (see Index)
1 tablespoon cider vinegar
3 tablespoons lemon juice
¼ teaspoon curry powder
1½ cups olive oil
4 ounces tuna
½ cup plain yogurt
1 pound tofu, diced
3 celery stalks, thinly sliced
1 sweet red pepper, diced
18 cherry tomatoes, halved
1 medium-size zucchini, diced
12 romaine lettuce leaves
½ cup alfalfa sprouts
2 tablespoons minced chives

1. Place the eggs, mustard, vinegar, lemon juice, curry powder, and ¼ cup of the oil in the container of a blender. Cover and process at blend. Immediately remove feeder cap and add the remaining oil in a steady stream. Stop machine if necessary and push the mixture down with a rubber spatula. Flake the tuna and add half to the thickened mixture. Process until smooth. Transfer mixture to a small bowl. Stir in remaining tuna and yogurt until mixed. Cover and chill until serving.

2. In a large mixing bowl, combine the tofu, celery, pepper, tomatoes, and zucchini. Gently toss with a fork.

3. Arrange lettuce on a serving plate. Pile tofu mixture in the center of the leaves. Top with the tuna sauce and sprinkle with the alfalfa sprouts and chives.

FISH-ON-THE-HALF-SHELL SALAD

Serves 6

3 medium-size avocados, halved
   and pitted
4 tablespoons lemon juice
½ cup Mayonnaise (see Index)
¼ teaspoon white pepper
3 tablespoons minced chives
2 tablespoons minced parsley
2 scallions, minced
1 cucumber, peeled
1½ pounds weakfish or flounder
   fillets, cooked, cooled, and
   flaked
½ cup alfalfa sprouts
Garnish
6 chicory leaves
6 thick slices tomato
6 lemon wedges

1. Enlarge the avocado hollows by removing a spoonful of the pulp from each half. Place the spoonfuls of pulp in a small mixing bowl and mash them with 1 tablespoon of the lemon juice. Sprinkle the avocado halves with the remaining lemon juice and set them aside. Add the mayonnaise, pepper, chives, parsley, and scallions to the mashed avocado and beat with a fork until thoroughly blended.

2. Cut the cucumber in half lengthwise. Use a spoon to scrape out the seeds. Chop the cucumber flesh into ¼-inch cubes. Stir the cucumber and fish into the mayonnaise mixture. Mound the salad in the avocado shells. Sprinkle with alfalfa sprouts.

3. Prepare each plate with an avocado half, a chicory leaf, a tomato slice, and a lemon wedge.

CURRIED COD AND POTATO SALAD

Serves 6

1½ pounds small new potatoes, cooked, cooled, and cut into ½-inch slices
1 cup shelled peas (about 1 pound), cooked and cooled
1½ pounds cod fillets, cooked, cooled, and flaked
6 scallions, thinly sliced on the diagonal
¾ cup Curried Vinaigrette (see Index)
1 small head escarole
3 tablespoons minced parsley

1. Put potatoes, peas, and fish in a large mixing bowl. Add the scallions and pour about ⅓ cup of the dressing over all. Gently toss until all ingredients are coated. Add more dressing, if desired. Cover with plastic wrap and chill.

2. Line a salad bowl with escarole leaves. Spoon the salad onto the leaves and sprinkle with parsley.

CUCUMBER AND DILLED FISH SALAD

Serves 6

2 cucumbers
¾ cup plain yogurt
1 tablespoon grated onions
2 tablespoons lemon juice
¼ teaspoon white pepper
¼ cup minced fresh dillweed or 1 tablespoon dried
2 pounds scrod fillets, cooked, cooled, and flaked
6 lettuce leaves
6 tomato slices

Garnish
1 large carrot, grated
6 lemon wedges

1. Score the cucumbers with the tines of a fork and discard the ends. Split them in half lengthwise, then cut them crosswise into ½-inch slices.

2. In a medium-size mixing bowl, whisk together the yogurt, onions, lemon juice, pepper, and dillweed. Add the sliced cucumbers. Toss to coat. Gently toss fish with the cucumber-yogurt mixture.

3. Arrange a leaf of lettuce, a tomato slice, and a mound of the fish salad on each plate. Sprinkle each portion of salad with grated carrot. Garnish with a lemon wedge.

Fruits and Greens Combination Salads

Independently of its exquisite flavor, the melon passed, among the Greeks and Romans, as being very beneficial to the stomach and head. It is possible that they may have gone a little too far; but then man is so ready to give imaginary qualities to what he loves, that we cannot wonder at their praises of this delicious plant, which we generally eat in the most simple manner.

Alexis Soyer, The Pantropheon, *1853*

AVOCADO, CHICORY, AND HONEYDEW SALAD

Serves 6

flesh of 1 avocado, cut into ½-inch cubes
1 tablespoon lemon juice
3 scallions, thinly sliced on the diagonal
1 head chicory or curly endive, leaves torn into bite-size pieces
1 small head Boston or Bibb lettuce, leaves torn into bite-size pieces
flesh of ½ honeydew melon, cut into ½-inch cubes
Curried Lime Dressing (see Index)

1. Toss avocado pieces in the lemon juice to prevent browning.

2. Toss scallions with the chicory and lettuce.

3. Combine the melon and avocado pieces and mix with the prepared greens. Toss with the dressing at the table.

184

FRUIT: THE PERMISSIBLE PLEASURE

Fruit, like flattery and sex, is one of the few things in life that, in addition to being pleasurable, is good for us. It's time we restored it to its former irresistible glory.

Fruit satisfies our sweet tooth naturally. It gives us sugar—but in a way and at a pace that our bodies have been designed to handle. (Refined sugar comes at us in too concentrated a form, the result of which can be feelings of weakness and actual hunger as the pancreas panics and produces more sugar-taming insulin than it should.) Fruit, because it has to be chewed and digested, and because it supplies its own natural sugar buffers in the form of fiber, provides the kind of gradual and usable energy boost that the twentieth-century candy bar cannot. (You can prove that for yourself simply by having a large piece of fruit the next time you might ordinarily have candy or a piece of pastry to ward off between-meal hunger. You'll find you'll get a lot more mileage from the fruit.)

	Calories	Total Carbohydrates (grams)	Grams of Dietary Fiber (per 100 grams)	Vitamin A % RDA	Vitamin C % RDA	Potassium (milligrams)
Apple	80	20	2.0	2.4	10	152
Apricots (3)	55	14	2.1	57.8	18	301
Avocado	370	13	2.0	12.6	50	1,303
Banana	100	26	3.4	4.6	20	440
Cantaloupe (½)	80	20	1.0	185.0	150	682
Cherries (1 cup)	105	26	1.7	33.2	20	317
Grapefruit (½)	50	13	0.6	10.8	73	116
Grapes (10)	35	9	0.4	1.0	3	87
Honeydew melon (½)	50	11	0.9	1.2	57	374
Orange	65	16	2.0	5.2	110	263
Peach	40	10	1.4	22.6	12	202
Pear	100	25	2.3	0.6	12	213
Pineapple (1 cup)	80	21	1.2	2.2	43	226
Plum	30	8	2.1	3.2	7	112
Raisins (1 cup)	420	112	6.8	0.6	2	1,106
Strawberries (1 cup)	55	13	2.2	1.8	147	244
Watermelon (1 slice)	110	27	N.A.	50.2	50	426
Doughnut	205	22	trace	0.5	0	34
Chocolate bar (1 ounce)	145	16	trace	1.6	trace	109
Ice cream (1 cup)	270	32	0	10.8	1	257
Boston cream pie (1 slice)	210	34	trace	2.8	trace	61

CITRUS ENDIVE SALAD

Serves 6

6 small Belgian endives
3 large navel oranges,
  segmented, seeds and
  membranes removed
2 small grapefruits, segmented,
  seeds and membranes removed
1 red onion

Dressing
1½ cups plain yogurt
1 teaspoon lemon juice
1 teaspoon honey

½ cup coarsely chopped walnuts

1. Halve the endives lengthwise. Then cut them lengthwise again into thin strips. Arrange the sliced endive in bunches at the ends of a serving platter.

2. Peel the onion and halve it lengthwise. Cut each section into ¼-inch slices.

3. In the center of the platter, arrange alternating layers of orange and grapefruit segments with the sliced onion.

4. Whisk the yogurt, lemon juice, and honey together until mixed. Drizzle the dressing over the fruits. Sprinkle the walnuts over the top. Serve immediately.

CRESS, MANGO, AND ROMAINE SALAD

Serves 6

1 head romaine lettuce, leaves torn
  into bite-size pieces
leaves from 1 bunch watercress
flesh of 3 mangoes, cut into ½-inch
  cubes
Ginger Cheese Dressing (see Index)
Garnish
4 scallions, finely sliced
seeds from 1 pomegranate

1. Toss together the lettuce and watercress. Place in a salad bowl or arrange on a platter. Cover with plastic wrap and refrigerate until serving time.

2. Place the mango pieces on top of the lettuce. Drizzle with the dressing and sprinkle the scallions and pomegranate seeds over the top. Serve immediately.

EGYPTIAN GRAPE SALAD

Serves 6

12 ounces feta cheese, drained if
  necessary
½ cup finely chopped sweet onion*
¼ cup lemon juice
¼ cup olive oil
freshly ground pepper
2 pounds seedless green grapes
1 head escarole, leaves separated
sprigs of mint

*Red Italian, Bermuda, and Spanish on-
ions are sweet varieties.

1. Crush the cheese with a fork and mix thoroughly with the onion, lemon juice, and oil. Season with pepper.

2. Combine the grapes with the cheese mixture by lightly tossing the two together.

3. Arrange escarole leaves on a platter. Top with grape-cheese mixture. Garnish with mint.

In the test tube, grapes show a surprising ability to inactivate viruses. Apparently, chemicals concentrated in the grape skin bind to viral proteins, rendering the viruses harmless.

FRUIT AND SPROUT SALAD

Serves 6

2 cups mung bean sprouts
1 small cucumber, scored and cut into ¾-inch cubes
3 freestone nectarines, diced
1 cup seedless green grapes, halved
1 scallion, thinly sliced
Vinaigrette Dressing (see Index)

1. To remove raw flavor from sprouts, place in a colander and pour boiling water over them. Drain, rinse with cold water, and drain again.

2. In a salad bowl, gently mix the sprouts with the cucumber, nectarines, grapes, and scallion.

3. Toss with the dressing at the table.

Orange or Grapefruit in Your Salad?

If either will do, consider these nutritional facts when deciding whether to use oranges or grapefruits in a salad. Oranges sometimes contain slightly more vitamin C than grapefruits do—and considerably more potassium and vitamin A. If your salad calls for the tang of grapefruit, try for the pink ones; they contain twice as much vitamin A as oranges do.

FLORIDA SALAD

Serves 6

1 small head romaine lettuce, torn into bite-size pieces
leaves from ½ bunch watercress
1 small zucchini, thinly sliced
1 small carrot, thinly sliced
3 button mushrooms, thinly sliced
flesh of 1 avocado, cut into ¾-inch cubes
1 tablespoon lemon juice

Dressing
½ cup olive oil
¼ cup rice wine vinegar
1 garlic clove, minced
1 teaspoon tamari soy sauce
1 teaspoon honey

2 pink grapefruits, segmented, seeds and membranes removed
1 sweet red pepper, diced

1. Toss together the lettuce, watercress, zucchini, carrot, and mushrooms.

2. Toss the avocado in lemon juice to prevent discoloration.

3. Combine the dressing ingredients in a large screw-top jar. Shake well to mix.

4. Cut the grapefruit segments in half and add them to the jar. Shake well.

5. Add the avocado and red pepper to the lettuce mixture. Pour dressing over all and toss to mix.

DATE-RAISIN WALDORF SALAD

Serves 6

4 Golden Delicious apples,
  quartered and diced
1 tablespoon lemon juice
1 cup diced celery
⅓ cup golden raisins
⅓ cup pitted chopped dates
Dressing
½ cup Mayonnaise (see Index)
¼ cup plain yogurt
2 teaspoons honey

6 Boston or Bibb lettuce leaves
½ cup coarsely broken walnuts

1. Toss apple pieces in the lemon juice to prevent discoloration.
2. In a salad bowl, combine the apples, celery, raisins, and dates.
3. In another bowl, whisk together the mayonnaise, yogurt, and honey. Pour the dressing over the apple mixture and toss lightly until all pieces are well coated.
4. Arrange a mound of salad on top of each lettuce leaf. Sprinkle with walnuts.

Bibb, oak-leaf, or Boston lettuce go well with a light oil and vinegar dressing or a cream dressing, because they are very tender and mild. Escarole, curly endive, and other hardier greens support a stronger, garlicky dressing.

FRUITED GREEN GODDESS SALAD

Serves 6

2 small heads romaine lettuce,
  torn into bite-size pieces
1 head Boston or Bibb lettuce,
  torn into bite-size pieces
flesh of 1 avocado, cut into ½-inch
  cubes
1 cup seedless green grapes
1 cup cubed honeydew melon
Dressing
½ cup Mayonnaise (see Index)
½ cup plain yogurt
2 tablespoons lemon juice
2 tablespoons rice wine vinegar
¼ cup chopped parsley
pinch dried tarragon
¼ teaspoon white pepper
1 garlic clove, minced

1. In a salad bowl, combine the lettuce with the avocado, grapes, and melon.
2. Combine the salad ingredients in a blender container. Process on high speed until smooth (about 30 seconds).
3. Pour the dressing over the salad and toss well.

PLUM SALAD

Serves 6

1 head escarole, torn into bite-size
   pieces
leaves from 1 bunch watercress
1 small red onion, thinly sliced
   into rings
6 plums, pitted and diced
½ cup coarsely chopped raw
   cashew nuts
Poppy Seed Dressing (see Index)

1. Gently toss together the escarole and the watercress.

2. Arrange the onion rings, plums, and nuts on top of the salad greens.

3. Toss with the dressing at the table.

SWEET CABBAGE SLAW

Serves 6

flesh of 1 small pineapple, cut into
   ½-inch cubes
1 small head cabbage, finely
   shredded
½ cup raisins
1 cup chopped walnuts
Dressing
½ cup Mayonnaise (see Index)
½ cup plain yogurt
2 tablespoons lemon juice
1 tablespoon honey
¼ teaspoon white pepper

1. In a salad bowl, combine the pineapple with the shredded cabbage, raisins, and walnuts. Toss to mix.

2. In another bowl, whisk together until smooth the dressing ingredients. Pour dressing over the salad and toss.

The Salade Mandala

Nature's Garden! A walk through it excites the senses and fills the body and brain with tranquillity.
JOHN R. CALELLA, *COOKING NATURALLY,* 1978

Poster art, like printed T-shirts, has become a cultural phenomenon. In the past several years, a truly beautiful example has made an appearance throughout the country. Titled *The Salade Mandala,* it pops up on walls of food cooperatives, natural foods stores, restaurant dining rooms, and our friends' homes. Like the lively Renaissance paintings of weddings and feasts, this visual jewel just teems with life, but here it is not burghers and maidens, but the plant kingdom, that the artist illuminates.

Bordered by summer, winter, fall, and spring skies, this multihued design is made up of four concentric circles embracing different aspects of the natural realm. Varied green shades carpet the outer circle on which vegetables, leafy greens, legumes, and herbs appear. A warm yellow ring is accented with protein-rich foods (nuts, seeds, and more). Aquamarine water beads separate it from a wide band divided into four colorful sections, each containing some grouping of fruits. A wreath of melons follows and adjoins the center, a brilliant orange sun. This *mandala* with its captivating affirmation of the plant domain prompted us one day to go in search of its creator, a person for whom the word *salade* obviously has special significance.

Just north of San Francisco in Marin County, a wood and glass structure seems to evolve out of a forested hillside. Tall comfrey leaves, dense mint branches, and large cactuses surround redwood decks that extend beyond several levels of living area. Stone steps wind from the upper portion down an ivy-covered incline to the shaded road. At the base, an eggplant-shaped shingle announces Villa Aubergine, home of John Calella, the draftsman for *The Salade Mandala.*

During our telephone arrangements, John strongly suggested that his concept of *salade* includes not only the taste of his dishes but the flavor of his entire day.

Therefore, at an early hour, we find ourselves jogging alongside a slender, hardy man of olive complexion. The route leads us for several miles through cool, winding lanes and back again to Villa Aubergine for quick showers and breakfast.

By 8:00 A.M., sunlight brilliantly floods the "bar," just one corner of a much larger food preparation area. Behind the handsome wooden counter, John scrubs vegetables at a small sink and puts them through a juicer. In minutes he pours creamy elixers—vegetable juices blended with seeds, almonds, and wheat germ—into tall-stemmed wine glasses.

In this inspiring location, John tests his own *salade* recipes and cooks frequently for an entourage of appreciative guests who have nicknamed him "Organic John."

Almost Saladlike Sauce

Our lunch on the patio at Villa Aubergine is a sunlit, multicolored display of fresh vegetables—both lightly cooked and raw. For the occasion, John has prepared homemade spinach-wheat spaghetti noodles to receive a fresh sauce from which firm mushroom slices and ruby-red tomato pieces emerge. A wide, shallow ceramic dish reveals marinated zucchini slices; a deeper one contains crisp, yellow wax beans and almonds in a delicate soy dressing, and, at the center, bright, lightly dressed greens and sprouts, so crunchy they break like ice, fill a clear glass bowl.

John Calella toasts a guest with a creamy elixer he makes from vegetable juices, blended with seeds, almonds, and wheat germ.

In a kitchen washed with sunlight, John prepares a simple, but sumptuous, salad.

The other diners at this meal—carpenters who are working on the house, several children, a musician, and a writer—seem delighted with the simple, uncomplicated combinations. No one dish at the table is the focal point; the various flavors, colors, and textures sensually and aesthetically complement one another.

Through formal work in physiology, biochemistry, and nutrition, John has learned to develop menus based on the chemical interaction of various foods in the body. He plans meals to enhance the subtle taste of the ingredients, to provide maximum nutritional benefit, and to offer digestive ease. "For hundreds of years out of boredom and then creativity we joined foods into soups, stews, and salads. Over centuries, thoughtless mixing and combining have brought about many of our prevailing digestive ailments and related diseases," he asserts.

For his first book, in which he presented these ideas and numerous delectable recipes, John set down the concept for *The Salade Mandala,* which a friend later transferred to canvas. "Bananas are not banana cream pie," he tells us. "*Salade* emphasizes foods from nature's garden as close to their pure state as possible." Many of the ideas incorporated in *Salade* are not new; they are a judicious compilation of logical nutritional theories that have been with us for ages. John's delicious Italian luncheon exemplifies some of them—no liquids served with the meal, avoidance of complicated combinations and heavy sauces, moderation with spices, elimination of prepared desserts, and a relaxing environment.

Salade, then, is a departure from our more common view of the combinations based on mayonnaise and oil and vinegar dressings. *Salade* is also more than plain fresh fruits and vegetables. It is, as our day has demonstrated, fresh air and sunshine, bounty and knowledge shared with friends, rest and relaxation, satisfying work, and nature's menu properly combined. "We can and must integrate the way we think and the way we live. Unless all are in harmony, we will have insufficient and inadequate nourishment for both the body and the spirit," says the designer of this *salade* course.

The following recipes are reprinted from *Cooking Naturally*. © Copyright 1978 by John R. Calella. Published by: And/Or Press, Berkeley, California.

COMMENTS ON THE RECIPES

The following ingredients that appear in some of these recipes may be unfamiliar to you. Most well-stocked natural foods stores will carry them.

Kelp—dried, granulated seaweed used as a seasoning.

Mineral Bouillon—an all-vegetable liquid concentrate made from whole wheat; corn; cane; lemon, orange, and papaya juice solids; soy lecithin; and dulse.

Mineral Powder—a dry powder prepared from uncooked green celery, tomatoes, spinach, red bell peppers, parsley, watercress, sesame seeds, and kelp, and flavored with yeast, orange aromatic herbs, and vegetable seasoning.

Safflower and Soya Butters—unsalted, uncolored, oil-base preparations that come in quarter-pound sticks like dairy butter. They are best when added to already cooked food just before eating. An adequate substitute is unsalted raw milk butter.

ALMOND PIE

Granulate 1 lb. almonds in your nutgrinder (or blender). Spread about a third of them on the bottom of a serving bowl. Slice:

1 pineapple, peeled (8 thin slices)
3 oranges, peeled (5 thin slices each)
¼ lb. strawberries (3 slices each)

Alternate layers of almonds and fruit in bowl, ending with pineapple.

SWEET POTATOES AND GREENS

Preheat oven to 450° for 10 minutes. Bake separately in tinfoil or together in a covered baking dish for 30 minutes:

1 large sweet potato
1 red onion

Clean, chop, and toss raw ingredients:

1 head romaine lettuce
½ bunch garden cress
½ bunch spinach
1 head bibb lettuce

Mix raw and cooked ingredients together.
Mix a dressing of:

1 teaspoon rosemary
1 tablespoon mineral powder
½ cup olive oil

BARLEY AND ME

Gather together these ingredients:

8 oz. barley
1 tablespoon mineral powder
1 teaspoon kelp
½ cube soya butter
½ bunch garden cress, finely chopped
¼ bunch parsley
3 green onions, chopped
1 bunch spinach
1 bunch escarole
1 oz. mineral bouillon
¼ lb. mushrooms, chopped
1 avocado, sliced
olive oil
water

Boil together 2 cups water, mineral powder, and kelp. Gently add barley to boiling water and lower the flame. Cook for 20 minutes covered; remove cover, and cook another 10 minutes over a very low flame. Then add soya butter, garden cress, parsley, and green onions. Stir well, recover pot, and set aside.

Saute in a wok the spinach and escarole with mineral bouillon, 1 oz. olive oil, and 2 oz. water. After cooking 3 to 5 minutes, add this to the barley. Mix in chopped mushrooms and sliced avocado; serve.

DANDELION SALAD

　2　*heads bibb lettuce*
½　*bunch dandelion greens*
½　*bunch celery*
½　*large red onion*
kernels from 3 ears uncooked corn

Wash all ingredients, dry them well, and chop into small bits. Put together the following in your blender, and mix well:

½　*medium avocado*
½　*medium red tomato, halved*
　1　*teaspoon kelp*
　1　*tablespoon mineral powder*
½　*bunch sweet basil*
½　*cup olive oil*

Pour dressing over greenery (though not really green in this case. Look at the beautiful mix of colors from the lettuce, onion, and corn. Eat with your eyes too!). Toss well and serve to four hungry friends.

Legume Salads

Basil was named basilikos *(royal) by the Greeks, because it was believed to be the secret ingredient in perfumes made for the nobility.*

BASIL AND BEAN SALAD

Serves 6

2 cups cooked beans*
1 Spanish onion, coarsely chopped
1 pint cherry tomatoes, halved
1 cucumber, chopped

Dressing
½ cup chopped parsley
2 tablespoons chopped basil
⅓ cup olive oil
2 tablespoons rice wine vinegar
1 tablespoon lemon juice
⅛ teaspoon black pepper

6 Boston or Bibb lettuce leaves

*Kidney beans, pinto beans, lima beans or other kinds of beans may be used in this recipe.

1. In a mixing bowl, combine the beans, onion, cherry tomatoes, and cucumber.
2. Combine the parsley, basil, oil, vinegar, lemon juice, and pepper in a blender container. Process at medium speed until smooth (about 30 seconds).
3. To serve, place a mound of bean salad on each lettuce leaf.

BLACK-EYED PEA SALAD IN TOMATO SHELLS

Serves 6

1¼ cups dried black-eyed peas,
    rinsed and soaked overnight in
    water to cover
  3 sprigs parsley
  1 celery stalk, halved
  1 sprig thyme
  1 garlic clove
  6 peppercorns
Mustard Vinaigrette (see Index)
  ¼ cup scallions, sliced on the
    diagonal
  2 tablespoons minced parsley
  ¼ cup minced basil
  2 shallots, minced
  1 tablespoon slivered lemon peel
  6 medium-size tomatoes

1. Drain the peas and discard the water.

2. Make a bouquet garni. Place the parsley sprigs, celery, thyme, garlic, and peppercorns in a cheesecloth sack. Place the sack in a 3-quart soup pot; add peas and cold water to cover by 2 inches. Bring to a boil, lower heat, cover, and simmer gently until tender (about 1½ hours). Drain; discard bouquet garni and cooking liquid.

3. In a large mixing bowl, mix the peas with the dressing. Add the scallions, parsley, basil, shallots, and lemon peel and gently toss. Cover with plastic wrap and chill.

4. Slice the stem ends from the tomatoes and scoop out the seeds. Scoop out and coarsely chop the pulp. Combine the pulp with the pea salad. Invert the tomato shells and let them drain on paper towels about 30 minutes. The shells may also be prepared a few hours in advance, if desired. Cover them with plastic wrap and allow them to drain in the refrigerator.

5. To serve, mound the pea salad in the tomato shells.

PEEL OR CUT ONIONS WITHOUT CRYING

Just start asking around, and you'll find out that there may be more methods for preventing tears during onion cutting than there are onions! Here are some you might want to try:

- Breathe only through your nose, with your mouth shut tight.
- Turn your head as far away as possible while you cut, so you don't breathe directly above the onion.
- Hold the onion under running water as you cut.
- Cut the onion without removing the stem end until last.
- Bite down on a crust of bread with one end protruding from your mouth.

LENTIL SALAD

Serves 6

1½ cups lentils, rinsed and soaked
  2 hours in water to cover
6 sprigs parsley
3 sprigs thyme
1 bay leaf
1 carrot

Dressing

2 tablespoons rice wine vinegar
1 teaspoon dry mustard
⅛ teaspoon pepper
¼ teaspoon ground coriander
2 shallots, minced
½ cup walnut oil or sesame oil
1 tablespoon lemon juice

¼ cup chopped parsley
1 tablespoon chopped chervil
1 cup coarsely chopped celery
½ medium-size red onion,
  coarsely chopped
1 teaspoon tamari soy sauce

1. Drain the lentils and combine them in a saucepan with a bouquet garni made by tying the parsley, thyme, and bay leaf together with a piece of thread. Add boiling water to cover (by at least 1½ inches) and add the carrot. Simmer, partially covered, until the lentils are tender but not mushy (35 to 45 minutes). Remove the carrot when it is tender and set it aside.

2. Prepare the dressing while the lentils are cooking. In a bowl, beat together the vinegar, mustard, pepper, coriander, and shallots. Add the oil in a stream and whisk until it is well combined. Stir in the lemon juice.

3. Dice the cooked carrot and stir it into the dressing. Stir in the parsley, chervil, celery, and onion.

4. Drain the lentils thoroughly and discard the bouquet garni. Place the lentils in a bowl and toss them with the tamari. Add the dressing and vegetables while the lentils are still warm and toss to coat. Marinate 2 hours at room temperature. Serve at room temperature or chilled.

PINTO BEAN AND RADISH SALAD

Serves 6

1¼ cups dried pinto beans, rinsed
  and soaked overnight in water
  to cover
2 garlic cloves
Vinaigrette (see Index)
1 bunch radishes, sliced ⅛ inch
  thick
¼ pound button mushrooms,
  quartered
1 small red onion, finely chopped
leaves from 1 pound spinach
½ cup alfalfa sprouts

1. Drain the beans and discard the water. Place the beans in a 3-quart saucepan with cold water to cover by 2 inches. Add the garlic cloves. Bring to a boil, lower heat, partially cover, and simmer gently until beans are tender (about 1½ hours). Drain and discard the garlic and cooking liquid.

2. Toss the dressing with the beans in a large mixing bowl. Allow them to cool to room temperature. Add the radishes, mushrooms, and onion. Toss gently. Cover with plastic wrap and chill.

3. To serve, arrange the spinach leaves on a serving plate. Mound the bean salad in the center of the leaves. Sprinkle the alfalfa sprouts over the beans.

MUSHROOM AND NAVY BEAN SALAD

Serves 6

1 cup dried navy beans, rinsed and soaked overnight in water to cover
4 cups boiling water

Dressing

2 tablespoons rice wine vinegar
2 tablespoons lemon juice
2 teaspoons French-Style Mustard (see Index)
1 garlic clove, minced
1 shallot, minced
⅛ teaspoon pepper
½ cup olive oil

1 pound mushrooms, thinly sliced
½ cup thinly sliced celery
1 tablespoon finely chopped parsley
½ teaspoon dried basil
2 scallions, thinly sliced on the diagonal

1. Drain the beans and discard the water, then cover and simmer them in the boiling water until tender (about 2 hours). Drain and cool slightly.

2. Whisk together the vinegar, lemon juice, mustard, garlic, shallot, pepper, and olive oil. Pour dressing over beans in a large bowl and toss to mix. Cover and chill.

3. Shortly before serving, stir in the remaining ingredients.

RAINBOW BEAN SALAD

Serves 6

1¼ cups dried mung beans, rinsed and soaked overnight in water to cover
2 garlic cloves
½ recipe for Vinaigrette (see Index)
¼ pound green beans, snapped into 1½- to 2-inch lengths
1 carrot, cut into ¼-inch slices
1 small yellow squash, cut into ½-inch slices
2 shallots, minced
1 tablespoon minced dillweed
12 cherry tomatoes

1. Drain beans and discard the water. Place the beans and garlic in a 3-quart soup pot and cover with fresh, cold water by 2 inches. Bring to a boil, lower heat, partially cover, and simmer gently until tender (about 1½ hours). Drain and discard the garlic and cooking liquid.

2. Toss the dressing with the beans in a large mixing bowl. Allow to cool to room temperature.

3. Place the green beans in a steamer together with the carrot slices. Steam until crunchy tender (about 10 minutes). Stir the cooked vegetables into the dressed mung beans. Allow to cool. Stir in the squash slices and the shallots. Add more dressing, if necessary. Cover with plastic wrap and chill until time to serve.

4. To serve, mound the salad on a serving plate. Sprinkle with dill. Arrange the cherry tomatoes around the edge of the salad.

A Creative Cafeteria Experience

Come to me all of you whose stomachs cry out and I will restore you. TRANSLATED FROM A LATIN MOTTO IN-SCRIBED ABOVE THE ENTRANCE TO THE FIRST EATING ESTABLISHMENT CALLED A RESTAURANT, OPENED BY M. BOU-LANGER IN PARIS, 1765.

Back in the late forties when I was four and five, my grandmother and I occasionally used to enjoy a bowl of chicken soup at a cafeteria on Market Street in Philadelphia. I was fascinated by the long self-service counter along which we slid our tray. We started at the silverware, halted at the windows of steaming food where a man dipped our soup, and momentarily stopped to look at the pretty molded salads set amid pebbles of ice. There were always neat rows of coconut cream pie and finally those shiny urns from which women poured steaming coffee. Sometimes we would sit for an hour over soup and watch all the people who came in and out of the room.

Through the years I have heard stories about, or have personally encountered, similar establishments—World War II military chow lines, Depression soup kitchens, and, of course, public school cafeterias specializing in canned tomato soup and leathery grilled cheese sandwiches. In the early sixties I witnessed a variation of the genre—the kosher chuckwagon dispensing Jewish-style food in a rustically decorated building.

Now a further progression of this type of self-service eatery exists in San Francisco, 3,000 miles and 30 years away from our early haunt on Market Street. In this particular restaurant, customers order drinks with names like "Orange Fantasy" and "Carobanana Shake," and delectable nut and vegetable pates supplant the standard meat loaf. Not one coconut cream pie with cardboard crust ever appears on the counter; all of the superlative desserts are made without any refined sweeteners. The breads

Immaculate, uncluttered, and comfortable—these are the happy characteristics of the Dipti Nivas dining room.

are homemade, whole grain products, and all the vegetables and fruits arrive fresh from California orchards and farms.

Abode of Light

Dipti Nivas (Sanskrit for "Abode of Light") is a spotlessly clean, bright cafeteria on Church Street. Patrons come from all walks of life—in-town professionals, blue-collar workers, students, families, retired citizens, and various ethnic groups who reside in the area. Two simply decorated adjoining rooms are bright with the daylight that comes through 15-foot glass windows. Here customers relax in wicker chairs at blonde wooden tables. The handsome sign that hangs above the outside doorway heralds vegetarian cuisine. But the melange of customers in this workaday restaurant proves that anyone, regardless of food preference, can break bread and be satisfyingly sustained.

Sisters Ratna King and Urmilla King Santana manage these gleaming surroundings. Seven years ago neither had any business experience. Today they run a highly organized operation, which the encircling community fully supports. Ratna smoothly handles most of the standard business procedures—payroll, ordering, hiring, overseeing. Since the restaurant's inception, Urmilla has assumed the job of establishing a well-rounded menu. "Urmilla has a second sense for what works with food," her sister relates. "Because she is married to Carlos Santana (renowned guitarist-musician) she brings back ideas from their tours all over the world. In her mind she can develop a recipe for a grain-stuffed cabbage roll from watching waiters carry plates of steaming *dolmas* in a cafe in Greece." Both women also put together a monthly newsletter that includes nutrition and recipe columns.

One of the surprising revelations for first-time diners is that the fare at Dipti Nivas is not only of the highest quality but is also just plain reasonable—not a common combination. "We won't go to table service because that would mean more overhead. We're much more interested in putting the money into ingredients. I employ as many as 28 full-time people to assemble all freshly prepared foods. We don't open cans around here, so that means a lot of cleaning and chopping," Ratna firmly asserts.

The steam table and limited space behind the narrow, 12-foot serving counter also have contributed in part to keeping Dipti Nivas's prices within reach of average purses. "Working in a small area and finding specific foods that keep well over steam have forced us to discipline ourselves. Early on we found we had to develop a fixed menu—casseroles, soups, cold desserts, a few excellent salads, selective sandwiches—that would work well here," Ratna notes. Now she, like all economical shoppers, orders specifically for these selections and, with lots of practice, has found where to get the best buys.

Soups and Salads

Ratna thinks of all of California as the garden patch from which she chooses her salad ingredients; yet, because of the close quarters, the menu board advertises just three nearly perfect choices—a green salad, a lovely fresh fruit one served with plain yogurt, and an unusual pate with tofu and fresh vegetables. Regular customers start with these and go on to make their own creations. Some combine the large green salad, a scoop of the pate, and a thick stream of Creamy Spinach Dressing that is a house specialty.

Dipti Nivas is a serious business venture that benefits from a professional approach coupled with a sense of mission.

"We won't go to table service because that would mean more overhead. We're much more interested in putting money into ingredients."

Chefs prepare 2 superb soups every day out of a log that includes at least 15 tested alternatives. Many titles have a familiar ring—borscht, vegetable barley, minestrone. Dipti Nivas' refinements, however, set their soups apart from conventional recipes. Unusual stocks, like those with soy sauce and nutritional yeast bases, often support vegetable ingredients. Dairy milk products do not keep well over the simmering water at the steam table, so they are replaced with satisfying noncurdling nut milks. Tomato Bisque and Cream of Mushroom Soup, both made with cashew milk, become true gourmet features vying with their heavy cream cousins. Most of the soups are so sustaining that patrons often make them the core of an entire meal, along with homemade bread and a salad.

The single, unifying force that lies at the heart of this business is the commitment of Ratna, Urmilla and her husband, and the majority of employees at Dipti Nivas as unobtrusive followers of Sri Chinmoy, an Indian spiritual master. His teachings motivate them to make their work an extension of their inner growth. The result is the fruit of their labor—exceptional food; clean, bright surroundings; reasonable prices; and radiant smiles. The restaurant-going public seems to appreciate those gifts.

CREAM OF MUSHROOM SOUP

Yields 2 quarts

1½ *pounds mushrooms, thinly sliced*
¼ *cup butter*
3 *garlic cloves, minced*
½ *pound cashews, coarsely chopped*
5 *cups water*
1 to 2 *nonsalted vegetable bouillon cubes, dissolved in small amount of boiling water*
¼ *cup minced parsley*
nutmeg to taste

1. In a 4-quart soup pot, saute the mushrooms in the butter until tender. Add the garlic. Saute on low heat 5 minutes.
2. In a blender, puree the cashews with the water until very smooth. Add to the mushroom mixture.
3. Add bouillon and cook on low heat until the soup begins to thicken. Stir frequently.
4. Add parsley and nutmeg.

CREAMY SPINACH DRESSING

Yields 1 cup

¼ *pound spinach, coarsely chopped*
2 *scallions, coarsely chopped*
⅛ *teaspoon dried tarragon*
¼ *cup safflower oil*
2 *tablespoons cider vinegar*
1 *teaspoon honey*

Puree all ingredients in a blender until velvety smooth.

TOFU PATE

Serves 6

1½ *pounds tofu, finely chopped or mashed*
3 *tablespoons tahini*
2 *tablespoons coarsely chopped sunflower seeds*
2 *celery stalks, finely chopped*
¼ *cup minced onions*
2 *tablespoons tamari soy sauce*

Combine all ingredients and mix well.

TOMATO BISQUE
Yields 2 quarts

3 scallions, thinly sliced
3 pounds tomatoes, finely chopped
2 tablespoons butter
⅓ cup tomato paste
½ pound cashews
5 cups water
1 nonsalted vegetable bouillon cube
1 teaspoon honey
½ to ¾ teaspoon cayenne pepper
½ teaspoon dried basil
1/16 to ⅛ teaspoon dried sage

1. Saute the scallions and tomatoes in butter 5 minutes. Add the tomato paste and simmer while you puree the cashews.

2. In a blender, puree the nuts with 3 cups of the water until smooth. Add remaining water and other remaining ingredients. Cook mixture on medium heat until it is thickened. Stir frequently.

Low-Calorie Salads

Cortland apples do not turn brown when sliced and, therefore, are well suited to salads.

APPLE AND RED CABBAGE SLAW

Serves 6

1 pound red cabbage, finely shredded
3 large carrots, grated
2 Cortland apples, diced
½ cup raisins
2 celery stalks, sliced into ¼-inch pieces
1 cup bean sprouts
¼ cup chopped parsley

Dressing
¼ cup lemon juice
1 tablespoon honey
1 tablespoon grated onions
2 teaspoons Prepared Mustard (see Index)
⅓ cup safflower oil

½ cup sunflower seeds

1. In a large salad bowl, combine cabbage, carrots, apples, raisins, celery, bean sprouts, and parsley.

2. In a cup, whisk together the lemon juice, honey, onions, and mustard. Gradually beat in the oil.

3. Pour the dressing over the salad mixture and toss to mix. Sprinkle with sunflower seeds.

BUNDLE UP YOUR GREENS

Here is a winning method for ensuring perfectly glorious, crisp, cold lettuce for every salad. It is one that is frequently used in preparing romaine for Caesar salad, but you can use it with any greens (such as escarole, endive, red-leaf lettuce):

1. Wash the greens and place them in a large colander. If the leaves are large and upright, stand them on end so that they drain well.
2. Place a single layer of greens on a cotton dish towel. Cover with another towel and another layer of greens. Continue the process until you have used all the lettuce.
3. Roll up the layers of towels and leaves like one large jelly roll. Secure both ends with rubber bands and place the roll in a plastic bag. Close the bag, and refrigerate the whole thing for at least several hours.
4. To use the lettuce, unroll the towels, remove the leaves you need for a salad, and then reroll. The remainder should stay table-ready for at least three days. The moisture in the refrigerator and that left in the leaves keeps the greens crisp, while the towels prevent surface moisture from rotting them.

CAESAR SALAD

Serves 8

2 heads romaine lettuce
1 garlic clove, split in 2
1 egg, raw or coddled 1 minute
2 tablespoons lemon juice
1 teaspoon pepper
1 teaspoon dry mustard
1 teaspoon tamari soy sauce
hot pepper sauce to taste
¾ cup grated Parmesan cheese
2 cups Garlic Croutons (see Index)

1. Wash the lettuce thoroughly and dry the leaves well. Wrap them in a towel and refrigerate them until you are ready to prepare the salad.

2. Rub split sides of garlic all over the inside of a chilled salad bowl. Mix the egg, lemon juice, pepper, mustard, tamari, and pepper sauce in the bottom of bowl. Slowly pour in the oil and, with a wire whisk, blend it with the other ingredients.

3. Break lettuce into bite-size pieces directly into the bowl. Use some of the rib of the leaves if it is tender.

4. Scatter the cheese and croutons over the lettuce. Immediately toss so that dressing at the bottom of the bowl evenly coats each piece of lettuce. Serve immediately.

Note: Traditionally, people like to assemble all the ingredients for this salad and put them together at the dinner table for the pleasure of their guests.

CARROT, CUMIN, AND FETA SALAD

Serves 6

1 pound carrots

Dressing
¼ cup lemon juice
¾ teaspoon ground cumin
½ cup safflower oil

1 pound feta cheese, drained and crumbled
¼ pound raisins
¼ cup minced parsley
2 tablespoons minced mint leaves

1. Grate the carrots on the large hole of a grater and place them in a large mixing bowl.
2. Combine the lemon juice, cumin, and oil in a small bowl and whisk until thoroughly combined. Pour dressing over the carrots and toss to mix. Arrange dressed carrots on a serving platter.
3. Top with the cheese and sprinkle with the raisins.
4. Combine the parsley and mint. Sprinkle over the salad. Cover and chill or serve at room temperature.

To Make a Sallet of All Kinds of Hearbes and Flowers

Take your hearbes and pick them very fine into faire water, and picke your flowers by themselves, and wash them all cleane, and swing them in a strainer, and when you put them into a dish, mingle them with Cowcumbers or Lemmans payred and sliced, and scrape Suger, and put in vinegar and Oyle, and throw the flowers on the top of the Sallet, and of every sorte of the aforesaid thinges, and garnish the dish about with the foresaide thinges, and hard Egges boyled and laid about the dish and upon the Sallet.

Thomas Dawson, The good huswifes Jewell, *1587*

CAULIFLOWER AND TOMATO SALAD

Serves 6

1 large head cauliflower, separated into florets
1 pint cherry tomatoes
1 medium-size red onion, thinly sliced
¼ cup minced basil

Dressing
¼ cup rice wine vinegar
1 tablespoon lemon juice
¼ teaspoon dry mustard
2 garlic cloves, minced
½ cup safflower oil
1 tablespoon chopped parsley
1 tablespoon chopped chives

leaves from 1 bunch watercress
freshly ground pepper

1. Steam the cauliflower in 1 inch of boiling water just until tender (about 5 minutes). Drain and chill.
2. In a large mixing bowl, combine the cauliflower, tomatoes, onion, and basil.
3. In a cup, whisk together the vinegar, lemon juice, mustard, and garlic. Gradually beat in the oil. Beat in the parsley and chives. Pour dressing over the salad and toss. Marinate at room temperature 1 hour.
4. Arrange watercress leaves on a serving platter. Mound the dressed salad in the center. Sprinkle with pepper.

Above the lower plants it towers,
The Fennel with its yellow flowers;
And in an earlier age than ours
Was gifted with wondrous powers
  lost vision to restore.

  Longfellow

The poet would find that even today some herbalists believe that fennel in soup or tea benefits the eyes
by strengthening them.

CELERY AND FENNEL SALAD

Serves 6

2 fennel bulbs
6 celery stalks
2 small zucchini
Dressing
¼ cup lemon juice
1 teaspoon dry mustard
2 teaspoons light honey
½ cup safflower oil

¼ cup sesame seeds, toasted

1. Remove the feathery leaves from the fennel bulbs. Using a pair of scissors, mince 2 tablespoons of the feathery leaves and set them aside. (The remaining portion may be used at another time.)

2. Using a vegetable peeler, remove the strings from the fennel bulbs and the celery. Cut the fennel bulbs, celery, and zucchini into julienne strips and combine them in a large mixing bowl.

3. In a cup, whisk together the lemon juice, mustard, and honey. Gradually beat in the oil. Pour the dressing over the julienne vegetables and gently toss. Sprinkle with the sesame seeds and the reserved fennel leaves.

LAYERED VEGETABLE MEDLEY

Serves 6

1 small head cauliflower, separated into florets
1 pound green beans, halved
3 small summer squash, cut into ¼-inch slices
1 bunch radishes, thinly sliced
Dressing
3 tablespoons rice wine vinegar
1 garlic clove, minced
½ teaspoon chili powder
½ cup safflower oil

2 tablespoons chopped basil

1. Steam the cauliflower in 1 inch of boiling water until tender (about 5 minutes). Drain and cool.

2. Steam the green beans in 1 inch of boiling water just until tender (about 5 minutes). Drain and cool.

3. Arrange the cauliflower in the bottom of a clear glass salad bowl. Place the green beans on top. Arrange the squash on top of the beans and the radishes on top of the squash.

4. In a cup, whisk together the vinegar, garlic, and chili powder. Beat in the oil. Pour dressing over the vegetables. Sprinkle with basil. Cover with plastic wrap and chill until serving time.

CUBED TOMATO ASPIC SALAD

Serves 6

1½ pounds tomatoes, peeled and cored
1 tablespoon unflavored gelatin
2 tablespoons lemon juice
2 tablespoons minced parsley
2 tablespoons minced basil
2 tablespoons minced celery leaves
1 small head romaine lettuce, shredded
2 medium-size cucumbers, cut into ⅛-inch slices
1 medium-size red onion, cut into ⅛-inch slices
⅓ cup alfalfa sprouts
6 small limes, cut into wedges

1. Coarsely chop the tomatoes on a large plate with a well so as not to lose the juice. Transfer the tomatoes and juice to a measuring cup (there should be 2 cups).

2. Place the tomatoes in a small saucepan and sprinkle the gelatin over the top. Let stand 5 minutes to soften. Bring just to a boil. Stir until gelatin is dissolved, then remove from heat. Cool to room temperature.

3. Rinse an 8×8-inch baking dish with cold water. Stir the lemon juice, parsley, basil, and celery leaves into the tomato mixture and transfer it to the dish. Cover with plastic wrap and refrigerate until set (about 4 hours).

4. Arrange the lettuce on a serving platter. Top with the cucumbers. Unmold the aspic and use a wet knife to cut it into 1-inch cubes. Arrange these on top of the cucumbers. Top with the onion slices and sprinkle with alfalfa sprouts. Serve cold with the lime wedges.

GAZPACHO TOFU SALAD

Serves 6

1½ pounds tofu, mashed
3 scallions, thinly sliced
1 garlic clove, minced
⅛ teaspoon hot pepper sauce
2 medium-size tomatoes, diced
1 cucumber, diced
1 green pepper, diced
6 escarole leaves
1 large sweet red pepper, sliced into 6 rings
2 tablespoons finely chopped basil

1. In a large mixing bowl, combine the tofu, scallions, garlic, pepper sauce, tomatoes, cucumber, and green pepper. Toss to mix.

2. Place an escarole leaf on each plate. Arrange a scoop of the tofu mixture on each leaf. Top with a red pepper ring and sprinkle with basil.

FRESH FRUIT AND YOGURT SOUP   For this recipe, see page 28

MARINATED VEGETABLE SALAD   For this recipe, see page 214

_____**Is It Peppermint or Spearmint?**_____

Peppermint and spearmint plants are often confused. Both bear dark green, deeply veined leaves that grow directly opposite one another. Spearmint leaves, however, are unevenly toothed, while peppermint leaves are evenly toothed. Spearmint leaves have the familiar taste of mint candy, gum, tea, and jelly. Peppermint leaves have a strong menthol taste.

Mint is one of the most democratic of plants. It makes itself available to almost everyone—country people and city dwellers alike. Gather it from meadows, fields, ditches, and along the sides of streams, and don't overlook the patch that might be in your own yard. Use it fresh as a soup herb, salad garnish, or refreshing tea. Dry some for winter use.

MEDITERRANEAN SPINACH SALAD

Serves 6

leaves from 2 pounds spinach
1 pint cherry tomatoes, halved
6 scallions, thinly sliced on the diagonal

Dressing
1 cup plain yogurt
2 tablespoons lemon juice
1 tablespoon olive oil
3 garlic cloves, minced
1 teaspoon dried thyme

1. In a large salad bowl, combine the spinach, tomatoes, and scallions.
2. In a small mixing bowl, combine the dressing ingredients. Whisk with a fork until blended.
3. Toss the salad with the dressing and serve immediately.

GARDEN PEA AND MINT SALAD

Serves 6

3 cups shelled peas (about 3 pounds)
2 scallions, thinly sliced on the diagonal

Dressing
2 tablespoons lemon juice
1 tablespoon honey
1 cup plain yogurt
⅓ cup finely chopped mint leaves

6 Boston lettuce leaves
1 large carrot, grated

1. Combine the peas and scallions in a medium-size mixing bowl.
2. Stir together the lemon juice and honey, then blend the mixture into the yogurt. Stir in the mint leaves. Toss pea mixture with the dressing.
3. Arrange a lettuce leaf on each plate. Place a scoop of the dressed peas on each leaf. Sprinkle each mound with grated carrot.

Green and Yellow Vegetables for Prostate

In a ten-year study of 122,000 Japanese men aged 40 and over, daily intakes of green and yellow vegetables were associated with a significantly lower mortality rate from prostatic cancer. The Japanese Cancer Association was told that vitamin A in the vegetables might be a contributing factor.

MARINATED VEGETABLE SALAD

Serves 6 to 8

2 cups cauliflower florets, broken into bite-size pieces
2 cups broccoli florets, broken into bite-size pieces
1 cup thinly sliced carrots
1 cup 1-inch green bean pieces
2 small yellow squash, cut into ¼-inch slices
2 small zucchini, cut into ¼-inch slices

Dressing
1 cup oil
1 cup cider vinegar
½ cup lemon juice
1 tablespoon grated onions
1 teaspoon dry mustard
1 garlic clove, minced
1 teaspoon dried oregano
½ teaspoon anise seed

1. Combine cauliflower, broccoli, carrots, and green beans in a steamer basket. Cook 5 minutes. Refresh in cold water.
2. Combine dressing ingredients in a 1-quart screw-top jar. Shake well to mix.
3. Combine steamed vegetables with the yellow squash and zucchini in a large bowl. Pour the dressing over and toss gently. Cover and refrigerate at least several hours before serving. Stir occasionally.

HAVE YOU TRIED TOFU IN SOUPS AND SALADS?

Tofu, otherwise known as bean curd or soy cheese, is the firm curd of soy milk once it separates from the whey. Relatively high in protein (an average serving of seven ounces supplies 30 percent of a person's daily requirement for protein) and low in fat and calories, it is a staple in oriental diets and is fast becoming one in American kitchens as well. Tofu lends itself to a variety of preparations—marinated in salads, cooked in soups, or pan-fried. The more you cook with it, the more possibilities for its use will open up to you.

MARINATED MUSHROOM AND TOFU SALAD

Serves 6

1½ pounds small mushrooms
2 celery stalks, cut into ¼-inch slices
2 fennel stalks, cut into ¼-inch slices
1 cup water
1 cup safflower oil
2 garlic cloves, minced
1 small bay leaf
1 teaspoon ground coriander seeds
juice of 2 lemons
1 pound tofu, cut into ½-inch cubes
tamari soy sauce to taste (optional)
6 Boston lettuce leaves
1 cup alfalfa sprouts

1. Combine the mushrooms, celery, and fennel in a large heat-resistant bowl.

2. In a small saucepan, combine the water, oil, garlic, bay leaf, and coriander seeds. Bring to a boil and pour over the mushroom mixture. Stir to mix and allow to cool to room temperature. Add the lemon juice and tofu and mix thoroughly. Season to taste with tamari, if used. Cover and chill.

4. To serve, arrange mushroom and tofu mixture on lettuce leaves. Discard the bay leaf. Sprinkle with alfalfa sprouts.

Meat Salads

Use the High-Fiber Champs in Soup or Salad

The championship title in the vegetable fiber sweepstakes goes to spinach. It is followed in descending order by corn, fresh peas, broccoli, zucchini, summer squash, green beans, celery, asparagus, raw cabbage, cucumbers, and onions. Add one or more of these to the next soup or salad you prepare and you automatically enhance its appeal, doing your heart and your digestion a favor in the bargain.

BEEFED-UP CHEF SALAD

Serves 6

1 medium-size flank steak
3 cups asparagus, sliced diagonally into 2-inch lengths
1 bunch broccoli
leaves from 1 pound spinach
¼ pound Roquefort cheese, crumbled
1 cup Garlic Croutons (see Index)
Raw Mushroom Vinaigrette (see Index)

1. Broil the flank steak as desired. Cool. Cut meat on the diagonal into very thin slices (approximately 2 to 3 inches long).

2. Bring a large pan of water to a boil. Blanch the asparagus 1 minute. Remove with a slotted spoon, reserving the water, and immediately refresh under cold running water. Drain well.

3. Remove the tough stalks from the broccoli and reserve them for another use. Cut the florets into bite-size pieces. Blanch these in the boiling asparagus water for 1 minute. Remove with a slotted spoon and immediately refresh under cold running water. Drain well.

4. In a large salad bowl, combine the sliced steak, asparagus, broccoli, and spinach. Sprinkle with cheese. Pour the dressing over all and toss gently.

216

HOMEMADE CROUTONS

Use either of these two easy methods to produce delicious toasted bread cubes for soups, salads, or even just for snacking:

Start with slices of day-old whole grain bread—any kind you like. Trim off the crusts if you wish. Cut each slice into ½-inch cubes.

For the top-of-the-stove method, heat a small amount of oil (preferably olive) in a heavy skillet. Use about 2 tablespoons oil for every 1 cup bread cubes. Add the croutons all at once and toss them with the oil. Saute them on medium heat until they are crisp all over. Stir the mixture frequently.

For baked croutons, toss bread squares in melted butter or oil, or brush the uncut slices with either one and then cut the slices into cubes. Spread the pieces evenly on an ungreased baking sheet, and toast them in a preheated 400°F oven for 10 to 12 minutes or until they are golden brown and crisp. Turn them occasionally so that they color on all sides.

SEASONED CROUTONS

When the bread cubes are almost done, toss them with a mixture of your favorite seasonings. Consider curry or chili powders; crushed, dried, or fresh basil, oregano, or thyme; or grated sharp cheese.

GARLIC CROUTONS

Saute a few crushed garlic cloves in the heated oil for a few minutes before adding the bread cubes. (Be careful they do not burn, or they will take on a bitter flavor.) Remove garlic, and proceed as with the basic recipe.

BEEF AND MUSHROOM SALAD

Serves 6

1 medium-size flank steak
¾ pound green beans
½ pound snow peas
2 cups boiling water
¼ pound small mushrooms, thinly sliced

Dressing

½ cup blue cheese, mashed with a fork
1 cup plain yogurt
3 tablespoons lemon juice
1 scallion, minced
¼ teaspoon freshly ground pepper

1. Broil the flank steak as desired. Cool. Cut meat into very thin slices on the diagonal. Cut the slices into matchsticks.

2. Steam the green beans in a covered pot of boiling water 5 minutes. Drain and refresh beans under cold running water. Cool.

3. Place the snow peas in a colander in the sink. Pour boiling water over them. Then place them under cold running water. Drain and cool. Cut each pea pod in half.

4. In a large salad bowl, combine the beef, beans, peas, and mushrooms.

5. In a small mixing bowl, whisk together the dressing ingredients. Serve dressing on the side.

LIVER SALAD WITH HOT VINEGAR DRESSING

Serves 6

2 tablespoons butter
1 pound chicken, duck, calf, or
   beef liver, cut into 1-inch pieces
freshly ground pepper
¼ pound mushrooms, cut into
   ⅛-inch slices
2 scallions, thinly sliced on the
   diagonal

Dressing

3 tablespoons walnut or sesame oil
4 shallots, minced
2 tablespoons cider vinegar
1 tablespoon water

1 head chicory
2 tablespoons minced parsley

1. Heat the butter to sizzling in a heavy skillet. Add the liver pieces, sprinkle with pepper, and saute on high heat about 5 minutes. Gently turn the liver so that it cooks on all sides. Transfer to a warm bowl.

2. Stir the mushrooms and scallions into the hot liver.

3. Add the oil and shallots to the drippings in the skillet. Cook 1 minute. Stir to loosen any particles in the pan. Add the vinegar and water, bring to a boil, and then immediately remove from heat. Pour the hot dressing over the liver and mushroom mixture; toss to coat.

4. Arrange the chicory on a serving platter. Mound the hot liver in the center and sprinkle with parsley. Serve warm.

ROQUEFORT CHICKEN SALAD

Serves 6

3 chicken breasts, skinned and
   boned
1 pound zucchini, cut into
   julienne strips
¼ pound mushrooms, thinly sliced
3 celery stalks, cut into julienne
   strips

Dressing

1 cup Mayonnaise (see Index)
juice of 1 lemon
1 teaspoon curry powder
1 tablespoon grated onions

leaves from 1 pound spinach
¼ pound Roquefort cheese,
   crumbled

1. Steam the chicken breasts in a covered skillet in 1 inch of boiling water about 20 minutes. Turn once. When cooked through, remove from pan and cool to room temperature. Tear the meat into shreds and set aside.

2. In a large mixing bowl, combine the zucchini, mushrooms, and celery. Stir in the chicken.

3. In a smaller bowl, whisk together the mayonnaise, lemon juice, curry powder, and onions. Pour over chicken mixture and toss to coat evenly.

4. Arrange the spinach leaves on a serving platter and mound the chicken mixture in the center. Sprinkle with the cheese.

CALIFORNIA CHICKEN AND ALMOND SALAD

Serves 6

3 cups cooked diced chicken
1½ cups coarsely chopped celery
2 scallions, finely chopped
½ cup almonds, coarsely chopped
Dressing
½ cup Mayonnaise (see Index)
½ cup plain yogurt
1 tablespoon lemon juice
flesh of 1 avocado, mashed
2 tablespoons minced dillweed

6 lettuce leaves

1. In a large mixing bowl, combine the chicken, celery, scallions, and almonds. Cover and chill.

2. In a small mixing bowl, whisk together the mayonnaise, yogurt, lemon juice, avocado, and dillweed. Beat until creamy. Cover and chill.

3. Just before serving, place a lettuce leaf on each plate. Toss the dressing and salad together and place a mound on each leaf.

POLYNESIAN TURKEY SALAD

Serves 6

2 cups cooked diced turkey
⅔ cup diced celery
½ cup coarsely chopped pecans
1 large apple, cored and diced
⅓ cup Mayonnaise (see Index)
1 small pineapple
6 escarole leaves

1. In a large mixing bowl, combine the chicken, celery, scallions, and almonds. Cover and chill.

2. Remove the rind from the pineapple, slice the pineapple into ½-inch rings, and remove the core from each. Place an escarole leaf on each salad plate. Select 6 of the best-shaped rings and place one on top of each leaf. Dice the remaining pineapple and mix it into the turkey salad.

3. Arrange a mound of salad slightly to one side of each pineapple ring.

BEEF-BULGUR SALAD

Serves 6

1½ cups bulgur
3 cups boiling water
1 sweet onion, peeled
2 tablespoons chopped parsley
1 tablespoon grated horseradish

Dressing

2 tablespoons sesame oil
1 tablespoon rice wine vinegar
1 tablespoon lemon juice
¼ teaspoon pepper
pinch dry mustard

12 thin slices cold cooked London broil

1. Place the bulgur in a large, heat-proof mixing bowl. Stir in the boiling water. Soak 1 hour or longer. Stir occasionally. Chill in the refrigerator.

2. Slice half the onion into thin rings and set them aside. Chop the remaining onion half and add it to the cold bulgur. Stir in parsley and horseradish.

3. In a small cup, whisk together the oil, vinegar, lemon juice, pepper, and mustard. Fold the dressing into the bulgur salad.

4. Arrange bulgur salad on individual plates and top each serving with 2 steak slices. Garnish with the onion rings.

CHICKEN AND EGGPLANT SALAD

Serves 6

1 4-pound chicken, quartered
4 cups water
1 unpeeled onion, halved
1 carrot, quartered
2 garlic cloves
1 bay leaf
1 medium-size eggplant (about 1 pound)

Dressing

½ teaspoon cornstarch
2 teaspoons tamari soy sauce
juice of 1 lemon
1 tablespoon finely grated ginger root
3 scallions, thinly sliced on the diagonal
2 tablespoons sesame seeds, toasted

1. Place the chicken parts, excluding the liver, in a 4-quart soup pot. Add the water, onion, carrot, garlic, and bay leaf. Bring to a boil, lower heat, cover, and simmer 45 minutes. Remove chicken and set aside to cool. Strain broth, return it to a smaller pan, and boil down until reduced to ¾ cup. Skim fat from surface and set broth aside to cool. Discard skin and bones from chicken, tear meat into shreds, and set aside.

2. Steam the whole, unpeeled eggplant on a rack over boiling water in a covered pot until it collapses (about 30 minutes). Remove from pan and cool. Peel off the skin and discard the excess seeds. Pull the eggplant fibers into shreds. Combine with the chicken.

3. Combine the cornstarch and tamari. Stir into the chicken broth. Bring to a boil. Cook and stir constantly until liquid is slightly thickened (about 5 minutes). Cool to room temperature. Stir in the lemon juice and ginger root. Pour this dressing over the chicken and eggplant and toss to coat.

4. Arrange dressed chicken and eggplant on a serving platter. Sprinkle with scallions and sesame seeds. Serve at room temperature.

KEY LIME CHICKEN SALAD

Serves 6

2 pounds skinned and boned chicken breasts
¼ cup butter
2 eggs, beaten
2 tablespoons minced chives
2 cups mung bean sprouts
2 cups boiling water

Dressing

1 cup Chicken Stock (see Index)
2 tablespoons light honey
finely grated peel and juice of 3 large limes
1¼ teaspoons cornstarch

2 scallions, thinly sliced on the diagonal
1 lime, halved lengthwise and cut into thin half-moon slices

1. Slightly flatten the chicken breasts by pounding them between sheets of wax paper. Melt the butter in a large skillet; add the chicken and turn it to coat with butter. Cover the chicken with a buttered round of wax paper. Cover the pan and cook on medium-low heat until the chicken is cooked through (about 10 minutes). Transfer the chicken to a plate, and when it is cool enough to handle, shred it into long strips.

2. Pour the beaten egg into the skillet containing the pan juices. Sprinkle the egg with the chives and, without stirring, cook over low heat until firm, but not browned. Turn the egg out onto a plate. Allow it to cool and cut it into shreds.

3. Place the bean sprouts in a strainer. Hold the strainer over the sink basin and pour the boiling water over them. Immediately refresh with cold running water. Drain well.

4. Place the Chicken Stock, honey, and lime peel in a small saucepan. Mix the lime juice and cornstarch together in a small cup and pour the mixture into the pan. Cook on medium heat while constantly stirring until mixture just begins to thicken (about 5 minutes). Cool slightly.

5. In a large mixing bowl, combine the chicken, egg, bean sprouts, and dressing. Gently toss ingredients to coat. Cover and chill.

6. To serve, arrange chicken mixture on a platter and sprinkle with the scallions. Garnish with lime slices.

The word salad *comes from the Latin word* sal, *meaning salt, and, it is believed, is derived from the early Roman custom of dipping chicory and lettuce into salt before eating them.*

MINTED LAMB SALAD

Serves 6

1½ pounds shoulder lamb chop
½ pound mushrooms, thinly
    sliced
1½ pints cherry tomatoes, halved
Dressing
  ¾ cup olive oil
  6 tablespoons lemon juice
  ¾ cup minced mint

  1 head Bibb lettuce, torn into
    bite-size pieces
leaves from ½ bunch watercress

1. Broil the lamb chop until it is medium-rare (the time will vary depending on the thickness of the chop and its distance from the broiler). Cool the chop. Trim off any fat and cut the meat into fine slivers.

2. Place the meat, mushrooms, and tomatoes in a large mixing bowl. In a small mixing bowl, combine the olive oil, lemon juice, and mint. Stir well to mix. Pour half of the dressing over all and toss to mix. Cover and chill until serving time.

3. Combine the lettuce and watercress in a salad bowl. Toss with the remaining dressing. Arrange the meat mixture over the dressed greens.

Salads from Leftovers

BAKED POTATO SALAD

BAKED POTATO SALAD_____

Serves 6

4 cold baked potatoes, peeled and
   sliced
1 cup coarsely chopped walnuts
4 celery stalks, thinly sliced
1 cup bean sprouts
3 tablespoons minced dillweed
2 tablespoons finely chopped
   parsley
4 radishes, coarsely chopped or
   sliced

Dressing
1 egg yolk
4 teaspoons French-Style Mustard
   (see Index)
¼ teaspoon curry powder
2 tablespoons lemon juice
1 cup olive oil

1. Combine the potatoes, walnuts, and celery in a large mixing bowl. Place the bean sprouts in a colander and pour boiling water over them. Refresh under cold running water. Drain. Add the bean sprouts to the bowl. Stir in the dillweed, parsley, and radishes.

2. Put the egg yolk, mustard, curry powder, and lemon juice into a small mixing bowl. Whisk until thoroughly combined. Slowly and gradually add the oil. Beat constantly with the whisk until mixture is thickened and smooth. Pour dressing over the salad ingredients and toss to mix. Cover and chill until serving time.

_____A Potpourri on a Plate_____

A salmagundi is a hodgepodge, a medley, a miscellany of items. To a chef it is a particular salad. You need a combination of attractively arranged ingredients—chopped meat, fish, onions, pickled vegetables, endive, and whatever else the inventive cook might have on hand—plus an oil, vinegar, and pepper dressing—to have a true salmagundi.

223

CHICKEN-EGG SALAD

Serves 6

4 medium-size ears corn
3 cups diced cooked chicken
½ cup finely chopped celery
1 small sweet red pepper, diced

Dressing

⅓ cup plain yogurt
⅓ cup Mayonnaise (see Index)
2 teaspoons lemon juice
1 teaspoon chili powder
1 teaspoon French-Style Mustard (see Index)

6 Boston lettuce leaves
3 hard-cooked eggs, sliced

1. In a large pan, steam corn over boiling water 5 minutes. Drain. When cool enough to handle, cut kernels from cobs and chill. Discard the cobs.

2. In a large mixing bowl, combine the chicken, celery, and pepper. In a small mixing bowl, whisk together the dressing ingredients. Combine mixtures and stir in the corn kernels.

3. Mound a portion of salad on each lettuce leaf and arrange egg slices on top.

EGG AND FISH SALAD

Serves 6

¼ cup Mayonnaise (see Index)
½ cup plain yogurt
1 tablespoon lemon juice
⅛ teaspoon crushed dried tarragon
1 shallot, mashed
¼ cup finely chopped spinach
¼ cup finely chopped watercress leaves
¼ cup finely chopped parsley
6 hard-cooked eggs
1 cup cold cooked fish, flaked
6 Boston lettuce leaves

1. In a small mixing bowl, combine the mayonnaise, yogurt, lemon juice, tarragon, and shallot. Whisk until blended. Stir in the spinach, watercress, and parsley. Cover and chill.

2. Cut the eggs in half lengthwise and remove the yolks. Force the yolks through a sieve with the back of a wooden spoon and allow them to fall into a small mixing bowl. Stir in the fish and just enough of the green mayonnaise to moisten and bind. Mound the mixture in egg white halves.

3. Place stuffed eggs on top of the lettuce leaves and serve with the remaining green mayonnaise on the side.

HOLIDAY TURKEY WALNUT SALAD

Serves 6

3 cups cooked turkey, cut into matchsticks
½ cup coarsely chopped walnuts
2 tablespoons minced shallots
1 sweet red pepper, cut into matchsticks

Dressing

1 egg yolk
2 tablespoons rice wine vinegar
2 teaspoons French-Style Mustard (see Index)
½ cup walnut oil

leaves from 3 bunches watercress
freshly ground pepper
½ cup alfalfa sprouts
toasted walnut halves

1. In a large mixing bowl, combine the turkey, chopped walnuts, shallots, and red pepper.

2. Whisk the egg yolk, vinegar, and mustard together in a small mixing bowl. Slowly beat in the oil until the dressing is creamy and smooth. Add dressing to the turkey mixture and toss to mix.

3. Arrange the watercress on a serving plate. Mound the turkey salad in the center. Sprinkle with pepper and alfalfa sprouts. Garnish with toasted walnut halves, if desired.

Note: Dressing can be served separately and added by individual diners.

LEFTOVER MEAT LOAF AND SPAGHETTI SQUASH SALAD

Serves 6

1 medium-size spaghetti squash (about 2 pounds)

Dressing

1 egg yolk
2 tablespoons cider vinegar
1 tablespoon French-Style Mustard (see Index)
2 garlic cloves, crushed
½ cup olive oil
¼ cup grated Parmesan cheese

2 cups cold cooked meat loaf, cut into ½-inch cubes
¼ cup chopped parsley

1. Preheat oven to 350°F.

2. Pierce the squash at both ends with a fork. Place it in a large baking pan and add hot water to a depth of 2 inches. Bake until the flesh can be easily pierced with a fork (about 1 hour). Remove from oven. When cool enough to handle, cut the squash in half lengthwise. Discard the seeds and any center pulp. Using a fork, pull the strands of flesh from the skin. Store in the refrigerator until ready for use.

3. In a small mixing bowl, lightly beat the egg yolk. Beat in the vinegar, mustard, garlic, oil, and cheese.

4. Toss the squash with the dressing in a serving bowl. Add the cubes of meat loaf and sprinkle with parsley.

LEFTOVER ROAST WITH PAN JUICE DRESSING

Serves 6

1½ pounds cold cooked roast beef, poultry, or lamb
1 pound new potatoes
3 scallions, sliced on the diagonal

Dressing
¼ cup cider vinegar
½ teaspoon tamari soy sauce
1 garlic clove, minced
⅓ cup sesame oil
¼ cup pan juices from the roast

freshly ground pepper
¼ cup minced parsley

1. Cut the meat into thin shreds or slices.
2. Boil the potatoes until tender (about 25 minutes). Drain and cool. Cut the potatoes into ½-inch cubes and combine them with the meat and scallions in a large mixing bowl.
3. In a small bowl, combine the vinegar, tamari, and garlic. While constantly beating, add the oil in a stream and then beat in the pan juices. Pour the dressing over the meat mixture and gently toss. Sprinkle with pepper and parsley.

RICE, ROAST, AND VEGETABLE SALAD

Serves 6

1½ cups brown rice
3¾ cups boiling water
1 carrot, cut into 1-inch julienne strips
1½ pounds cold cooked roast beef, lamb, or pork, cut into fine julienne strips
1 sweet red pepper, cut into slivers
1 green pepper, cut into slivers
6 scallions, thinly sliced
1 cup Mayonnaise (see Index)
¼ cup minced dillweed

1. Simmer the rice, covered, in boiling water on low heat 30 minutes. While the rice is simmering, cut the carrot into 1-inch lengths. Cut each piece lengthwise into 3 slices. Cut the slices into matchsticks.
2. Sprinkle the carrot sticks over the cooking rice, recover, and cook 5 minutes longer. Remove from heat (do not lift cover) and allow to stand 20 minutes. Remove cover and fluff. Chill, covered, until serving time.
3. In a large mixing bowl, combine the rice and carrot with the meat, peppers, scallions, and mayonnaise. Toss well to mix. Transfer to a serving platter and sprinkle with the dillweed.

Note: If you have leftover gravy, store it, covered, in the refrigerator. Just before serving, remove any solidified fat from the surface. Stir up to ½ cup gravy into the salad.

ROAST CHICKEN-SWEET POTATO SALAD

Serves 6

1½ pounds sweet potatoes
2 large Granny Smith apples, cut into ½-inch cubes
½ cup golden raisins
2 cups cold roast chicken, diced
3 tablespoons minced chives
Curried Vinaigrette (see Index)
6 lettuce leaves

1. Place the potatoes in a saucepan with enough cold water to cover them. Bring to a boil, lower heat, cover, and simmer until tender (35 to 40 minutes). Drain and let them cool slightly but peel them while they are still somewhat warm. Cut them into ½-inch cubes and immediately toss with ¼ cup of the dressing. Cool to room temperature.

2. Add the apples, raisins, chicken, and chives to the sweet potato mixture. Add more dressing to taste. Cover and chill until serving time.

3. Place a scoop of salad on top of each lettuce leaf.

Salads of Nuts and Seeds

In the South, "salad" may mean cooked greens served hot. Some southerners refer to "turnip salad" and "mustard salad" when they mean hot turnip greens or mustard greens.

CARAWAY AND ROOT VEGETABLE SALAD

Serves 6

1 pound carrots
1 pound turnips, diced

Dressing

5 tablespoons rice wine vinegar
1 tablespoon caraway seeds, crushed
2 teaspoons light honey
2 teaspoons French-Style Mustard (see Index)
½ cup olive oil

1. Cut the carrots in half lengthwise, then cut the halves into ½-inch slices. Place the carrots with the turnips in a 4-quart soup pot and cover with cold water. Bring to a boil, lower heat, cover, and simmer until tender (3 to 4 minutes). Drain the vegetables in a colander, refresh them under cold running water, pat them dry with a clean towel, and place them in a salad bowl.

2. Combine the vinegar, caraway seeds, honey, and mustard in a small stainless steel or enamel butter warmer. Heat until the vinegar starts to bubble around the edges. Remove from heat and cool slightly. Transfer vinegar mixture to a small screw-top jar. Add the oil, cover, and shake vigorously until mixed. Pour dressing over the vegetables and toss. Cover with plastic wrap and chill for at least 6 hours.

_____Cauliflower Is Worth the Trouble_____

Mark Twain said, "Cauliflower is nothing but cabbage with a college education." People who gladly coddle their cauliflower because of its special character would disagree. Growers know from experience that the beautiful white domes require a little more attention than their cabbage cousin. Cool temperatures, a moist environment, and a blanket of their own leaves tied up around them during the hottest days of summer all ensure light, unblemished, perfect heads. No true lovers of garden-fresh cauliflower florets tossed in a light vinaigrette dressing would ever begrudge the extra care.

CAULIFLOWER AND TOMATO SALAD WITH PIGNOLIAS

Serves 6

2 pounds tomatoes, peeled, seeded, and finely chopped
2 garlic cloves, minced
2 tablespoons lemon juice
½ cup olive oil
⅛ teaspoon cayenne pepper
10 basil leaves, finely chopped
¼ cup minced parsley
½ cup pignolias (pine nuts)
1 large head cauliflower, broken into florets

1. Place the tomatoes in a glass or ceramic bowl. Mix in the garlic, lemon juice, oil, cayenne, basil, and parsley. Cover and allow to stand at room temperature 2 hours. Stir occasionally. Chill 1 hour.

2. Spread the pignolias on a baking pan and toast them in a 300°F oven until golden (10 to 15 minutes). Stir occasionally. Cool and set aside.

3. Steam the cauliflower over boiling water in a large covered pan just until tender (about 7 minutes). Cool, cover, and chill.

4. To serve, arrange the cauliflower on a serving dish. Pour the tomato sauce over it and sprinkle with pignolias.

PASTA PIGNOLIA SALAD

Serves 6

1¼ pounds whole wheat pasta shells
1 tablespoon oil
10 plum tomatoes
2 garlic cloves, minced
12 basil leaves, chopped
1 small red onion, finely chopped
1 sweet red pepper, cut into julienne strips
1 cup pignolias (pine nuts)
½ cup olive oil
¼ cup grated Parmesan cheese

1. Cook the pasta *al dente* in a large pot of boiling water with the tablespoon of oil added.

2. Meanwhile, cut tomatoes in half and remove the stems and core. Cut each half into 4 long wedges and place them in a glass bowl. Add the garlic, basil, onion, pepper, and pignolias. Stir in olive oil.

3. When pasta is finished, immediately toss with vegetable mixture. Cover and chill at least 2 hours.

4. Before serving, toss again and garnish with Parmesan cheese.

CHESTNUT, PUMPKIN, AND WATERCRESS SALAD

Serves 6

1 small pumpkin, halved and seeded
1 pound chestnuts; roasted, steamed, or blanched; and skinned

Dressing

3 tablespoons rice wine vinegar
1 tablespoon lemon juice
1 teaspoon French-Style Mustard (see Index)
1 shallot, finely minced
½ cup walnut oil

leaves from 2 bunches watercress
2 tablespoons minced parsley

1. With a 1-inch melon-ball cutter, scoop out enough balls from the flesh of the pumpkin to measure 2 cups. Steam the balls in a vegetable steamer, over 1 inch of boiling water, until they are tender (10 to 15 minutes). Remove from heat, drain, and cool slightly. Combine the pumpkin balls and chestnuts in a mixing bowl.

2. In a screw-top jar, combine the vinegar, lemon juice, mustard, shallot, and oil. Shake vigorously to mix and pour dressing over the vegetables. Toss gently, cover, and chill until serving time.

3. Arrange the watercress on a serving plate. Mound the chestnut and pumpkin mixture in the center of the plate. Sprinkle with the parsley.

GREEN BEAN ALMONDINE SALAD

Serves 6

1¼ pounds green beans
2 medium-size sweet red peppers

Dressing

¼ cup sesame oil
¼ cup lemon juice
¼ cup rice wine vinegar
2 teaspoons coriander seeds
2 whole cloves
1 teaspoon grated onions
½ bay leaf
¼ teaspoon dried thyme
¼ teaspoon celery seed

Garnish

¼ cup finely chopped parsley
½ cup almonds, blanched, skinned, and slivered

1. Steam the green beans in a covered pan of boiling water 3 minutes. Drain.

2. Place the peppers under the broiler and cook. Turn often until charred and blistered on all sides. Place the peppers in a brown paper bag and seal it. Let stand until cool (about 10 minutes). Remove the peppers from the bag and discard bag. Peel the peppers, remove the core, and discard the seeds. Cut the peppers in half lengthwise and then slice each half into strips ¼-inch wide.

3. Place the dressing ingredients in a 2-quart soup pot. Bring to a boil, lower the heat, and add the beans and peppers. Cover tightly and cook 7 minutes. Shake the pan occasionally. Transfer to a heat-resistant bowl and allow to cool. Chill. Discard the bay leaf and cloves. Sprinkle with parsley and almonds.

Nuts are a concentrated food source of proteins, unsaturated fats, the B-complex vitamins, vitamin E, calcium, iron, potassium, magnesium, phosphorus, and copper. Once they are shelled, nuts should be stored in the refrigerator in airtight containers to preserve their freshness and to prevent oxidation and rancidity of their fat content.

NUTTY AVOCADO FRUIT SALAD

Serves 6

flesh of 2 avocados, cut into ½-inch
    cubes
2 bananas, sliced into ¼-inch
    rounds
¼ teaspoon cardamom
juice of 2 limes
1 Golden Delicious apple, cut into
    ½-inch cubes
1 cup seedless green grapes
⅓ cup pitted and coarsely chopped
    dates
1 cup coarsely chopped walnuts
½ cup shredded fresh coconut

1. Combine the avocados and bananas in a large mixing bowl. Sprinkle the cardamom and then the lime juice over the fruit. Toss gently.
2. Stir in the apple, grapes, dates, and walnuts.
3. Transfer mixture to a serving bowl. Sprinkle with the shredded coconut.

Seed Your Salads

Pumpkin, sesame, and sunflower seeds are jam-packed with valuable nutrients—such as the B-complex; vitamins A, D, and E; phosphorus; calcium; iron; fluorine; iodine; potassium; magnesium; zinc; and unsaturated fatty acids. Sesame seeds are high in calcium. Sunflower seeds contain up to 50 percent protein.

SESAME SPINACH SALAD

Serves 6

Dressing
1 egg yolk
¼ cup rice wine vinegar
1 tablespoon lemon juice
¼ cup sesame oil
½ cup safflower oil
¼ cup plain yogurt
2 tablespoons finely chopped basil
½ cup sesame seeds, toasted

leaves from 1½ pounds spinach
½ pound mushrooms, cut into
    ⅛-inch slices
2 Cortland apples, diced into
    ½-inch cubes

1. In a blender container, combine the egg yolk, vinegar, lemon juice, both oils, yogurt, basil, and ¼ cup of the sesame seeds. Blend until thick and smooth. Cover and chill at least 4 hours. Remove from refrigerator 15 minutes before serving.
2. Arrange the spinach in a salad bowl. In another bowl, toss the mushrooms and apples with the dressing. Pour over the spinach. Sprinkle with the remaining sesame seeds.

WALNUT VINAIGRETTE SALAD

Serves 6

4 cups water
1 thick slice of onion
1 teaspoon tamari soy sauce
2½ cups walnut halves
1 bunch radishes, cut into
⅛-inch slices

Dressing

3 tablespoons rice wine vinegar
1 tablespoon French-Style
Mustard (see Index)
2 teaspoons honey
½ cup walnut oil

1 head escarole, torn into bite-
size pieces

1. In a 3-quart saucepan, bring the water, onion, and tamari to a boil. Add the walnut halves, lower heat, cover, and simmer 10 minutes. Drain and discard the liquid. When the nuts are cool, combine mixture with the radishes.

2. Beat the vinegar and mustard together in a cup. Beat in the honey and oil. Pour dressing over the nut-radish mixture.

3. Place the escarole in a salad bowl. Use a slotted spoon to hold the nut-radish mixture while you drain the dressing over the escarole. Toss the escarole to coat it with dressing. Arrange the nut-radish mixture over the dressed greens.

Temple Beautiful

Let thy Kitchen be thy apothecary and let foods be thy medicine.
HIPPOCRATES

The scent of freshly grated nutmeg dominates the entire room. In moments the unmistakable aroma of cumin is present. Soon the scent of ginger, then cardamom, then coriander mingle with the others. Eight tall plastic buckets rest atop a long wooden counter. Seven more sit on an enamel-top table in the middle of the room. Chopped vegetables of varying types, textures, and colors fill them. Large glass jars revealing thick, creamy substances stand among the containers. Five people are working in the room, one a child of eleven whose mother is tying a print bandanna around her long hair. A man with a European accent pokes his head through the crack of the door. "So sorry to disturb you," he whispers, "but is there anything I can do?" A spirited woman answers appreciatively, "Oh, sure, vacuum the dining room or fluff the pillows in the living room. I didn't get to it yet."

In a kitchen without a working refrigerator, stove, or oven, Ellen and her friend David are preparing dinner for 40 to 80 guests. The other three are a family who have

Steve and Ellen Haasz open their doors to a wide variety of visitors. Some drop in regularly to dine; others, some of whom travel long distances to enjoy the exceptional food, come only occasionally.

come as students to observe the activities. All of this is in preparation for a special dinner—a salad smorgasbord—that is served three times every week.

On Tuesday, Wednesday, and Thursday nights, Steven and Ellen Haasz open the doors of their eclectically decorated Victorian residence to a wide variety of visitors. Some drop in regularly to dine; others have to make a special long-distance trip for several hours of conviviality and exceptional food. The bill of fare is fresh, raw vegetable and grain dishes accentuated with special seasonings and satisfying, unusual sauces.

Noncooking Classes

Steven and Ellen have chosen to answer most of the numerous questions about this unique approach to food through their noncooking classes. Upon reservation, a limited number of people sit in on the last hour of dinner preparation which climaxes a full day of chopping and grinding. Ellen tells the participants, "What you will get to see now is that things are kind of loose. We'd like you to know that it's possible to be as comfortable and creative with noncooking as many people are with cooking." (She gives each person mimeographed sheets of basic information and popular recipes to take home.)

Students arrive at 5:30 P.M. They find a clear area in the kitchen from which they watch the proceedings until someone signals them to assist in the final mixing of ingredients. David has just finished using the most important appliance in the room, a large commercial grinder. Making use of the various blades, he chops all the vegetables (except tomatoes) and grinds large quantities of nuts and seeds. In this efficient, sparsely equipped room, pots, pans, and skillets are nonexistent.

Miracle Chef

At 5:45 P.M. Ellen arrives from a full day of teaching high-school English. She is the master chef who has come to put the final touches on all of the dishes. Seven years of experimentation have taught this tireless woman which combinations of veg-

Ellen can turn chopped vegetables into "chili," "spaghetti," or "chop suey."

Guests at Temple Beautiful help themselves to an all-raw buffet dinner.

etables, herbs, spices, oils, and special sauces offer good nutrition and produce rave reviews. Miraculously turning buckets of chopped vegetables into "chili," "spaghetti," or "chop suey," she talks as she works: "Just because someone wants to eat healthfully, he need not deprive himself of one of the greatest joys in life—delicious food. We prepare food that not only cleans and rebuilds the body, but tastes exciting and satisfying." (Simply by adding three or four ingredients, she turns containers of carrots into "pumpkin pie" or "hash browns.") "It isn't that we try to simulate traditional foods, but when someone tells us that one of our cabbage combinations tastes like chicken salad, or chili, we adopt the name. We want people to feel at home."

The time has come to pour the sauces and to mix together the ingredients in each pail. Chefs and students alike roll up their sleeves, wash their hands and arms, and dig down into the varying textures—crisp, smooth, thick, fine, coarse. Ellen tastes each mixture and makes a final quality judgment.

Feast for Forty

At precisely 6:30 P.M., an announcement brings the guests to the two large banquet tables in the dining room. Chopsticks, commodious bowls, and the 15 colorful entrees span the top of an antique buffet at the side of the room. Seeing is not believing at this feast. A group at one end of the table talks about the delicious potatoes in the "hash browns." A little girl who has come fully prepared to dislike "all this stuff" spends a good portion of the evening indulging her yen for the "Mock Chicken Salad." "The euphemisms," says Ellen, "have turned out to be very important. Without the familiar names some people would never try some of these mixtures—ones they often end up adoring."

Dinner never formally concludes; it tapers off. A professor departs to teach an evening class; two actors leave for a performance; a group of college students goes off to study; several families depart to put their children to bed. Everyone donates four dollars in the small cash box to cover the Haaszes' basic food costs.

By 10:00 P.M. the Haaszes are winding up their cooking class. Their students have a few final queries. "Limited to such few food categories," they inevitably ask, "what special techniques do you use to turn these simple ingredients into such gourmet meals?" Several essential factors elevate these foods to superlative company dishes. The ingredients must be of the highest quality, since they will be unchanged by heat or complex preparations. They also must be cut in a way that makes them appealing. A number of techniques—chopping, dicing, grinding, and mincing—are used to expose the full flavor of the food and create interesting textures. In addition, a wide variety of herbs and spices—all freshly, finely ground every day—give each dish its distinctive character. "Basil is our favorite, but we love them all—dill, savory, celery seed, cinnamon," says Ellen enthusiastically.

The Haaszes use sprouts of nuts, seeds, and wheat berries to add crisp textures and vital nutritional elements to their menus, but most important, these three foods are also the basis for their indispensable sauces. Raw nuts and seeds, finely ground and covered with a soaked wheat water called Rejuvelac, produce a mildly fermented product, not unlike yogurt. These sauces offer people the gravitational bulk that they normally receive from many cooked foods. They are also full of protein and easy to digest in this form. "The taste often takes getting used to. But you learn to love them. Some say they are 'addicted' to them," Ellen tells her listeners.

Life Food

Underlying the Haaszes' warm hospitality and meticulous attention to quality and technique is a personal philosophy. Steven states it simply, "The body obtains nourishment from four sources: light, air, water, and food. But the only food that cleans and regenerates the body is 'life' food—uncooked food replete with the vitamins, minerals, and enzymes that nature provides." Ellen adds, "We offer people an opportunity to see that they don't have to deny themselves the unequaled pleasure of taste just because they want to eat healthfully."

MOCK CHICKEN SALAD
Serves 4

2 large cakes tofu
½ cup finely grated celery
½ cup finely minced onion
1 cup mung bean sprouts
½ cup finely grated cabbage
¼ cup tamari soy sauce
pepper, cayenne pepper to taste, or Hot
   Chili Oil (see recipe in this section)
1 garlic clove, freshly squeezed
2 tablespoons olive oil
½ teaspoon sesame oil
½ cup pumpkin seeds (optional)
½ to 1 cup cashew or sunflower sauce
   (see Nut or Seed Sauce below)

Garnish
8 sprigs parsley
cherry tomatoes

1. Mash tofu and mix in all other ingredients except sauce and garnishes. Add sauce and toss throughout mixture.
2. Place mixture in a deep glass casserole dish and garnish with parsley and cherry tomatoes.

NUT OR SEED SAUCE
Yields about 1 quart

1 cup raw nuts or seeds (such as
   sunflower or alfalfa seeds, cashew or
   filbert nuts)
2 cups Rejuvelac (see recipe below)

1. Blend nuts or seeds with liquid until a silky-smooth consistency results.
2. Place in a glass or ceramic container and let sit in a warm place for 8 hours. The quantity will increase in size by one third.
Note: If using sunflower seeds, the whey will separate from the curd. For a thin sauce, stir the two together; for a thick one, siphon out the liquid and retain the curd layer.

REJUVELAC
Yields 3½ cups

1 cup wheat berries
1 quart spring water

1. Soak berries in water in ceramic or glass container for 48 hours.
2. Strain through a stainless steel strainer. The liquid is Rejuvelac. This procedure may be repeated with the same berries for 7 more days. Soak only for 24 hours on successive soakings.
Note: At the end of their use, feed the berries to the birds or use them in the compost pile.

HOAGIE SALAD

Serves 4

½ *cup wheat berries*
spring water
3 *cups shredded lettuce*
3 *cups shredded spinach*
2 *cups of any of these or any*
combination thereof—finely
chopped: cucumber, radish, bell
pepper, fresh parsley, carrot,
parsnip, zucchini, cauliflower,
broccoli
1 *cup finely minced onions*
1 *cup olive oil*
2 *teaspoons Hot Chili Oil (see*
recipe below)
6 *teaspoons lemon juice*
4–6 *teaspoons dried oregano*
1 *teaspoon dried marjoram*
juice from 2 garlic cloves
4 *tomatoes, cut into chunks*

1. Soak wheat berries overnight in enough spring water to cover well. The next morning drain berries and put them aside.
2. In a large wooden salad bowl, toss together the lettuce, spinach, chopped vegetables, and onions.
3. Mix together oils, lemon luice, herbs, and garlic juice and pour over vegetables.
4. Fold in wheat berries and tomatoes.

HOT CHILI OIL

Yields 1 cup

4 to 5 *whole, unseeded hot red or green*
chili peppers
1 *cup raw green olive oil*

1. Grind peppers and add to oil. Allow to soak overnight.
2. Strain oil from peppers. Use oil in Mock Chicken Salad, Hoagie Salad, or other preparations of your choice.

Salads That Keep

CRUNCHY AVOCADO MOUSSE

Serves 6

3¼ cups degreased Chicken Stock
  (see Index)
2 tablespoons unflavored gelatin
2 avocados, halved and pitted
juice of 1 lime
2 tablespoons minced chives
½ cup bean sprouts
½ cup finely chopped celery
1 bunch watercress

1. Lightly oil a 6-cup decorative mold. Place the mold in a larger bowl partly filled with ice and a little cold water.

2. Place the stock in a 2-quart saucepan. Sprinkle the gelatin over the top and allow to stand 5 minutes to soften. Place pan on medium heat and stir gently until gelatin is dissolved. Remove from heat and cool to room temperature. Spoon a thin layer of the stock into the bottom of the prepared mold and allow it to set (since the mold is in a basin of ice water, this should take only a few minutes).

3. Slice one-half of one of the avocados into crescents about ⅛ inch thick. Arrange these on top of the set stock in the mold and gently ladle another small amount of stock over the avocado pattern to set the design.

4. Mash the remaining avocados and whisk them into the remaining stock. Stir in the lime juice, chives, bean sprouts, and celery.

5. Separate the watercress leaves from the stems. (Save the leaves for garnish.) Chop the stems into ⅛-inch lengths and stir them into the avocado mixture. Transfer the mixture to the mold. Cover and chill until set (about 7 hours).

6. Unmold mousse before serving and garnish with the watercress leaves.

239

SPROUTS ADD FLAVOR
AND NUTRITIONAL DYNAMITE

Did you know that sprouting nuts, seeds, grains, and legumes triggers an incredible explosion of all their original vitamin values? Experiments by University of Pennsylvania scientists proved that soybean sprouts increased the basic ascorbic acid (vitamin C) content of soybeans by more than 500 percent in 72 hours! At Yale, researchers discovered that oat sprouts, just at the point that their tiny green leaves started to appear, had increased the original riboflavin (vitamin B_6) reading of oats by 2,000 percent.

For only pennies from your pocket and minutes of your time, you can grow your own sprouts. It's so easy to do and it's such fun to watch the miracle of germination and growth happening right before your eyes. In three to six days, you'll have a jar of flavorful food just jam-packed with vitamins, minerals, protein, and enzymes.

Mung beans and alfalfa seeds are two good starting choices for sprouting, but later you'll want to branch out into soybeans, lentils, whole dried peas, and many more alternatives.

Begin by soaking two tablespoons mung beans or one tablespoon alfalfa seeds overnight (8 to 12 hours) in enough water to cover them. (You'll need fewer alfalfa seeds because they expand more.) Use an ordinary wide-mouth glass jar. Cover the top of the jar with nylon stocking, several thicknesses of cheesecloth, or pliable fiberglass screening (sold for windows at hardware stores). Use a rubber band to secure any of these. Place the jar in a dark place, under the kitchen sink or in a cabinet.

After the soaking period, drain the water through the screening. (Because the liquid is nutritionally valuable, save it for use in stocks or treat your plants to a rejuvenating drink.) Two times each day, pour fresh water in the jar, swish it around, and drain it off immediately.

Sprouts are usually ready to use three to six days after germination. Their flavor, texture, and nutritional value will depend on the degree of growth and the stage at which they most appeal to you. After you've experimented enough times, you'll learn to halt the activity of the seed or bean when it reaches the stage you like. As a rule of thumb for good flavor, refer to this guide:

alfalfa seeds	1 to 2 inches
lentil beans	1 inch
mung beans	1 to 3 inches
peas or soybeans	2 inches
rye, wheat, or other grains	allow to develop only to the length of the seed
sunflower seeds	¼ inch

Throughout the sprouting process, keep your crop in a dark place until the last day of sprouting. At that time, place the container in a sunny window for about four hours. Chlorophyll will begin to develop in the first set of leaves. Store sprouts in the refrigerator in a covered plastic container or glass jar. Keep them no longer than a week and use them freely, for they fit in everywhere—in soups, stews, salads, and sandwiches.

BRUSSELS SPROUTS SALAD

Serves 6

1½ pounds Brussels sprouts
Dressing
¼ cup rice wine vinegar
½ cup sesame oil
2 garlic cloves, finely minced
1 tablespoon minced chervil
   leaves

leaves from 1 pound spinach
1 pint cherry tomatoes, halved
¼ cup minced parsley

1. Remove any tough outer leaves from Brussels sprouts. Trim off the stem ends. Wash thoroughly. Bring 2 inches of water to boil in a 1-quart soup pot. Add the sprouts, return to a boil, lower heat, cover, and simmer until tender (about 10 minutes). Drain.

2. In a small bowl, whisk together the vinegar, oil, garlic, and chervil. Pour dressing over the hot sprouts and allow to cool to room temperature. Turn occasionally. Chill, covered, up to 4 days. Stir occasionally.

3. To serve, arrange spinach on a platter or in a salad bowl. Toss the tomatoes with the Brussels sprouts and mound on top of the spinach. Sprinkle with parsley.

CELERY HEARTS A LA GREQUE

Serves 6

2 pounds celery hearts
1 cup water
1 cup olive oil
¼ cup cider vinegar
juice of 1 lemon
10 coriander seeds
10 white peppercorns
½ bay leaf
½ teaspoon fennel seed
1 garlic clove, peeled

1. Separate the stalks from each bunch of celery hearts and cut them diagonally into 1½-inch lengths.

2. In a 2-quart saucepan, combine the remaining ingredients. Add the celery and bring to a boil. Lower the heat, cover, and simmer 3 minutes. Remove from heat and cool to room temperature.

3. Transfer the celery and liquid to a shallow serving dish. Cover and chill overnight.

MARINATED CUCUMBER AND RADISH SALAD

Serves 6

4 medium-size cucumbers, thinly
   sliced
1 bunch radishes, thinly sliced
¼ cup rice wine vinegar
2 tablespoons lemon juice
3 tablespoons olive oil
¼ cup minced chives

1. Combine the cucumbers and radishes. Combine the vinegar and lemon juice and pour over the vegetables. Cover and marinate up to 2 days.

2. When ready to serve, drain off most of the liquid. Stir in the oil and chives.

JULIENNE OF ROOT VEGETABLES

Serves 6

½ pound Jerusalem artichokes
2 small turnips
3 medium-size carrots
Dressing
¼ cup cider vinegar
1 tablespoon minced tarragon
1 scallion, finely sliced
½ cup olive oil

leaves from 1 head chicory

1. Slice the artichokes and turnips and then cut the slices into matchsticks.
2. Cut the carrots into 1-inch lengths. Cut each piece lengthwise into 3 slices. Cut each slice into matchsticks. Combine the vegetables in a medium-size mixing bowl.
3. In a small bowl, whisk together the vinegar, tarragon, scallion, and oil. Pour dressing over the vegetables and stir to mix. Cover and store in the refrigerator up to 2 days. Stir occasionally.
4. To serve, arrange the chicory leaves on 6 plates. Stir the marinated vegetables and place a portion on each plate.

RED AND GREEN PEPPER SALAD

Serves 6

3 large sweet red peppers
3 large sweet green peppers
Dressing
3 tablespoons lemon juice
½ cup olive oil
1 garlic clove, smashed
1 tablespoon minced basil
1 tablespoon minced parsley

1. Cut the peppers from top to bottom into ½-inch strips, discarding the seeds and stems. Place pepper strips in a medium-size pan of boiling water and simmer them 5 minutes. Drain in a colander and immediately run cold water over to refresh and cool them. Drain again and dry on paper towels. Place peppers in a large mixing bowl.
2. In a small mixing bowl, combine the dressing ingredients. Whisk to mix. Pour dressing over the peppers and toss to coat. Cover and marinate the pepper strips for several hours at room temperature or several days in the refrigerator.

To Peel or Not to Peel—Is That the Question?

The answer is: Don't peel unless you must! In root vegetables, the nutrients which are concentrated directly under the skin are lost in peeling. So it is to your advantage to retain vegetable skins unless their removal is crucial to the appearance of the dish or the skin is tough, bitter, or too uneven to be thoroughly cleaned.

UNDERGROUND SLAW

Serves 6

1 pound small turnips
3 medium-size carrots
3 medium-size parsnips
juice of 1 lemon
1 medium-size red onion, finely
   chopped

Dressing
½ cup plain yogurt
½ cup Mayonnaise (see Index)
¼ cup minced dillweed

1. Using the large hole of a hand grater, grate the turnips, carrots, and parsnips into a large mixing bowl. Sprinkle with the lemon juice and toss to mix. Stir in the onion.

2. In a small mixing bowl, combine the dressing ingredients. Mix well. Add to the grated vegetables and toss well. Cover and refrigerate for up to 3 days.

LAYERED BEET AND YOGURT MOLD

Serves 6

White Yogurt Layer
1 tablespoon unflavored gelatin
¼ cup lemon juice
2 cups plain yogurt
1 cup finely minced celery

Red Beet Layer
1 tablespoon unflavored gelatin
½ cup tomato juice
1 cup degreased Beef Stock (see
   Index)
1½ cups cooked beets, chopped
   into ⅜-inch cubes
2 tablespoons minced chives
2 tablespoons finely chopped
   parsley

1. Lightly oil a 6-cup decorative mold and set aside.

2. Make the white layer. Sprinkle the gelatin over the lemon juice in a small heat-resistant cup and let stand 5 minutes to soften. Place cup in a pan of very hot water until gelatin dissolves. In a large mixing bowl, whisk yogurt and dissolved gelatin together until smooth. Stir in the celery and transfer the mixture to the prepared mold. Cover with plastic wrap and chill until firm but not completely set.

3. Meanwhile, prepare the red layer. Sprinkle the gelatin over the tomato juice in a small heat-resistant cup. Place cup in a pan of very hot water until gelatin dissolves. Measure the stock into a medium-size mixing bowl and stir the dissolved gelatin into it. Cover and chill. Stir occasionally until nearly set or until the mixture forms a mound when dropped from a spoon. Stir in the beets, chives, and parsley.

4. Remove mold containing the white layer from the refrigerator. It should be firm but not completely set. Gently spoon the beet mixture over the white layer. Cover and chill until completely set (about 6 hours).

5. Unmold gelatin onto a plate or platter before serving.

GAZPACHO ASPIC

Serves 6

2 tablespoons unflavored gelatin
1 cup Beef Stock (see Index)
¼ cup lemon juice
2¼ cups tomato juice
1 large green pepper, finely chopped
1 large sweet red pepper, finely chopped
2 medium-size cucumbers, peeled, seeded, and coarsely chopped
3 green onions, thinly sliced
2 tablespoons minced parsley

1. Lightly oil a 6-cup decorative mold and set it aside.

2. Sprinkle the gelatin over the stock in a small saucepan and allow to stand 5 minutes to soften. Place on medium heat. Stir gently until gelatin dissolves. Remove from heat and allow to cool to room temperature. Transfer to a large mixing bowl. Stir in the lemon juice and tomato juice. Cover and chill until mixture is the consistency of unbeaten egg white. Stir occasionally.

3. Mix the remaining ingredients into the loosely set gelatin mixture. Turn into the mold. Cover and chill until set (about 6 hours).

4. Unmold before serving.

Jerusalem artichokes, tubers of the sunflower family, are very similar in appearance and taste to new potatoes. These knobby vegetables are rich in sugar and must be washed rapidly if their delectable taste is to be retained. Be careful not to overcook them or to steam them at too high a temperature; they get tough easily. Raw Jerusalem artichokes have the texture of cabbage stalks and are especially delicious in salads.

INDIAN APPLE SOUP   For this recipe, see page 28

SPINACH-STRAWBERRY SALAD   For this recipe, see page 251

Unexpected Salad Combinations

BANANA-SWEET POTATO SALAD

Serves 6

5 sweet potatoes, peeled, cooked, and cut into ⅜-inch cubes
4 large bananas, cut into ½-inch slices
3 Golden Delicious apples, cut into ⅜-inch cubes
½ cup golden raisins
½ cup coarsely chopped walnuts
Dressing
juice of 1 lemon
½ cup peanut oil
¼ cup honey

1. Combine potatoes, bananas, apples, raisins, and walnuts in a large bowl.
2. In a blender, process the dressing ingredients until smooth. Pour over the salad ingredients. Toss well to coat.

BERRIED TURKEY SALAD

Serves 6

4 cups cooked diced turkey
1 cup raw cashews
1 cup blueberries
4 scallions, thinly sliced
1 cup Mayonnaise (see Index)
2 teaspoons curry powder
1 tablespoon lime juice
leaves from 2 bunches watercress

1. In a large bowl, combine the turkey, cashews, blueberries, and scallions.
2. In a small bowl, mix mayonnaise, curry powder, and lime juice. Add to turkey mixture. Toss gently to coat.
3. Place watercress leaves in the bottom of a salad bowl. Heap the turkey salad in the center of the leaves.

"They were probably sour anyway," says the fox in one of Aesop's fables, upon failing to reach a bunch of grapes. So a person who disparages something beyond his capacity to attain is said to take a "sour grapes" attitude.

CHICKEN COCONUT SALAD

Serves 6

2 cups cooked brown rice
3 tablespoons sesame oil
1 tablespoon lime juice
3 cups diced cooked chicken
1 sweet red pepper, diced
½ cup coarsely chopped celery
1 cup halved seedless green grapes
½ cup Mayonnaise (see Index)
½ cup plain yogurt
2 teaspoons curry powder
6 tablespoons shredded coconut

1. In a large bowl, combine the rice, oil, and lime juice. Toss well to coat. Stir in the chicken, pepper, celery, and grapes.
2. Combine mayonnaise, yogurt, and curry powder. Mix well.
3. Add mayonnaise mixture to chicken-rice mixture and toss well. Cover and chill 1 hour.
4. Sprinkle with coconut before serving.

CURRIED ORANGE AND TUNA SALAD

Serves 6

¾ pound fresh tuna, baked at 350°F for 40 minutes or until flaky or 2 6½-ounce cans water-packed tuna, drained and flaked
1 cup cold cooked brown rice
½ cup finely chopped celery
1½ teaspoons lemon juice
5 teaspoons Mayonnaise (see Index)
5 teaspoons plain yogurt
¼ cup cottage cheese
1 teaspoon curry powder
3 navel oranges, segmented

Garnish
sliced scallions
peanuts or cashews
shredded coconut
raisins

1. In a bowl, lightly toss the tuna, rice, celery, and lemon juice.
2. In another bowl, whisk together mayonnaise, yogurt, cottage cheese, and curry powder until blended. Toss with the salad ingredients.
3. Arrange the orange segments on 6 salad plates. Place a scoop of tuna salad in the center of the segments. Serve the garnish ingredients in small bowls on the side.

HERBED APPLE AND CORN SALAD

Serves 6 to 8

1½ cups corn (about 3 ears),
   cooked and cooled
6 okra, thinly sliced
2 Golden Delicious apples, diced

Dressing

½ cup olive oil
3 tablespoons cider vinegar
1 tablespoon water
1 teaspoon Prepared Mustard
   (see Index)
3 tablespoons evenly mixed
   chopped parsley, chives, and
   watercress
1 small onion, coarsely chopped

6 Boston lettuce leaves

1. Place the corn in a mixing bowl. Add the okra and apples to the corn.
2. Combine the olive oil, vinegar, water, mustard, herbs, and onion in a small screw-top jar. Shake well to mix. Toss with salad ingredients.
3. Arrange lettuce leaves on individual salad plates. Scoop a portion of the apple-corn mixture into the center of each leaf.

NECTARINE-POTATO SALAD

Serves 6

2 pounds new potatoes, scrubbed,
   boiled, and cut into ½-inch
   cubes
1 cup green beans, cut into
   ½-inch lengths
½ cup peas (about ½ pound)
3 scallions, thinly sliced
3 nectarines, cut into ½-inch
   cubes

Dressing

½ cup Mayonnaise (see Index)
½ cup plain yogurt
1 tablespoon Prepared Mustard
   (see Index)

1 tablespoon minced dill
1 tablespoon minced parsley

1. Place the potatoes in a large salad bowl.
2. Steam the green beans and peas together in a small amount of boiling water, just until crunch-tender (about 10 minutes). Cool and add to salad bowl. Add the scallions.
3. Add the nectarines to the salad bowl.
4. Make a dressing by combining the mayonnaise, yogurt, and mustard. Add to the salad and toss well. Sprinkle with the dill and parsley.

Most Europeans, who regularly drink wine with their meals, serve the salad last in order to prevent the salad vinegar from interfering with the wine. (At least, that is the idea that started the tradition.)

_____Fruit Facial_____

After enjoying the rapturous flavor of the papaya in salad or soup, save the shell and use it for the facial of a lifetime. Rub the inside surface on your face and neck and let it dry to make a mask. The papain (an enzyme) in it will act on dead cells and freckles if you leave it on for 15 minutes or so. Wash it off with warm water and behold a silky, glowing complexion that feels and looks younger.

PAPAYA-VEGETABLE SALAD

Serves 6

2 small zucchini, cut into julienne
  strips
3 celery stalks, thinly sliced
½ cup bean sprouts
3 scallions, thinly sliced
½ cup coarsely chopped walnuts

Dressing

¼ cup oil
2 tablespoons lemon or lime juice
1 tablespoon honey
1 tablespoon finely chopped fresh
  basil or 1 teaspoon dried

3 papayas, halved and seeded
1 tablespoon lemon or lime juice

1. In a mixing bowl, toss together the zucchini, celery, bean sprouts, scallions, and walnuts.

2. In a small screw-top jar, combine the oil, lemon juice, honey, and basil. Shake well to mix. Add to zucchini-celery mixture and toss to coat.

3. Sprinkle papaya halves with the lemon juice. Spoon a portion of the vegetables into each cavity. Serve chilled.

POACHED FISH AND FRUIT SALAD

Serves 6

3 pounds white fish fillets, such
  as sole, flounder, or scrod
juice of ½ lemon
¼ cup lime juice
¼ cup Mayonnaise (see Index)
¼ cup plain yogurt, beaten well
2 tablespoons honey
1 tablespoon finely chopped mint
1½ teaspoons grated, peeled ginger
  root
1 pound seedless green grapes
2 navel oranges, segmented
1 scallion, thinly sliced
6 Boston lettuce leaves
½ cup slivered almonds

1. Arrange the fillets in a single layer in a buttered saucepan. Sprinkle with the lemon juice. Add just enough cold water to the pan barely to cover the fish. Bring to a boil, lower heat, cover, and simmer very gently until the fish flakes easily (10 to 15 minutes). Cool fish in its poaching liquid by placing saucepan in a larger pan of ice water or ice cubes, then chill.

2. Combine lime juice, mayonnaise, yogurt, honey, mint, and ginger root in a small mixing bowl.

3. Drain and flake the cooled fish. Combine fish, grapes, orange segments, and scallion slices in a large bowl. Toss the fish mixture with the dressing.

4. Heap a portion of the fish salad onto each lettuce leaf. Sprinkle each with slivered almonds.

SPINACH-STRAWBERRY SALAD

Serves 6

leaves from 2 pounds spinach
2 cups hulled and halved
    strawberries
1 cup thinly sliced mushrooms
3 ounces Roquefort cheese,
    crumbled
Poppy-Seed Dressing (see Index)*

*For this recipe, make dressing with framboise vinegar, if available. This can be found in gourmet or specialty stores.

1. Place spinach in a large salad bowl. Add the strawberries, mushrooms, and cheese. Cover with plastic wrap and refrigerate until serving time.

2. Toss with dressing just before serving.

ORANGE AND RADISH SALAD

Serves 6

6 romaine lettuce leaves
3 navel oranges, peeled and sliced
    into thin discs
2 red onions, sliced into ½-inch
    rings
3 bunches red radishes
Vinaigrette Dressing (see Index)

1. Arrange the lettuce leaves on 6 individual serving plates. Arrange the orange slices on top of the lettuce. Sandwich the onion slices between the orange slices.

2. Grate the radishes and moisten them with a small amount of dressing. Sprinkle the grated radish over the orange and onion slices. Additional dressing may be served on the side, if desired.

Forest Food

Learn of the green world what can be thy place.
EZRA POUND, CANTO LXXXI

Formal gardens are not this lady's cup of tea. In their stead she prefers the small woodland plots that lie just beneath her kitchen window. From them she picks the leaves and ragged scarlet pompoms from the bee balm for her morning beverage. The clear stream flowing beside her cabin holds out crisp, deep green watercress and, at its banks, tender, young wild leeks. The base of an imposing maple tree beds a mass of yellow, velvet-stemmed mushrooms. All these are the nucleus of an early breakfast.

On part of 300 forested acres in New York state, Lynn Anderson and thirteen other adults and children have chosen to erect the separate family dwellings that form the Rainbow Farm Community. Lynn lives in a charming wood frame structure located just off the lane that winds its way through the clearing.

Everyone shares in the responsibilities involved in making the farm a viable settlement. Each person participates in building construction, gardening, and road maintenance. Adults work at jobs in nearby towns to finance cooperatively owned equipment, such as a recently purchased snow plow and tractor. Individual skills,

Lynn Anderson pauses as she
gathers the makings of a meal.

whether they surface at the farm or are part of a person's particular occupation, are
both stimuli and tools for the entire group.

   Lynn's specialty has always been food. In the late sixties, she ran a small restaurant in Woodstock, New York, which was so successful that she was encouraged
to publish a collection of the recipes used there. In summer months, a large proportion
of the vegetables and greens on the menu came from the restaurant's garden and the
outlying woods. Some evenings, roadside day lilies and wild burdock root were listed.

   Lynn devotes a lot of time to researching and writing about wild plants, and she
constantly experiments in the kitchen with the products of her daily foraging. Her
friends at the farm readily testify to her abilities: "We just go to Lynn whenever we
can't identify a plant," says one. "She's got an uncanny ability to make something
superb out of a few wild greens and vegetables," another tells us.

   What is unique about Lynn's approach to gathering is that she actually "culti-
vates" wild vegetation. Many mornings and evenings she returns from a walk with an

Lynn relaxes as she enjoys one of her own creations.

Lynn's friends all agree that she can make something superb out of a few greens and vegetables.

armful of greens to set out in the rich earth surrounding her cabin. Visitors are often surprised to find her transplanting dandelion, wild ginger, and mustard among her annual nasturtiums, asters, and marigolds. The final surprise is her sprinkling of compost on the weeds as well as the flowers. "Good composted weeds make good edible weeds," she tells her friends.

Lynn also has encouraged her compatriots to leave selected patches of weeds like wintercress and lamb's-quarters growing together with the cultivated vegetables in the cooperative garden. Each season, sheep sorrel flourishes amid the onions, and dense blankets of purslane surround the greens. "Purslane is both ground cover and food," she says. "It may take over parts of the garden, but it doesn't hurt anything."

Lynn Anderson's quiet, easy manner when she talks about gathering plants and turning them into imaginative meals belies her boundless enthusiasm. In the following pages, we offer you some of her carefully designed recipes and her useful comments on the wild edibles they contain.

HOW TO BEGIN FORAGING

Begin foraging with friends who have some knowledge of wild edibles. First-hand learning of what and how to eat from nature is the best way to go. Books are an important backup for adding to the things you learn. If you must use them, if no people are around to start you on your way, use more than one book and cross-refer to broaden your picture of wild plants; some books are strong on information, some on illustration. You need a wide range of both in the beginning stages of foraging to clear up the confusion that can be caused by depending on just one author's eye view of wild foods. Be discriminating and sensible when trying new plants. Never eat anything of doubtful identification. A good first step is to familiarize youself with the poisonous plants of your area. The departments of conservation and agriculture are good sources of free literature to use as guidelines to foraging.

Some plants, such as dandelions, asparagus, and day lilies, may already be familiar. Start with them, learn how and what to do with them, then go on to a few more as you get more confident in your identifications. Spring is a great time to start. Watercress is bright and green where early rains have created gentle, constant water runoffs, and the wild onion family, unmistakable with its strong aromas, provides garlic, onions, leeks, and chives to add zip to our meals.

EARLY SPRING SALAD

Serves 4 to 6

watercress, chopped just a bit to free
  sprigs from main stem—enough to
  make about 4 cups
green tops of 6 to 8 wild leeks, coarsely
  chopped
 1 cup alfalfa sprouts
 ½ cup chopped day lily shoots
 ¼ cup chopped dandelion greens
Sesame-Lemon Dressing (see recipe
  below)

Spring is the time of fresh, green salads, and this is one of my favorites; in fact, I eat variations of it every day until the season runs out.

Toss ingredients together and coat lightly with the dressing.

SESAME-LEMON DRESSING

 ⅓ cup oil (a mixture of olive and a
  lighter oil is good)
juice of 1 lemon
 2 tablespoons roasted sesame seeds,
  crushed or ground
 2 teaspoons tamari soy sauce

Shake ingredients in a jar or combine in blender.

Watercress is found in patches where water runs constantly and gently, usually in level, low areas. It should never be pulled out by the roots but, instead, snipped off in sprigs above the roots which should then be patted back into the patch to protect them from drying out and dying. In this way, we can insure the propagation of the plant. Never overpick one area of a patch; take a sprig from here and there all around the patch. This, too, aids the growth of watercress.

By early summer, new lettuce and bright radishes are available in markets and gardens. If you're lucky enough to have a garden nearby, you will find many edible weeds growing alongside the cultivated crops. Don't overlook them. The arrow- or lance-shaped leaves of sheep sorrel give a delicious, lemony bite to salads. Low-growing, shiny-leafed purslane is a tasty, colorful green, and lamb's-quarters, unmistakable with its dusty green leaves and lavender dust on top, is truly a delicacy. This is a salad to try and enjoy.

SUMMER GARDEN SALAD
Serves 4

1 cup coarsely chopped mixed wild greens from the garden—sheep sorrel, lamb's-quarters, and purslane

3 cups mixed bite-size lettuce leaves—ruby, buttercrunch, or looseleaf

6 red radishes, 5 thinly sliced in rounds and the last cut to make a radish rose

2 to 3 scallions, white part thinly sliced in rounds, green tops finely chopped

2 day lily flowers, petals separated from center

Dill Yogurt Dressing (see recipe below)

Toss greens and sliced radishes in a serving bowl. Arrange the orange day lily petals in a floral ray on top of salad. Scatter mixed scallion pieces over petals and place radish rose in the center. Pass the dressing at the table.

DILL YOGURT DRESSING
Yields about 1 cup

½ cup yogurt

¼ cup olive oil or other oil

1 tablespoon finely chopped fresh dill or 1 teaspoon dried dillweed

pinch freshly ground black pepper

dash cayenne pepper

Mix by hand with wire whisk or fork.

The first day lily shoots appear in early spring. Like watercress, day lilies like watery areas, though they will flourish in almost any place, dry or wet. These shoots can be pinched off and chopped into salads to add an almost sweet and succulent flavor. Usually, it doesn't in the least disturb the abundant growth to pluck a few plants. As the leaves mature, they take on a fibrous quality, making them unsatisfactory for salads, but as a soup green they are delicious. By mid-June the flower buds are produced and can be eaten raw or cooked, as can the open flowers. A truly giving and beautiful plant.

BURDOCK ROOT AND RICE SALAD

Serves 6

Marinade

½ *cup olive oil*
juice of 1 lemon
  1 *tablespoon tamari soy sauce*
  1 *garlic clove, crushed*
  1 *teaspoon dillseed or cumin seed, crushed or ground*

½ *cup sunflower seeds*
  3 *burdock roots, 8 to 12 inches long and ½ inch diameter or less, thinly sliced on the diagonal*
  2 *cups cooked rice, chilled*
¼ *cup parsley, finely chopped*
½ *cup mushrooms, thinly sliced (edible wild mushrooms such as collybia, morel, or meadow mushroom are an exquisite addition to this salad, or cultivated mushrooms are just fine)*
¼ *cup onion or wild leek bulbs, diced or ¼ cup chives, minced*
  6 *lettuce leaves*
  2 *tomatoes, cut into thin wedges*
  2 *medium-size carrots, grated*

As late summer rolls around, the first-year roots of many wild plants reach a mature eating size like their counterparts in the garden. Though wild carrot, parsnip, and burdock roots can be dug and eaten throughout the spring and summer, they are most easily located in late summer when the second-year, or seed-producing, plants are a signal that the new crop is nearby, and you are sure to find masses of tiny plants scattered beneath the old ones. Don't let the small leaves fool you, however; below these little leaves grow roots as long as 1½ feet. A pickax is a must to dig deeply into the earth and turn up these long, thin roots. Scrub them well with a vegetable brush and you are ready to cook and eat a real treat. Burdock root is a favorite of mine in soups, sauteed with other vegetables, or in salads like this one.

1. Blend or mix marinade ingredients; set aside.
2. Roast sunflower seeds in heavy skillet until lightly browned; remove and cool.
3. In same pan, steam burdock roots in a little water until just tender (10 to 15 minutes). Pour off any remaining water and immediately add marinade to burdock root which has been placed in a large mixing bowl. Set aside to cool.
4. Meanwhile, prepare remaining ingredients. Toss together rice, sunflower seeds, parsley, mushrooms, and onions or chives; add marinating burdock root and toss again until all vegetables are well coated with marinade.
5. Place lettuce leaves on 6 serving plates and spoon salad mixture onto each one. Arrange tomato wedges in a circular floral pattern on top of each and center a mound of grated carrot for a finishing touch.

The wild leek is easily distinguished from chives by its flat, broad leaf. This is one of the first green plants to appear on the sides of otherwise brown mountain slopes and water runoffs. It is a water lover like cress and day lilies, but can be found on much higher ground in clumps or singly (unlike chives which always grow in a cluster). Early in the season, the greens are the most delicate part, though the small butts can be eaten, also. As the plant matures, the bulb grows just like an onion and reaches a size more adequate for pickling and preserving. At that time, the leaves are turning yellow and dying.

The easiest way to pick leeks is with a small pickax so the bulbs can be easily turned up out of the ground; pulling only breaks off the tops. Chives, on the other hand, should be snipped or pinched off at the bottom of each stalk without disturbing the roots. In this way, new growth is encouraged.

MILKWEED-TOFU SALAD

Serves 2

½ cup young milkweed pods, sliced on the diagonal

1 large cake tofu or 2 small, diced in ½-inch cubes

2 medium-size carrots, cut in matchstick slivers

1 medium-size onion, sliced in thin rings

1⅓ cups olive or other oil

2 tablespoons cider vinegar

1 tablespoon tamari soy sauce

1 small garlic clove, crushed

1 scant teaspoon ground ginger root

6 lettuce leaves

As the growing season continues, the versatile, common milkweed plant sends forth its pods. While they are still small, green, and somewhat firm to the touch, they have many uses—cooked alone or in combination with other vegetables. The following is a cool, main-meal salad for those hot summer days.

Lightly steam milkweed pods until they just begin to turn bright green. Cool. Toss together with tofu, carrots, onion, oil, vinegar, tamari, garlic, and ginger root; allow to marinate at least one hour. (The longer it sits, the more saturated the ingredients become with marinade flavor.) Arrange lettuce leaves in 2 salad bowls to form cups and spoon salad into centers.

Dressings

DILLED FETA DRESSING

Yields 2 cups

1 cup diced feta cheese
½ cup milk
½ cup plain yogurt
2 tablespoons minced dillweed

Process all ingredients in a blender until smooth. Chill before serving.

Note: This dressing poured over sliced tomatoes is a delight.

FRENCH-STYLE MUSTARD

Yields 1 cup

¼ cup freshly ground brown mustard seed (grind to personal preference—the finer the grind, the smoother the mustard)
5 tablespoons dry mustard
½ cup hot water
¾ cup champagne vinegar
2 tablespoons cold water
2 large onion slices
2 teaspoons honey
1 teaspoon molasses
2 garlic cloves, peeled and halved
¼ teaspoon dill seed
¼ teaspoon cinnamon
¼ teaspoon allspice
¼ teaspoon dried tarragon, crumbled
⅛ teaspoon cloves

1. Soak the mustard seed and dry mustard in the water and ¼ cup of the vinegar at room temperature at least 3 hours.

2. Combine the remaining ingredients in a small saucepan. Bring to a boil, boil 1 minute, remove from the heat, cover, and let stand 1 hour.

3. Transfer the soaked mustard mixture to a blender. Strain the spice infusion into the mustard mixture. Press the spices against the sides of the strainer to extract all the flavor. Process until the mixture is the consistency of a coarse puree.

4. Pour the mixture into the top of a double boiler, set over simmering water, and cook until thickened (20 to 25 minutes). The mustard will thicken a bit more when chilled.

5. Remove mustard from the heat and pour into a jar. Let cool, uncovered, and then put a top on it and store in the refrigerator.

259

———————————**Zingy Salad Green**———————————

"Arugula," "rocket," "roquette," "rocket cress," "rugula," "rucola," "ruchetta," and "ruca" are only some of the names aficionados use to describe a particular pepper-flavored green. Well known in European countries, where it is as popular as endive, arugula is now becoming a choice American salad ingredient. Similar to watercress, a few leaves among a bowl of greens introduce a zingy, unique taste. Although arugula is not available everywhere, well-stocked greengrocers and Italian foods specialty markets often carry it.

ARUGULA AND WALNUT DRESSING

Yields 1¾ cups

1 cup firmly packed arugula
  leaves*
¾ cup olive oil
2 tablespoons lemon juice
1 garlic clove, minced
½ cup coarsely chopped walnuts

*Watercress may be substituted for the arugula.

Process the arugula, oil, lemon juice, and garlic in a blender container until smooth. Add the walnuts and process off and on until they are just crunchy. Refrigerate until serving.

Note: Chilled steamed vegetables or tomatoes are well matched to this dressing.

BLENDER TOMATO JUICE DRESSING

Yields 1½ cups

½ cup safflower oil
¼ cup sesame oil
⅓ cup tomato juice
2 tablespoons lemon juice
1 shallot, finely chopped
⅛ teaspoon cayenne pepper
1 teaspoon celery seed

Process all ingredients in a blender until smooth. Chill before serving.

Note: This dressing is especially suited to mixed vegetable or green salads. It also makes an unusual dressing for cold fish salads.

CURRIED LIME DRESSING

Yields 2 cups

1 cup olive oil
½ cup lime juice
½ cup honey
1 tablespoon grated lime rind
2 teaspoons celery seed
1 teaspoon curry powder

Process in blender until smooth. Refrigerate until serving.

Note: Serve on green salad, fruit salad, or cottage cheese.

GINGER CHEESE DRESSING

Yields 1½ cups

1 cup cottage cheese
¼ cup milk
3 tablespoons lemon or lime juice
3 tablespoons honey
¾ teaspoon ginger

Process all ingredients in a blender until smooth. Chill before serving.

Note: This dressing adds interest and variety to fruit salads. Add more milk (about 2 tablespoons) if a thinner dressing is desired.

GORGONZOLA DRESSING

Yields 2 cups

1 cup Mayonnaise (see Index)
½ cup tomato juice
1 tablespoon lemon juice
1 teaspoon tamari soy sauce
1 garlic clove, minced
¼ teaspoon cayenne pepper
⅔ cup grated Gorgonzola cheese*

*The cheese will be easier to handle if frozen before grating.

In a mixing bowl, whisk the mayonnaise, tomato juice, lemon juice, tamari, garlic, and cayenne until blended. Whisk in the cheese. Refrigerate until serving time.

NO-COOK HOLLANDAISE DRESSING

Yields 1 cup

¼ cup lemon juice
1 tablespoon French-Style Mustard (see recipe in this section)
2 egg yolks
¾ cup olive oil

Combine the lemon juice, mustard, and egg yolks in a bowl. Whisk until blended. Gradually whisk in the oil in a stream. Refrigerate until serving.

Note: This dressing combines well with avocado and seafood salads.

POPPY-SEED DRESSING

Yields 1⅔ cups

1 cup oil
⅓ cup honey
⅓ cup cider vinegar
1 tablespoon poppy seed
1 teaspoon dry mustard
¼ teaspoon dried tarragon

Process all ingredients in blender until smooth. Refrigerate until serving.

Note: Serve over green salad, fruit salad, or cottage cheese.

To clear your breath of onion or garlic odor, chew on a fresh coffee bean.

HERBAL GARLIC YOGURT DRESSING

Yields 2 cups

¾ cup Mayonnaise (see Index)
¾ cup plain yogurt
1 garlic clove, minced
2 tablespoons finely chopped onions
½ cup chopped parsley
¼ cup minced dill
¼ teaspoon dried tarragon
3 tablespoons cider vinegar

Process all ingredients in a blender until smooth. Chill before serving.

Note: This dressing combines well with salads containing cucumbers.

Maximizing Mayonnaise

If the recipe calls for a whole egg, make your mayonnaise in a food processor or blender—you'll get a fluffier product than if you beat it by hand. Blender-made mayonnaise is also slower to separate during storage. (Add a dollop of previously made mayonnaise during preparation to reinforce the binding still more.) Should the mayonnaise separate, slowly beat the mayonnaise into a new egg yolk, or a teaspoon of prepared mustard, or a tablespoon of either water or vinegar. This most useful and popular of cold sauces comes by its name honestly—from the old French word for egg yolk, moyeu.

MAYONNAISE (BLENDER)

Yields 1½ cups

2 egg yolks, lightly beaten
2 tablespoons lemon juice or vinegar
½ teaspoon dry mustard
1⅓ cups oil
2 teaspoons boiling water

1. Warm the blender container in hot water and dry thoroughly.

2. Combine the yolks, lemon juice, and mustard in the container. Blend at medium speed about 1 minute.

3. Gradually add the oil, a few drops at a time, until ⅓ cup oil has been incorporated into the yolks.

4. At this point the remaining oil can be added 1 tablespoon at a time, until all the oil has been used.

5. To insure against the mayonnaise separating, blend in the boiling water.

6. Store in a covered glass jar in the refrigerator.

Note: For best results, have all ingredients at room temperature.

MAYONNAISE (HAND-BEATEN)

Yields 1¼ cups

2 egg yolks, lightly beaten
2 tablespoons lemon juice or vinegar
½ teaspoon dry mustard
1⅓ cups oil
2 teaspoons boiling water

1. Warm a glass or stainless steel bowl and a wire whisk in hot water. Dry thoroughly.

2. Add the egg yolks to the bowl with 1 tablespoon of the lemon juice and the dry mustard. Beat to mix well.

3. Continue beating constantly as you add the oil, 1 drop at a time. Be sure the yolks are absorbing the oil; this may require that you stop adding the oil and just beat the yolks for a few seconds.

4. After about ⅓ cup of the oil has been incorporated into the yolks, the remaining oil can be added by the tablespoon. Beat well after each addition of oil.

5. When the mayonnaise is thick and stiff, beat in the remaining lemon juice to thin it out.

6. To insure against the mayonnaise separating, blend in the boiling water.

7. Store mayonnaise in a covered glass jar in the refrigerator.

Note: For best results, have all ingredients at room temperature.

PREPARED MUSTARD

Yields ½ cup

¼ cup dry mustard
¼ cup hot water
3 tablespoons white vinegar
⅛ teaspoon garlic powder
pinch dried tarragon
¼ teaspoon molasses

1. Soak mustard in water and 1 tablespoon of the vinegar at least 2 hours.

2. Combine the remaining vinegar and the garlic and tarragon in a separate bowl and let stand 30 minutes.

3. Strain the tarragon from the second vinegar mixture and add the liquid to the mustard mixture.

4. Stir in the molasses.

5. Pour the mustard into the top of a double boiler and set pan over simmering water. Cook until thickened (about 15 minutes). The mustard will thicken a bit more when chilled.

6. Remove from the heat and pour into a jar. Let cool uncovered, and then put a lid on it and store in the refrigerator.

RAW MUSHROOM VINAIGRETTE

Yields 2 cups

1 pound mushrooms, thinly sliced
½ cup thinly sliced scallions
1 garlic clove
½ cup finely chopped parsley
1 tablespoon finely chopped basil
½ cup olive oil
¼ cup lemon juice

Place all ingredients in a wide-mouth screw-top jar, cover, and shake to mix. Refrigerate at least 2 hours. Remove garlic before serving.

Note: This dressing is excellent over green salads or chilled steamed vegetables such as green beans or cauliflower.

RUSSIAN DRESSING

Yields about 4 cups

1 cup yogurt
2 cups mayonnaise
1 cup catsup
2 teaspoons horseradish

Combine yogurt and mayonnaise with wire whisk. Stir in catsup and horseradish. Store in covered quart glass jar in refrigerator.

VINAIGRETTE

Yields ¾ cup

3 tablespoons cider vinegar
1 teaspoon honey
½ cup olive oil

In a screw-top jar, shake the vinegar and honey together until combined. Add the oil and shake until thoroughly mixed.

Variations

Curried Vinaigrette: Add ½ teaspoon curry powder and 1 minced shallot to the vinegar and honey. Shake well before adding the oil.

Garlic Vinaigrette: In a bowl, crush 1 garlic clove with ¼ teaspoon white pepper to a paste. Stir in the vinegar and honey. Transfer mixture to a screw-top jar; add the oil and shake well. Prepare at least 2 hours before serving.

Herbal Vinaigrette: Add 2 teaspoons each of finely minced chives, parsley, basil, and tarragon to any of the above vinaigrette dressings.

Mustard Vinaigrette: Shake 1 teaspoon dry mustard together with the vinegar and honey. Add the oil and shake.

Tomato Vinaigrette: Add 1 tablespoon tomato paste to Mustard Vinaigrette or Garlic Vinaigrette.

SESAME—DISTINCTIVE SUBTLE FLAVOR

Sesame paste (frequently referred to as tahini) and sesame oil are two popular products of the small, glossy, oval-shaped sesame seeds. In soups and salads their distinctive taste has no equal.

When sesame seeds are ground they become tahini, a product similar in consistency to peanut butter. It is sold in Middle Eastern markets and, lately, in most natural foods stores. A portion of the paste diluted with some soup stock and then added back to the pot gives the soup a creamy texture. Some people deliberately substitute tahini for cream in their soups as a way to avoid the saturated fat cream contains. If you mix tahini with water and lemon juice plus seasonings, it can be used as an unusual, nutty-tasting salad dressing or vegetable dipping sauce.

Light sesame oil provides a high-quality, good-tasting base for oil and vinegar dressings. The darker variety, made from roasted seeds and often sold in oriental grocery stores, is used primarily as a condiment. Just a few drops added to a soup, a salad dressing, or even to the other oil in which you toast croutons imparts a definite, unmistakable flavor.

Don't overlook the delightful crunchiness roasted or unroasted sesame seeds add when generously scattered over a salad or soup.

TAHINI DRESSING

Yields 2¾ cups

1 cup tahini*
1 cup water
3 tablespoons lemon juice
3 tablespoons tamari soy sauce
1 large garlic clove, pressed
1 teaspoon ground cumin
½ teaspoon cayenne pepper
½ teaspoon minced coriander
  leaves (optional)
¼ teaspoon dark sesame oil
  (optional)

*The oil and the ground sesame seed may separate from one another in the container. Stir them together well before proceeding with the recipe.

1. Put tahini in a large mixing bowl. Whisking constantly, gradually pour in the water until mixture becomes smooth.

2. Add lemon juice, tamari, garlic, cumin, cayenne, and coriander, if used, and stir them well into the tahini. Add sesame oil if you desire a more dominant sesame taste.

Note: Use this dressing with sturdy greens such as romaine and firm vegetables such as cabbage, broccoli, and carrots.

ZESTY ITALIAN HERB DRESSING

Yields 2 cups

1½ cups oil
½ cup wine vinegar
2 garlic cloves, pressed
½ teaspoon dried basil
½ teaspoon dried oregano
¼ to ½ cup grated Parmesan
    cheese (optional)
freshly ground black pepper to taste

Combine ingredients in a jar. Shake well. Refrigerate overnight before serving.

Metric Conversion Chart

Customary American	Metric
Mass	
1 ounce	28 g
4 ounces	115 g
8 ounces	225 g
16 ounces	450 g
Volume	
¼ teaspoon	1 ml
½ teaspoon	2 ml
1 teaspoon	5 ml
1 tablespoon	15 ml
¼ cup	60 ml
½ cup	125 ml
1 cup	250 ml
1 quart	1 l

Customary American	Metric
Length	
½ inch	1.0 cm
1 inch	2.5 cm
4 inches	10.0 cm
8 inches	20.0 cm
12 inches	30.0 cm
Temperature	
250°F	120°C
300°F	150°C
350°F	175°C
400°F	200°C
450°F	230°C

Index

Italicized page numbers refer to color illustrations.

C

D

E

F

Fennel Soup, 94
Fish
    Asian Fish Soup, 34
    Bluefish and Green Bean Salad, 180
    Cucumber and Dilled Fish Salad, 183
    Curried Cod and Potato Salad, 183
    Curried Orange and Tuna Salad, 248
    Egg and Fish Salad, 224
    Filleting of, 70–71
    Fish Chowder, 118
    Fish Head Soup, 125
    Fish-on-the-Half-Shell Salad, 182
    Hungarian Fish Chowder, 66
    New England Fish Chowder, 72
    Poached Fish and Fruit Salad, 250
    Seafood Slaw, 181
    Squid Salad, 181
    Steamed Combo, 73
    Tofu Tuna Salad, 182
Fish Stock, 13, 21
    Tom's, 72
Florentine Egg Soup, 53
Florida Salad, 187
Flowers, added to salads, 163
Foraging, 255
French Dressing, 157
French Sorrel Soup, 87
French-Style Mustard, 259
Fresh Basil Soup, 106
Fresh Double Pea Soup, 134
Fresh Fruit and Yogurt Soup, 28, *211*
Fresh Herbed Green Pea Soup, 38
Fresh Pea and Lettuce Soup, 111
Fresh Snapper Soup, 116
Fresh Vegetable Miso Soup, 131
Fresh Vegetable Tamari Soup, 129

Fruit
    for salads, 185
    testing ripeness of, 156
Fruit French Dressing, 157
Fruit salads
    Avocado, Chicory, and Honeydew, 184
    Citrus Endive, 186
    Cress, Mango, and Romaine, 186
    Date-Raisin Waldorf, 188
    Egyptian Grape, 186
    Florida, 187
    Fruit and Sprout, 187
    Fruited Green Goddess, 188
    Nutty Avocado, 231
    Plum, 189
    Poached Fish and Fruit, 250
Fruit soups
    Apple Vichyssoise, 25
    Banana Coconut, 26
    Cashew, Grape, and Pear, 26
    Fresh Fruit and Yogurt, 28, *211*
    Indian Apple, 28, *245*
    Plum, 27
    Prune, 29
    Tomato Orange, 27

G

Garbanzo Soup, 38
Garden Pea and Mint Salad, 213
Garlic, adding to salad, 159
Garlic Broth, 33

H

I

J

Japanese Chicken and Mushroom Soup, 66
Jellied stocks, 14–15
Julienne of Root Vegetables, 242

K

Kale Lentil Soup, 106
Key Lime Chicken Salad, 221
King, Ratna, 201–3
Kohlrabi Soup, 80
Kombu-Fish Stock, 120
Kombu-Potato Stock, 120
Kombu-Soba Soup with *Nori,* 120
Kombu Soup Stock, 120
Kombu-Watercress Soup, 120

L

Lamb
    Meatball Soup, 56
    Minted Lamb Salad, 222
Lamm, Kathie, 97–102
Layered Beet and Yogurt Mold, 243
Layered Minestrone, 130
Layered Vegetable Medley, 209
Leek and Potato Soup, Spanish, 93
Leftover Meat Loaf and Spaghetti Squash
    Salad, 225
Leftover Roast with Pan Juice Dressing, 226

Legumes
    Baked Bean Soup, 122
    Basil and Bean Salad, 196
    Bean and Rice Salad, 175
    Black-Eyed Pea Salad, 197
    Bluefish and Green Bean Salad, 180
    Chick-Pea Blender Soup, 37
    Curried Black Bean Soup, 142
    Fresh Double Pea Soup, 134
    Fresh Herbed Green Pea Soup, 38
    Fresh Pea and Lettuce Soup, 111
    Garbanzo Soup, 38
    Garden Pea and Mint Salad, 213
    Green Bean Almondine Salad, *75,* 230
    Italian Lima Bean Soup, 39
    Lima Bean Soup, 40
    Mushroom and Navy Bean Salad, 199
    Pea and Pod Soup, 78
    Pinto Bean and Radish Salad, 198
    Pinto Bean and Sausage Soup, 40
    Pinto Bean Soup, *41,* 103
    Rainbow Bean Salad, 199
    Southern Bean and Rice Soup, 56
    Succotash Chowder, 53
    Sweet Corn and Beans, 50
    Three-Bean Chili, 176
    Three-Bean Soup, 43
    White Bean Soup Supreme, 35
Lentils
    Greek Lentil Soup, 132
    Kale Lentil Soup, 106
    Lentil Salad, 198
    Spicy Mexican Lentil Soup, 140
Lettuce
    Fresh Pea and Lettuce Soup, 111
    Stuffed Lettuce Soup, 123
Lewis Street Roquefort Cheese Dressing, 74
Lima Bean Soup, 40
    Italian, 39

Y

Z